Standards Practice Book

For Home or School

Grade 2

INCLUDES:

- Home or School Practice
- Lesson Practice and Test Preparation
- English and Spanish School-Home Letters
- Getting Ready for Grade 3 Lessons

Printed in the U.S.A.

ISBN 978-0-547-58814-8

28 0928 20 19

4500757893 D E F G

Number Sense and Place Value

Critical Area Extending understanding of base-ten notation

1 Number Concepts

Domains Operations and Algebraic Thinking
Number and Operations in Base Ten

Common Core Standards CC.2.OA.3, CC.2.NBT.2, CC.2.NBT.3

2 Numbers to 1,000

Domains Number and Operations in Base Ten

Common Core Standards CC.2.NBT.1, CC.2.NBT.1a, CC.2.NBT.1b, CC.2.NBT.3, CC.2.NBT.4, CC.2.NBT.8

CRITICAL AREA Addition and Subtraction

COMMON CORE

Critical Area Building fluency with addition and subtraction

3 Basic Facts and Relationships

Domains Operations and Algebraic Thinking

Common Core Standards CC.2.OA.1, CC.2.OA.2, CC.2.OA.4

4 2-Digit Addition

Domains Operations and Algebraic Thinking
Number and Operations in Base Ten

Common Core Standards CC.2.OA.1, CC.2.NBT.5, CC.2.NBT.6, CC.2.NBT.9

5 2-Digit Subtraction

Domains Operations and Algebraic Thinking
Number and Operations in Base Ten

Common Core Standards CC.2.OA.1, CC.2.NBT.5, CC.2.NBT.9

6 3-Digit Addition and Subtraction

Domains Number and Operations in Base Ten

Common Core Standards CC.2.NBT.7

CRITICAL AREA Measurement and Data

COMMON CORE **Critical Area** Using standard units of measure

7 Money and Time

Domains Measurement and Data
Common Core Standards CC.2.MD.7, CC.2.MD.8

8 Length in Customary Units

Domains Measurement and Data
Common Core Standards CC.2.MD.1, CC.2.MD.2, CC.2.MD.3, CC.2.MD.5, CC.2.MD.6, CC.2.MD.9

9 Length in Metric Units

Domains Measurement and Data

Common Core Standards CC.2.MD.1, CC.2.MD.2, CC.2.MD.3, CC.2.MD.4, CC.2.MD.5, CC.2.MD.6

10 Data

Domains Measurement and Data

Common Core Standards CC.2.MD.10

Geometry and Fractions

Critical Area Describing and analyzing shapes

11 Geometry and Fraction Concepts

Domains Geometry

Common Core Standards CC.2.G.1, CC.2.G.2, CC.2.G.3

End-of-Year Resources

Getting Ready for Grade 3

These lessons review important skills and prepare you for Grade 3.

Chapter 1

School-Home Letter

Dear Family,

My class started Chapter 1 this week. In this chapter, I will learn about place value of 2-digit numbers and even and odd numbers.

Love, ___________________________

Vocabulary

digits 0, 1, 2, 3, 4, 5, 6, 7, 8, and 9 are digits.

even numbers 2, 4, 6, 8, 10 . . .

odd numbers 1, 3, 5, 7, 9 . . .

Home Activity

Give your child a group of 20 small objects, such as beans. Have your child count the objects and tell how many. Then have your child pair the objects and tell whether the number is *even* or *odd*. Repeat with a different number of beans.

Literature

Look for this book at the library. Ask your child to point out math vocabulary words as you read the book together.

One Hundred Hungry Ants
by Elinor J. Pinczes.
Houghton Mifflin, 1993.

Capítulo 1

Carta para la casa

Querida familia:

Mi clase comenzó el Capítulo 1 esta semana. En este capítulo, aprenderé sobre el valor posicional de los números de 2 dígitos y números pares e impares.

Con cariño, ______________________

Vocabulario

dígitos 0, 1, 2, 3, 4, 5, 6, 7, 8 y 9 son dígitos.

números pares 2, 4, 6, 8, 10 . . .

números impares 1, 3, 5, 7, 9 . . .

Actividad para la casa

Dé a su hijo un grupo de 20 objetos pequeños, como unos frijoles. Pídale que cuente los objetos y que diga cuántos hay. Luego, pídale que los agrupe y diga si el número es *par* o *impar*. Repita con un número distinto de frijoles.

Literatura

Busque este libro en la biblioteca. Pídale a su hijo que señale palabras del vocabulario de matemáticas mientras leen juntos el libro.

One Hundred Hungry Ants
por Elinor J. Pinczes.
Houghton Mifflin, 1993.

Name ______________________________

HANDS ON
Lesson 1.1

Algebra • Even and Odd Numbers

COMMON CORE STANDARD CC.2.OA.3
Work with equal groups of objects to gain foundations for multiplication.

Shade in the ten frames to show the number. Circle even or odd.

1. 15

even odd

2. 18

even odd

3. 11

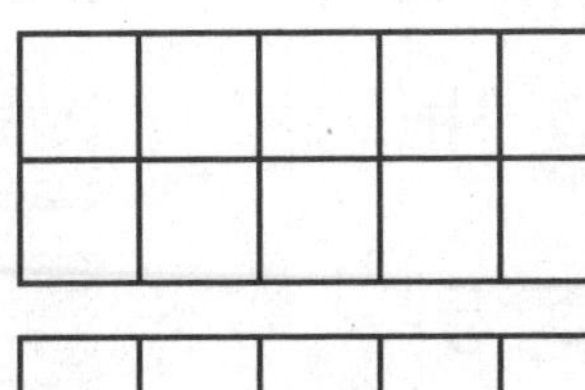

even odd

4. 17

even odd

5. 13

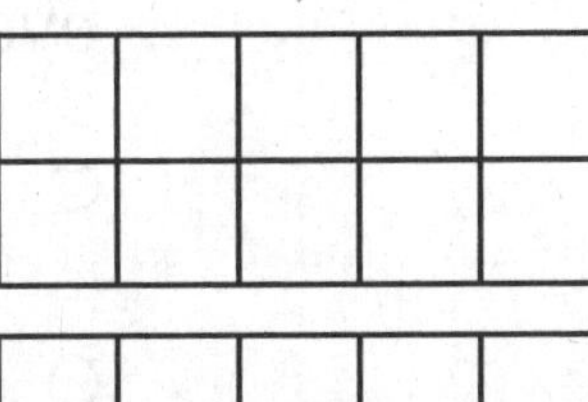

even odd

6. 20

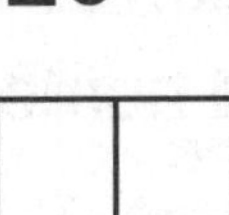

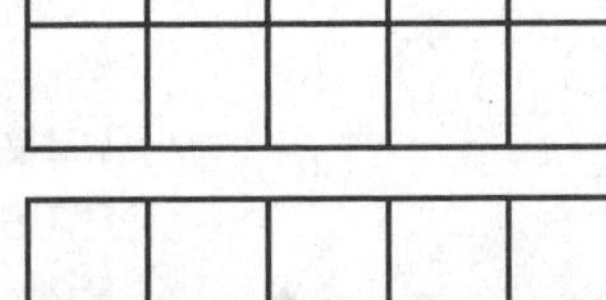

even odd

PROBLEM SOLVING

7. Mr. Dell has an odd number of sheep and an even number of cows on his farm. Circle the choice that could tell about his farm.

9 sheep and 10 cows

10 sheep and 11 cows

8 sheep and 12 cows

Lesson Check (CC.2.OA.3)

1. Which of these numbers is an even number?

○ 3

○ 4

○ 5

○ 9

2. Which of these numbers is an odd number?

○ 2

○ 6

○ 7

○ 8

Spiral Review (CC.2.OA.3)

3. Which of these numbers is an odd number? (Lesson 1.1)

○ 10

○ 8

○ 3

○ 4

4. Which of these numbers is an even number? (Lesson 1.1)

○ 7

○ 6

○ 5

○ 1

5. Which of these numbers is an even number? (Lesson 1.1)

○ 9

○ 7

○ 5

○ 2

6. Which of these numbers is an odd number? (Lesson 1.1)

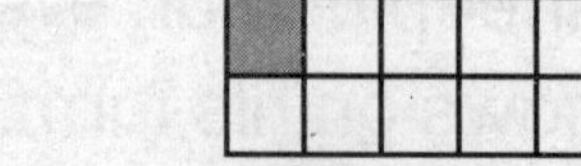
○ 1

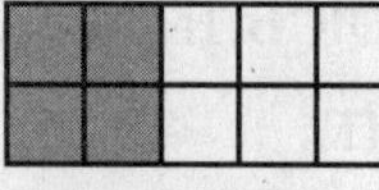
○ 4

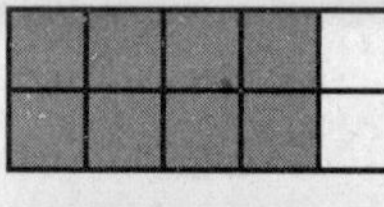
○ 8

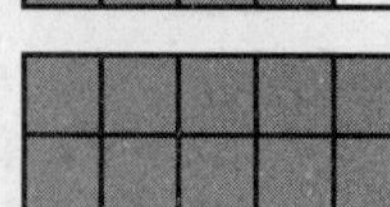
○ 10

Name ______________________

Algebra • Represent Even Numbers

COMMON CORE STANDARD CC.2.OA.3
Work with equal groups of objects to gain foundations for multiplication.

Shade in the frames to show two equal groups for each number. Complete the addition sentence to show the groups.

1. 8 ___ = ___ + ___

2. 18 ___ = ___ + ___

3. 10 ___ = ___ + ___

4. 14 ___ = ___ + ___

5. 20 ___ = ___ + ___

6. 12 ___ = ___ + ___

PROBLEM SOLVING

Solve. Write or draw to explain.

7. The seats in a van are in pairs. There are 16 seats. How many pairs of seats are there?

____ pairs of seats

Lesson Check (CC.2.OA.3)

1. Which sum is an even number?

○ 9 + 9 = 18
○ 9 + 8 = 17
○ 8 + 7 = 15
○ 6 + 5 = 11

2. Which sum is an even number?

○ 1 + 2 = 3
○ 3 + 3 = 6
○ 2 + 5 = 7
○ 4 + 7 = 11

Spiral Review (CC.2.OA.3)

3. Which is an even number?

(Lesson 1.1)

○ 7
○ 9
○ 10
○ 13

4. Which is an odd number?

(Lesson 1.1)

○ 4
○ 11
○ 16
○ 20

5. Ray has an odd number of cats. He also has an even number of dogs. Which can be Ray's pets?

(Lesson 1.1)

○ 3 cats and 1 dog
○ 3 cats and 3 dogs
○ 4 cats and 2 dogs
○ 5 cats and 2 dogs

6. Which sum is an even number?

(Lesson 1.2)

○ 2 + 3 = 5
○ 3 + 4 = 7
○ 4 + 4 = 8
○ 7 + 8 = 15

Name ______________________________

Understand Place Value

COMMON CORE STANDARD CC.2.NBT.3
Understand place value.

Circle the value of the underlined digit.

1. 
23
20 2

2. 
48
8 80

3. 18
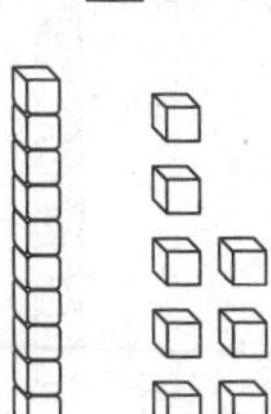
10 1

4. 43
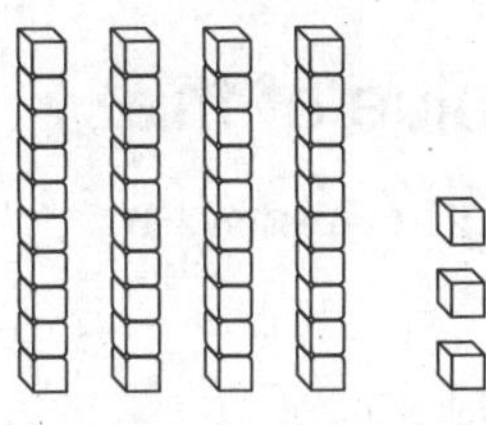
40 4

5. 54
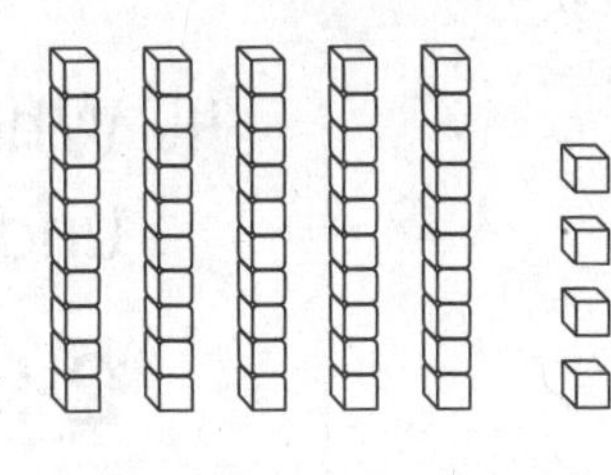
5 50

6. 65
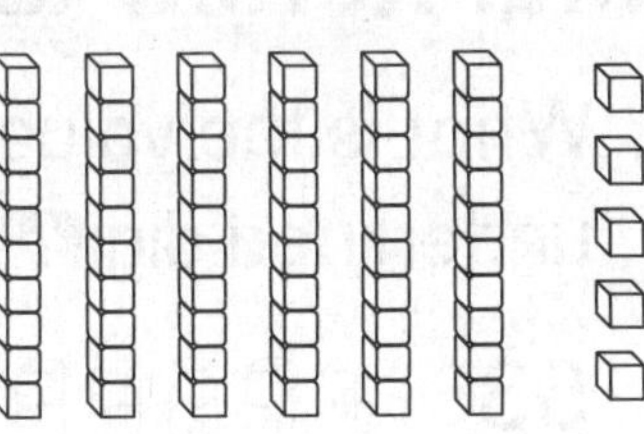
50 5

7. 70
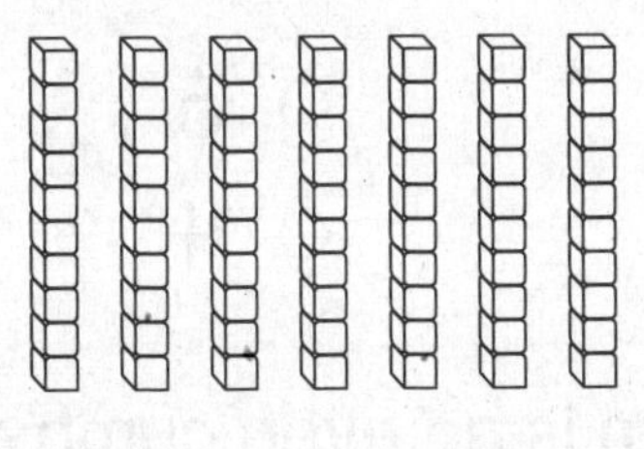
7 70

8. 37
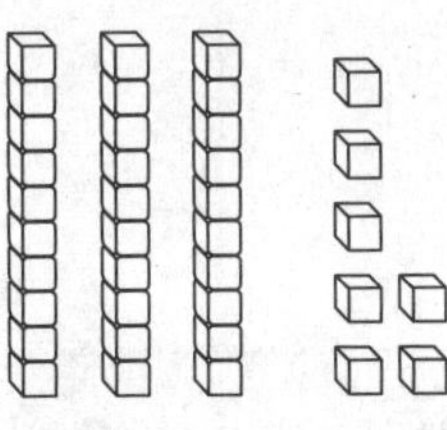
70 7

9. 22
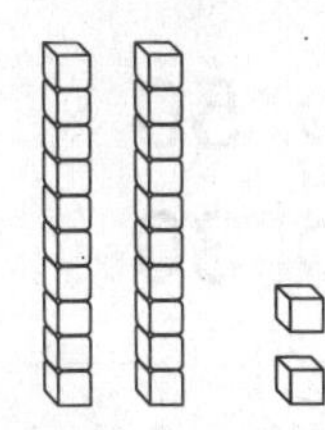
20 2

PROBLEM SOLVING

Write the 2-digit number that matches the clues.

10. My number has a tens digit that is 8 more than the ones digit. Zero is not one of my digits.

My number is ____.

Lesson Check (CC.2.NBT.3)

1. What is the value of the underlined digit?

3<u>2</u>

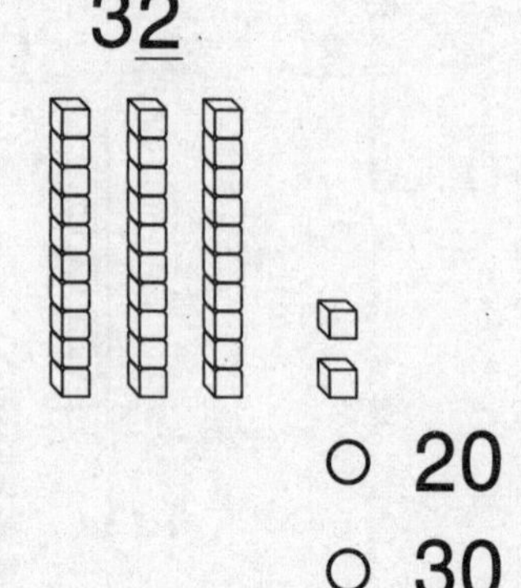

- ○ 2
- ○ 3
- ○ 20
- ○ 30

2. What is the value of the underlined digit?

<u>2</u>8

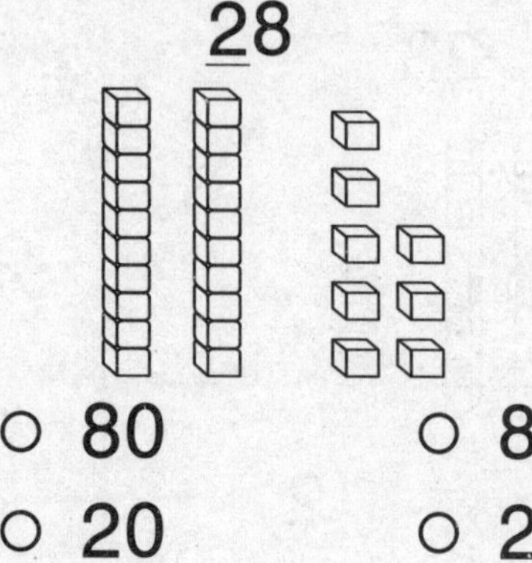

- ○ 80
- ○ 20
- ○ 8
- ○ 2

Spiral Review (CC.2.OA.3, CC.2.NBT.3)

3. What is the value of the underlined digit? (Lesson 1.3)

<u>5</u>3

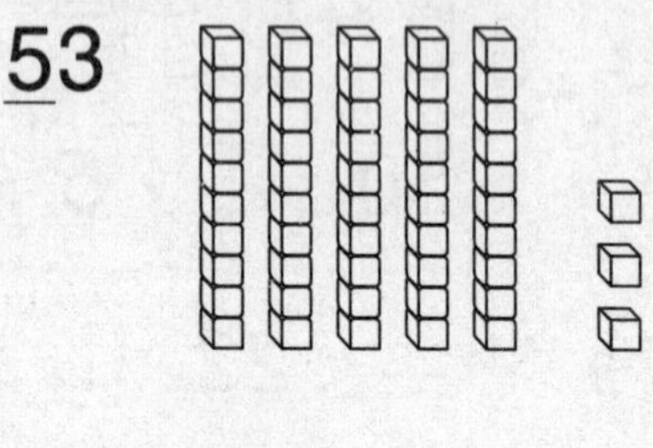

- ○ 50
- ○ 30
- ○ 8
- ○ 5

4. What is the value of the underlined digit? (Lesson 1.3)

2<u>4</u>

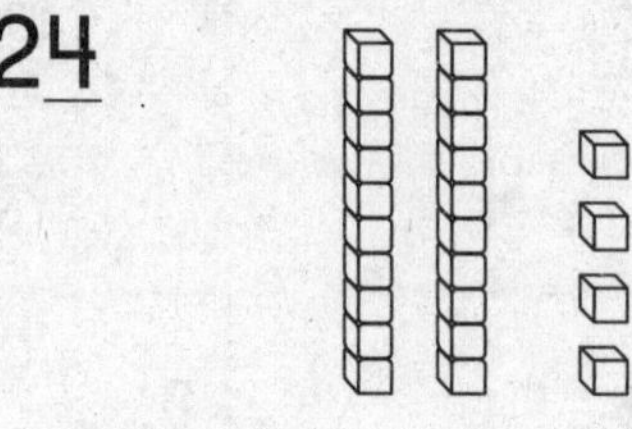

- ○ 40
- ○ 20
- ○ 6
- ○ 4

5. Which of these choices is an even number of pens and an odd number of pencils? (Lesson 1.1)

- ○ 7 pens 7 pencils
- ○ 5 pens 4 pencils
- ○ 2 pens 3 pencils
- ○ 2 pens 2 pencils

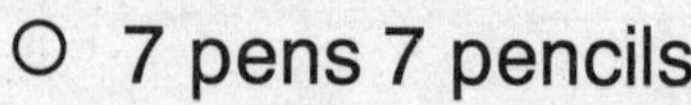

6. Which sum is an even number? (Lesson 1.2)

- ○ $5 + 2 = 7$
- ○ $6 + 3 = 9$
- ○ $7 + 4 = 11$
- ○ $7 + 7 = 14$

Name ___________________________________

Expanded Form

COMMON CORE STANDARD CC.2.NBT.3
Understand place value.

Draw a quick picture to show the number. Describe the number in two ways.

1. 68

____ tens ____ ones

____ + ____

2. 21

____ tens ____ one

____ + ____

3. 70

____ tens ____ ones

____ + ____

4. 53

____ tens ____ ones

____ + ____

5. 35

____ tens ____ ones

____ + ____

6. 47

____ tens ____ ones

____ + ____

PROBLEM SOLVING

7. Circle the ways to write the number shown by the model.

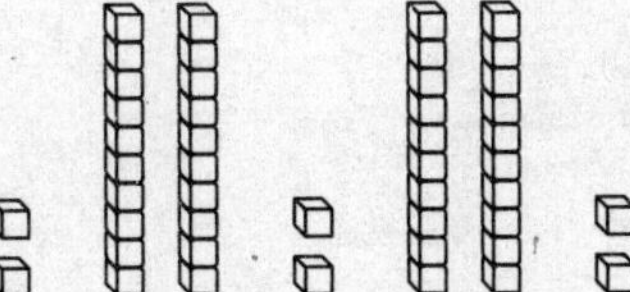

4 tens 6 ones	40 + 6	64
6 tens 4 ones	60 + 4	46

Lesson Check (CC.2.NBT.3)

1. Which is a way to describe the number 92?

○ 9 tens
○ 2 tens 9 ones
○ 9 tens 2 ones
○ 11 tens

2. Which is a way to describe the number 45?

○ 4 tens 5 ones
○ 5 tens 4 ones
○ 4 tens 0 ones
○ 4 tens 9 ones

Spiral Review (CC.2.NBT.3)

3. What is the value of the underlined digit? (Lesson 1.3)

<u>4</u>9

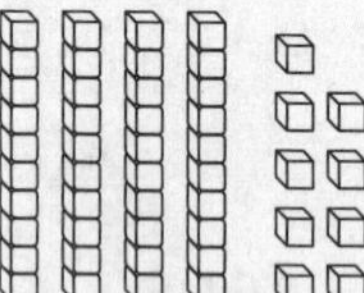

○ 90 ○ 9
○ 40 ○ 4

4. What is the value of the underlined digit? (Lesson 1.3)

3<u>4</u>

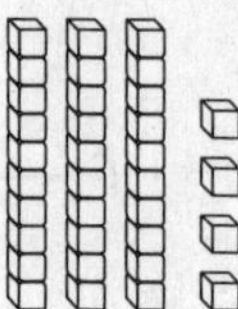

○ 40 ○ 4
○ 30 ○ 3

5. Which is another way to describe the number 76? (Lesson 1.4)

○ 7 tens
○ 6 tens 7 ones
○ 7 tens 6 ones
○ 7 tens 13 ones

6. Which is another way to describe the number 52? (Lesson 1.4)

○ 7 tens 2 ones
○ 2 tens 5 ones
○ 5 tens
○ 5 tens 2 ones

Name ____________________

Different Ways to Write Numbers

COMMON CORE STANDARD CC.2.NBT.3
Understand place value.

Write the number another way.

1. 32

____ tens ____ ones

2. forty-one

____

3. 9 tens 5 ones

____

4. 80 + 3

____

5. 57

____ tens ____ ones

6. seventy-two

____ + ____

7. 60 + 4

____

8. 4 tens 8 ones

____

9. twenty-eight

____ + ____

10. 80

____ tens ____ ones

PROBLEM SOLVING

11. A number has the digit 3 in the ones place and the digit 4 in the tens place. Which of these is another way to write this number? Circle it.

3 + 4　　40 + 3　　30 + 4

Lesson Check (CC.2.NBT.3)

1. Which is another way to write 3 tens 9 ones?
   - ○ 93
   - ○ 30 + 90
   - ○ 90 + 3
   - ○ 39

2. Which is another way to write the number eighteen?
   - ○ 8 + 1
   - ○ 81
   - ○ 10 + 8
   - ○ 10 + 80

Spiral Review (CC.2.NBT.3)

3. Which is another way to write the number 47? (Lesson 1.5)
   - ○ 70 + 4
   - ○ 40 + 7
   - ○ 4 + 7
   - ○ 40 + 70

4. Which is another way to write the number 95? (Lesson 1.5)
   - ○ 50 + 9
   - ○ 90 + 50
   - ○ fifty-nine
   - ○ ninety-five

5. What is the value of the underlined digit? (Lesson 1.3)

   6<u>1</u>

   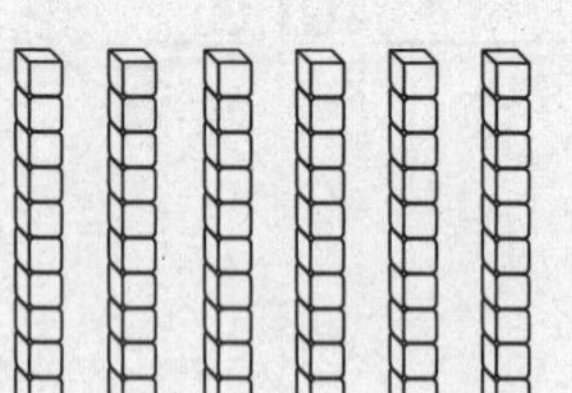

   - ○ 1
   - ○ 6
   - ○ 7
   - ○ 10

6. What is the value of the underlined digit? (Lesson 1.3)

   <u>1</u>7

   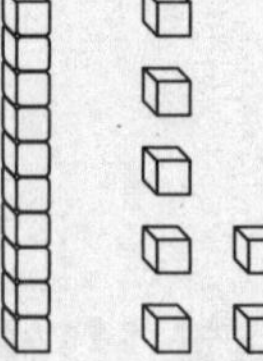

   - ○ 1
   - ○ 7
   - ○ 10
   - ○ 70

Name ______________________

Algebra • Different Names for Numbers

COMMON CORE STANDARD CC.2.NBT.3
Understand place value.

The blocks show the number in different ways. Describe the blocks in two ways.

1. 24

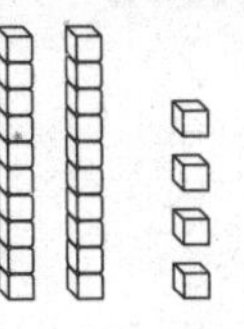

____ tens ____ ones

____ + ____

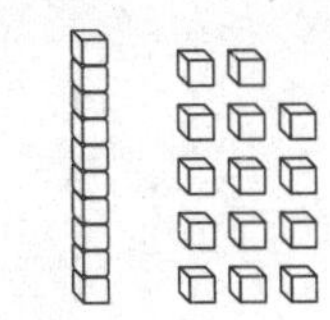

____ ten ____ ones

____ + ____

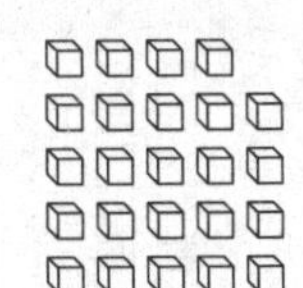

____ tens ____ ones

____ + ____

2. 36

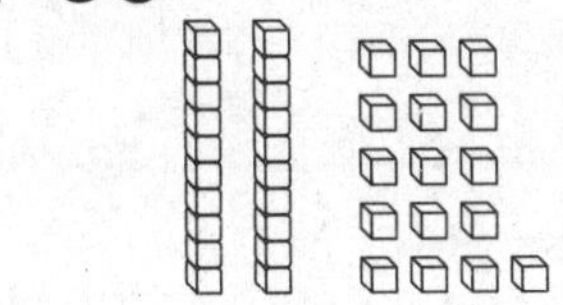

____ tens ____ ones

____ + ____

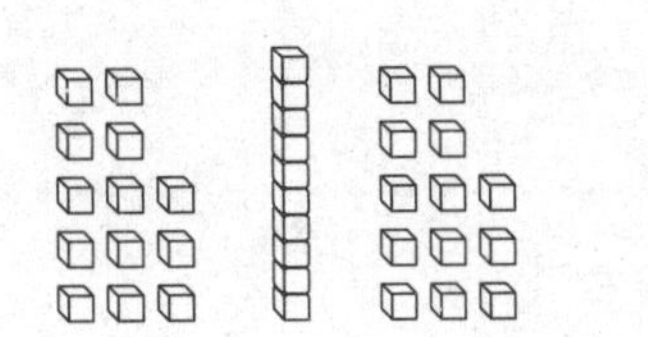

____ ten ____ ones

____ + ____

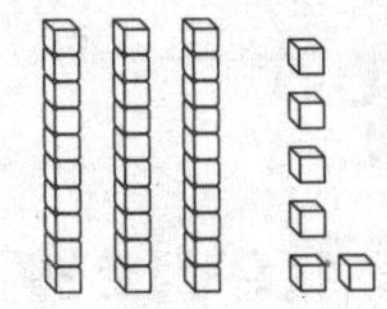

____ tens ____ ones

____ + ____

3. 45

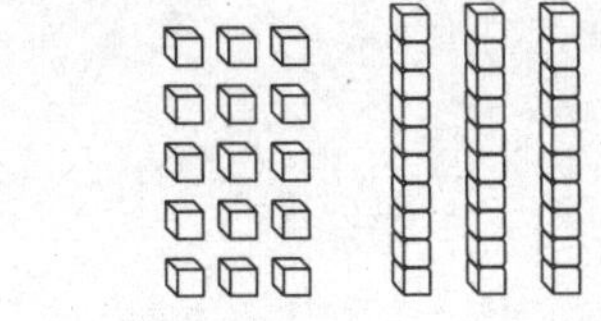

____ tens ____ ones

____ + ____

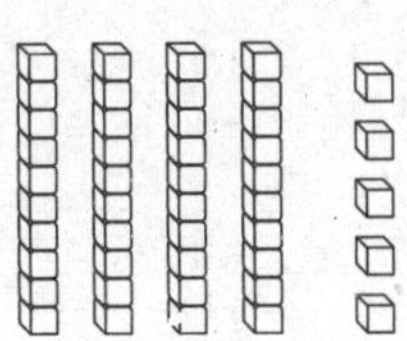

____ tens ____ ones

____ + ____

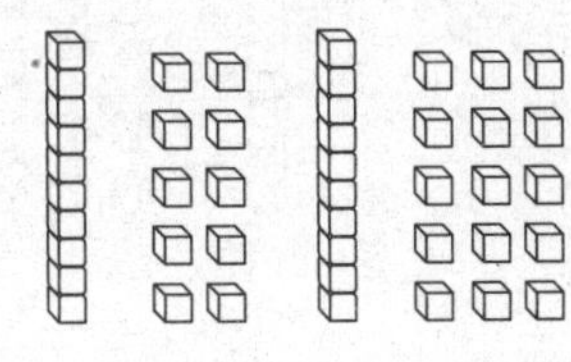

____ tens ____ ones

____ + ____

PROBLEM SOLVING

4. Toni has these blocks. Circle the blocks that she could use to show 34.

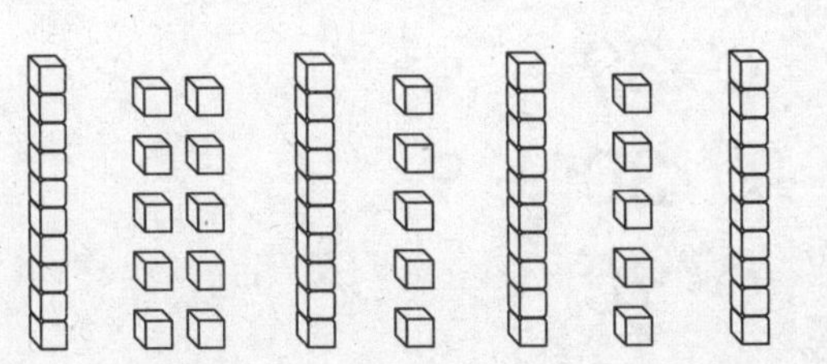

Lesson Check (CC.2.NBT.3)

1. What number is shown with the blocks?

2 tens 13 ones

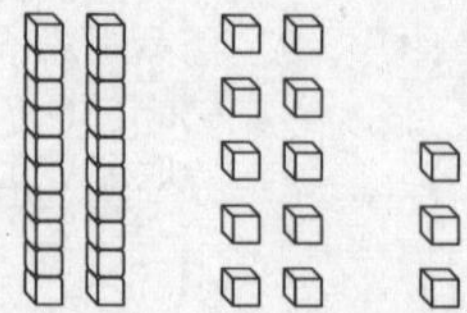

- ○ 33
- ○ 34
- ○ 43
- ○ 63

2. What number is shown with the blocks?

1 ten 16 ones

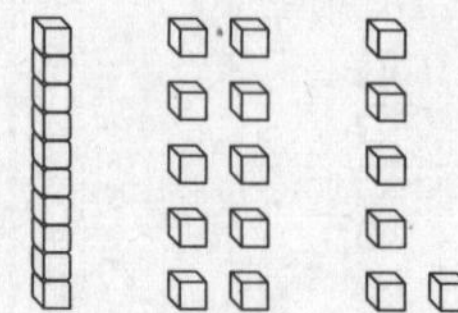

- ○ 16
- ○ 26
- ○ 31
- ○ 36

Spiral Review (CC.2.NBT.3)

3. What number is shown with the blocks? (Lesson 1.6)

1 ten 17 ones

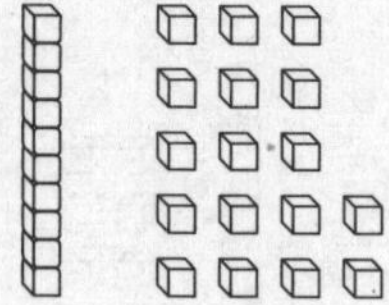

- ○ 17
- ○ 27
- ○ 42
- ○ 57

4. What is the value of the underlined digit? (Lesson 1.3)

2<u>9</u>

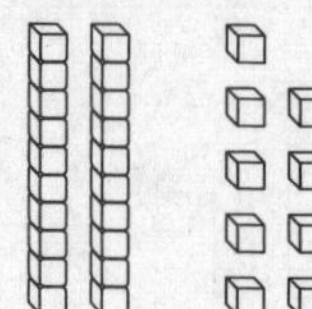

- ○ 2
- ○ 20
- ○ 9
- ○ 90

5. Which is another way to write 9 tens 3 ones? (Lesson 1.5)

- ○ 39
- ○ 30 + 9
- ○ 90
- ○ 93

6. How many tens and ones are in the number 50? (Lesson 1.4)

- ○ 0 tens 5 ones
- ○ 2 tens 3 ones
- ○ 5 tens 0 ones
- ○ 5 tens 5 ones

Name ______________________________

Problem Solving • Tens and Ones

COMMON CORE STANDARD CC.2.NBT.3
Understand place value.

Find a pattern to solve.

1. Ann is grouping 38 rocks. She can put them into groups of 10 rocks or as single rocks. What are the different ways Ann can group the rocks?

Groups of 10 rocks	Single rocks

2. Mr. Grant needs 30 pieces of felt. He can buy them in packs of 10 or as single pieces. What are the different ways Mr. Grant can buy the felt?

Packs of 10 pieces	Single pieces

3. Ms. Sims is putting away 22 books. She can put them on the table in stacks of 10 or as single books. What are the different ways Ms. Sims can put away the books?

Stacks of 10 books	Single books

TEST PREP

Lesson Check (CC.2.NBT.3)

1. Mrs. Chang is packing 38 apples. She can pack them in bags of 10 or as single apples. What choice is missing from the list of ways Mrs. Chang can pack the apples?

Bags of 10 apples	Single apples
2	18
1	28
0	38

- ○ 3 bags, 0 single apples
- ○ 1 bag, 18 single apples
- ○ 3 bags, 8 single apples
- ○ 4 bags, 8 single apples

Spiral Review (CC.2.NBT.3)

2. What is the value of the underlined digit? (Lesson 1.3)

<u>5</u>4

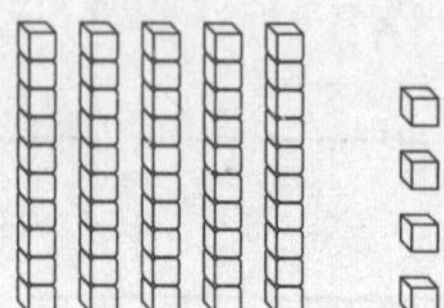

- ○ 50
- ○ 40
- ○ 5
- ○ 4

3. What number is shown with the blocks? (Lesson 1.6)

2 tens 19 ones

- ○ 21
- ○ 29
- ○ 34
- ○ 39

4. Which is another way to write the number 62? (Lesson 1.5)

- ○ 2 tens 6 ones
- ○ 20 + 6
- ○ sixty-two
- ○ 60 + 20

5. What number can be written as 8 tens 6 ones? (Lesson 1.5)

- ○ 68
- ○ 86
- ○ 114
- ○ 140

Name ______________________

Counting Patterns Within 100

COMMON CORE STANDARD CC.2.NBT.2
Understand place value.

Count by ones.

1. 58, 59, ____, ____, ____, ____, ____

Count by fives.

2. 45, 50, ____, ____, ____, ____, ____

3. 20, 25, ____, ____, ____, ____, ____

Count by tens.

4. 20, ____, ____, ____, ____, ____, ____

Count back by ones.

5. 87, 86, 85, ____, ____, ____

PROBLEM SOLVING

6. Tim counts his friends' fingers by fives. He counts the fingers on six hands. What numbers does he say?

   5, ____, ____, ____, ____, ____

Lesson Check (CC.2.NBT.2)

1. Which group of numbers shows counting by fives?

   - ○ 17, 18, 19, 20, 21
   - ○ 70, 75, 80, 85, 90
   - ○ 20, 30, 40, 50, 60
   - ○ 65, 64, 63, 62, 61

2. Which group of numbers shows counting by tens?

   - ○ 10, 11, 12, 13, 14
   - ○ 20, 25, 30, 35, 40
   - ○ 60, 70, 80, 90, 100
   - ○ 10, 9, 8, 7, 6

Spiral Review (CC.2.OA.3, CC.2.NBT.2, CC.2.NBT.3)

3. Which group of numbers shows counting back by ones? (Lesson 1.8)

   - ○ 21, 20, 19, 18, 17
   - ○ 25, 30, 35, 40, 45
   - ○ 88, 89, 90, 91, 92
   - ○ 30, 40, 50, 60, 70

4. A number is shown with 2 tens and 15 ones. Which of these is a way to write the number? (Lesson 1.6)

   - ○ fifteen
   - ○ twenty
   - ○ twenty-five
   - ○ thirty-five

5. Which of these is another way to describe 72? (Lesson 1.4)

   - ○ 70 + 20
   - ○ 70 + 2
   - ○ 20 + 7
   - ○ 7 + 2

6. What sum is an even number? (Lesson 1.2)

   - ○ 2 + 5 = 7
   - ○ 3 + 6 = 9
   - ○ 9 + 9 = 18
   - ○ 5 + 6 = 11

Name ______________________________

Counting Patterns Within 1,000

COMMON CORE STANDARD CC.2.NBT.2
Understand place value.

Count by fives.

1. 415, 420, ________, ________, ________, ________

2. 675, 680, ________, ________, ________, ________, ________

Count by tens.

3. 210, 220, ________, ________, ________, ________, ________

4. 840, 850, ________, ________, ________, ________, ________

Count by hundreds.

5. 300, 400, ________, ________, ________, ________, ________

Count back by ones.

6. 953, 952, ________, ________, ________, ________, ________

PROBLEM SOLVING

7. Lee has a jar of 100 pennies.
She adds groups of 10 pennies to the jar.
She adds 5 groups. What numbers does she say?

________, ________, ________, ________, ________

TEST PREP

Lesson Check (CC.2.NBT.2)

1. Which group of numbers shows counting by tens?
   - ○ 875, 870, 865, 860, 855
   - ○ 191, 192, 193, 194, 195
   - ○ 160, 170, 180, 190, 200
   - ○ 115, 120, 125, 130, 145

2. Which group of numbers shows counting by hundreds?
   - ○ 850, 860, 870, 880, 890
   - ○ 620, 625, 630, 635, 640
   - ○ 150, 149, 148, 147, 146
   - ○ 400, 500, 600, 700, 800

Spiral Review (CC.2.NBT.2, CC.2.NBT.3)

3. Which group of numbers shows counting by fives? (Lesson 1.9)
   - ○ 245, 250, 255, 260, 265
   - ○ 105, 104, 103, 102, 101
   - ○ 355, 455, 555, 655, 755
   - ○ 550, 560, 570, 580, 590

4. Which group of numbers shows counting back by ones? (Lesson 1.8)
   - ○ 17, 18, 19, 20, 21
   - ○ 71, 70, 69, 68, 67
   - ○ 25, 20, 15, 10, 5
   - ○ 40, 50, 60, 70, 80

5. Which is another way to describe 45? (Lesson 1.4)
   - ○ 45 tens 0 ones
   - ○ 9 tens 5 ones
   - ○ 5 tens 4 ones
   - ○ 4 tens 5 ones

6. Which is another way to write 7 tens 9 ones? (Lesson 1.5)
   - ○ ninety-seven
   - ○ eighty-nine
   - ○ 79
   - ○ 16

Name ______________________________

COMMON CORE STANDARDS CC.2.OA.3, CC.2.NBT.2, CC.2.NBT.3

Chapter 1 Extra Practice

Lesson 1.1 (pp. 13–16)

Shade in the ten frames to show the number.
Circle **even** or **odd**.

1. 17

even odd

2. 20

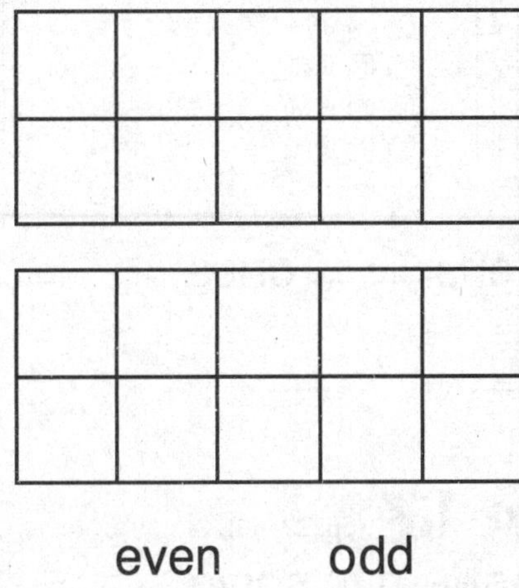

even odd

Lesson 1.3 (pp. 21–24)

Circle the value of the underlined digit.

1. 5<u>7</u>

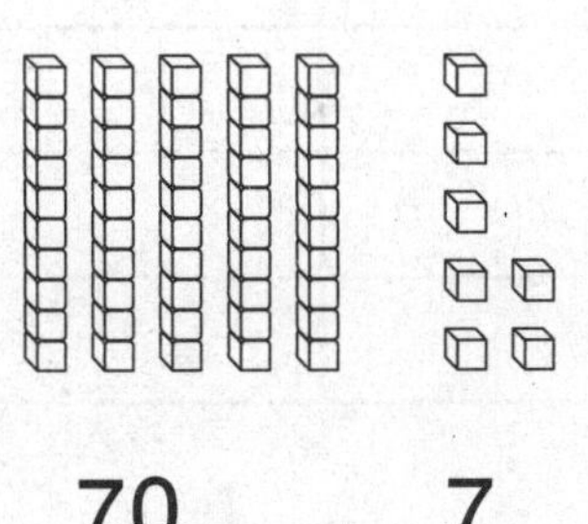

70 7

2. <u>9</u>3

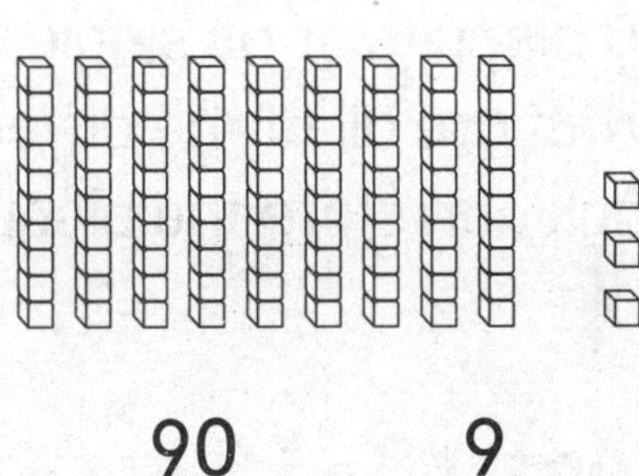

90 9

Lesson 1.4 (pp. 25–28)

Draw a quick picture to show the number.
Describe the number in two ways.

1. 22

_____ tens _____ ones

_____ + _____

2. 67

_____ tens _____ ones

_____ + _____

Lesson 1.6 (pp. 33–36)

The blocks show the numbers in different ways.
Describe the blocks in two ways.

1. 48

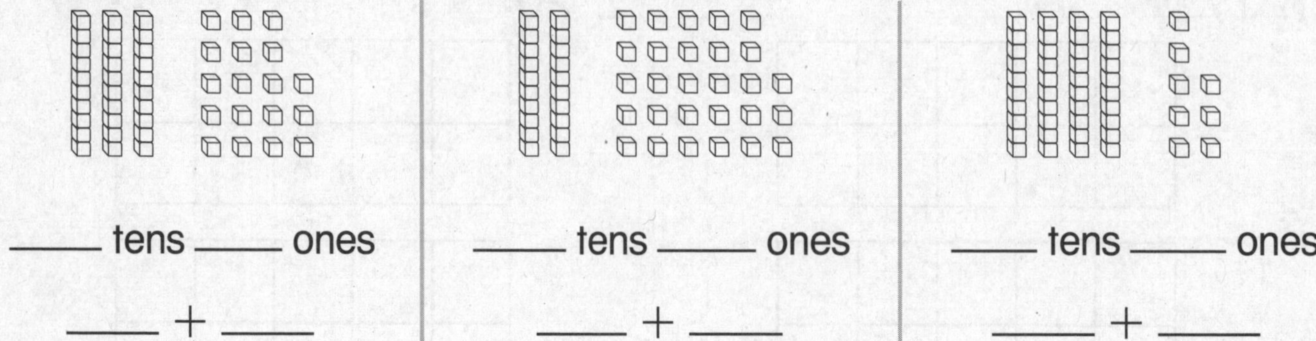

____ tens ____ ones	____ tens ____ ones	____ tens ____ ones
____ + ____	____ + ____	____ + ____

Lesson 1.7 (pp. 37–40)

Find a pattern to solve.

1. Jack baked 38 biscuits. He can store them in boxes of 10 biscuits or as single biscuits. What are all of the different ways Jack can store the biscuits?

Boxes of 10 biscuits	Single biscuits

Lessons 1.8 - 1.9 (pp. 41–48)

Count by tens.

1. 50, ______, ______, ______, ______, ______

Count back by ones.

2. 37, 36, 35, 34, ______, ______, ______

Count by fives.

3. 455, 460, ______, ______, ______, ______, ______

Count by hundreds.

4. 100, 200, ______, ______, ______, ______, ______

Chapter 2

School-Home Letter

Dear Family,

My class started Chapter 2 this week. I will learn about place value of numbers to 1,000. I will also learn about comparing these numbers.

Love, ____________________

Vocabulary

compare To describe whether numbers are equal to, less than, or greater than one another

hundred A group of 10 tens

is equal to 145 is equal to 145

= 145 = 145

is greater than 131 is greater than 121

> 131 > 121

is less than 125 is less than 185

< 125 < 185

thousand A group of 10 hundreds

Home Activity

Have your child look through magazines for 3-digit numbers and cut them out. Work together to write a word problem using two of these numbers, gluing the cut-out numbers in place. Have your child solve the problem.

Charles collected 127 leaves. Ann collected 240 leaves. Who collected the greater number of leaves?

Literature

Reading math stories reinforces learning. Look for these books in the library.

A Place for Zero
by Angeline Sparagna LoPresti and Phyllis Hornung. Charlesbridge Publishing, 2003.

More or Less
by Stuart J. Murphy. HarperCollins, 2005.

Capítulo 2

Carta para la casa

Querida familia:

Mi clase comenzó el Capítulo 2 esta semana. Aprenderé sobre el valor posicional de los números hasta 1,000. También aprenderé a comparar estos números.

Con cariño, ______________________

Vocabulario

comparar Describir si los números son iguales a, menores que o mayores que otro número

centena Un grupo de 10 decenas

es igual a 145 es igual a 145

= 145 = 145

es mayor que 131 es mayor que 121

> 131 >121

es menor que 125 es menor que 185

< 125 < 185

millar Un grupo de 10 centenas

Actividad para la casa

Pídale a su hijo que busque números de 3 dígitos en revistas y que los recorte. Luego, trabajen juntos para escribir un problema usando dos de estos números y péguenlos en algún lugar. Pídale a su hijo que resuelva el problema.

Carlos juntó 127 hojas.
Ana juntó 240 hojas.
¿Quién juntó el mayor número de hojas?

Literatura

Leer cuentos de matemáticas refuerza el aprendizaje. Busque estos libros en la biblioteca.

A Place for Zero
por Angeline Sparagna LoPresti and Phyllis Hornung.
Charlesbridge Publishing, 2003.

More or Less
por Stuart J. Murphy
HarperCollins, 2005.

Name ______________________

Group Tens as Hundreds

COMMON CORE STANDARDS CC.2.NBT.1a, CC.2.NBT.1b
Understand place value.

Write how many tens. Circle groups of 10 tens. Write how many hundreds. Write the number.

1. ______ tens
______ hundreds
______

2. ______ tens
______ hundreds
______

3. ______ tens
______ hundreds
______

PROBLEM SOLVING

Solve. Write or draw to explain.

4. Farmer Gray has 30 flowerpots. He plants 10 seeds in each pot. How many seeds does he plant?

______ seeds

Lesson Check (CC.2.NBT.1a, CC.2.NBT.1b)

1. Which number has the same value as 40 tens?
   - ○ 4010
   - ○ 400
   - ○ 40
   - ○ 4

2. Which number has the same value as 80 tens?
   - ○ 8
   - ○ 80
   - ○ 800
   - ○ 8010

Spiral Review (CC.2.OA.3, CC.2.NBT.2, CC.2.NBT.3)

3. Which of these is a way to show the number 63? (Lesson 1.6)
   - ○ 5 tens 13 ones
   - ○ 5 tens 3 ones
   - ○ 3 tens 6 ones
   - ○ 1 ten 63 ones

4. Which group of numbers shows counting by fives? (Lesson 1.8)
   - ○ 5, 6, 7, 8, 9
   - ○ 5, 10, 15, 20, 25
   - ○ 50, 60, 70, 80, 90
   - ○ 50, 51, 52, 53, 54

5. Carlos has 58 pencils. What is the value of the digit 5 in this number? (Lesson 1.3)
   - ○ 5
   - ○ 8
   - ○ 13
   - ○ 50

6. Which sum is an even number? (Lesson 1.2)
   - ○ $2 + 3 = 5$
   - ○ $4 + 4 = 8$
   - ○ $5 + 6 = 11$
   - ○ $8 + 7 = 15$

Name ______________________

Explore 3-Digit Numbers

COMMON CORE STANDARD CC.2.NBT.1
Understand place value.

Circle tens to make 1 hundred. Write the number in different ways.

1. 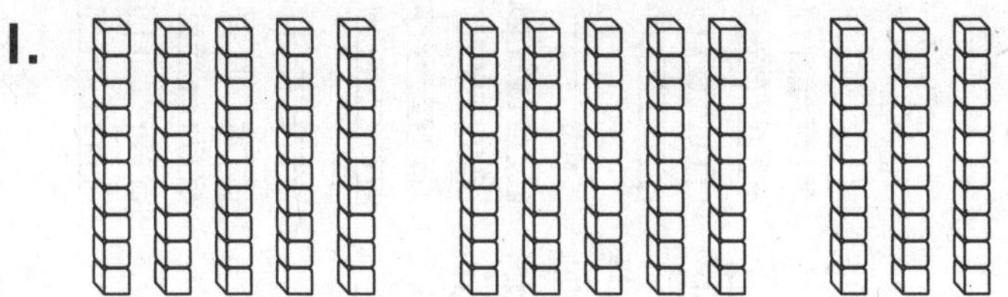

______ tens

______ hundred ______ tens

______

2. ______ tens

______ hundred ______ tens

______

3. 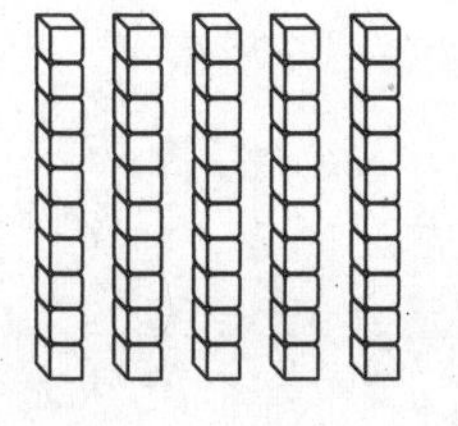

______ tens

______ hundred ______ tens

______

PROBLEM SOLVING

Solve. Write or draw to explain.

4. Millie has a box of 1 hundred cubes. She also has a bag of 70 cubes. How many trains of 10 cubes can she make?

______ trains of 10 cubes

Lesson Check (CC.2.NBT.1)

1. Which has the same value as 12 tens?

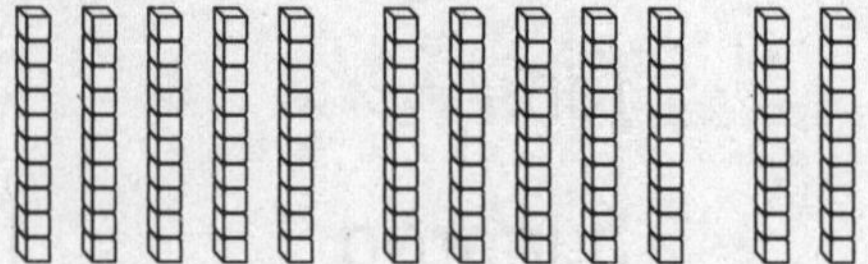

○ 2 hundreds 2 tens
○ 1 hundred 2 tens
○ 2 tens 1 one
○ 1 ten 2 ones

2. Which has the same value as 15 tens?

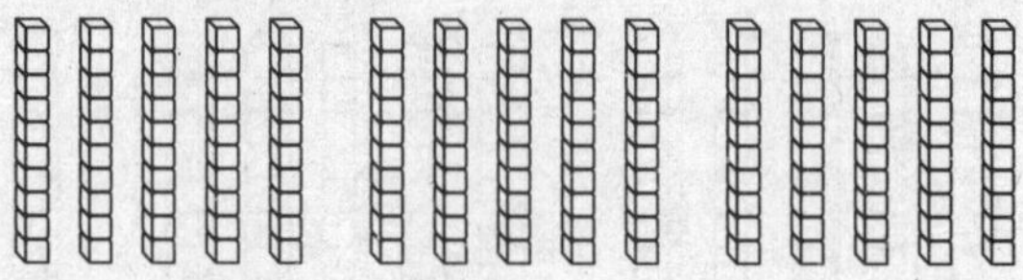

○ 1 ten 5 ones
○ 5 tens 1 one
○ 1 hundred 5 tens
○ 5 hundreds 1 ten

Spiral Review (CC.2.OA.3, CC.2.NBT.3)

3. Which of these is an odd number? (Lesson 1.1)

○ 18
○ 10
○ 9
○ 4

4. Which of these is a way to show the number 35? (Lesson 1.6)

○ 2 tens 15 ones
○ 3 tens 0 ones
○ 3 tens 15 ones
○ 5 tens 3 ones

5. Which of these is another way to describe 78? (Lesson 1.4)

○ 7 + 8
○ 70 + 8
○ 70 + 80
○ 80 + 7

6. Which is another way to write the number 55? (Lesson 1.5)

○ 15 + 5
○ 25
○ fifty
○ 5 tens 5 ones

Name ______________________________

HANDS ON
Lesson 2.3

Model 3-Digit Numbers

COMMON CORE STANDARD CC.2.NBT.1
Understand place value.

Write how many hundreds, tens, and ones.
Show with ▦ ▬ ▪. Then draw a quick picture.

1. 118

Hundreds	Tens	Ones

2. 246

Hundreds	Tens	Ones

3. 143

Hundreds	Tens	Ones

4. 237

Hundreds	Tens	Ones

PROBLEM SOLVING

5. Write the number that matches the clues.
   - My number has 2 hundreds.
   - The tens digit is 9 more than the ones digit.

   My number is ________.

Hundreds	Tens	Ones

Lesson Check (CC.2.NBT.1)

1. What number is shown with these blocks?

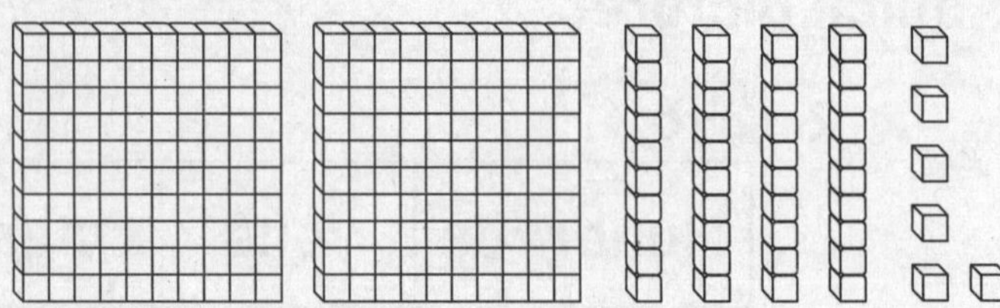

Hundreds	Tens	Ones

246 ○ 264 ○ 462 ○ 642 ○

Spiral Review (CC.2.OA.3, CC.2.NBT.1a, CC.2.NBT.1b, CC.2.NBT.3)

2. Which number has the same value as 28 tens? (Lesson 2.1)

○ 28
○ 280
○ 2800
○ 2810

3. Which of these is another way to describe 59? (Lesson 1.4)

○ 90 + 50
○ 90 + 5
○ 50 + 9
○ 5 + 9

4. Which of these is an odd number? (Lesson 1.1)

○ 11
○ 12
○ 18
○ 20

5. Which of these is a way to show the number 73? (Lesson 1.6)

○ 3 tens 7 ones
○ 7 tens 3 ones
○ 30 tens 7 ones
○ 70 tens 3 ones

Name ______________________________

Hundreds, Tens, and Ones

COMMON CORE STANDARD CC.2.NBT.1
Understand place value.

Write how many hundreds, tens, and ones are in the model. Write the number in two ways.

1.

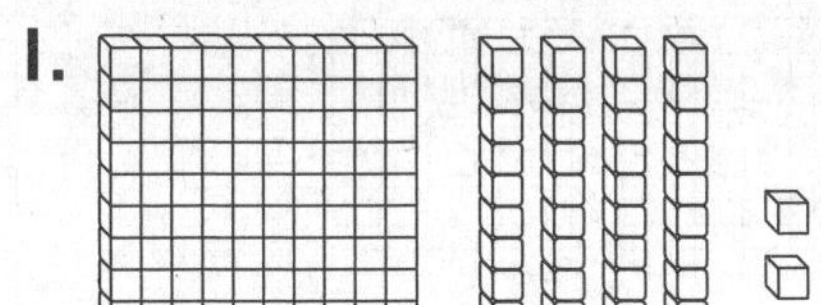

Hundreds	Tens	Ones

______

______ + ______ + ______

2.

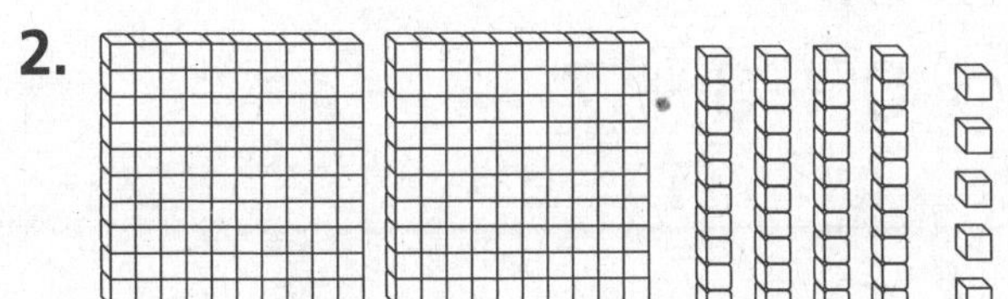

Hundreds	Tens	Ones

______

______ + ______ + ______

3.

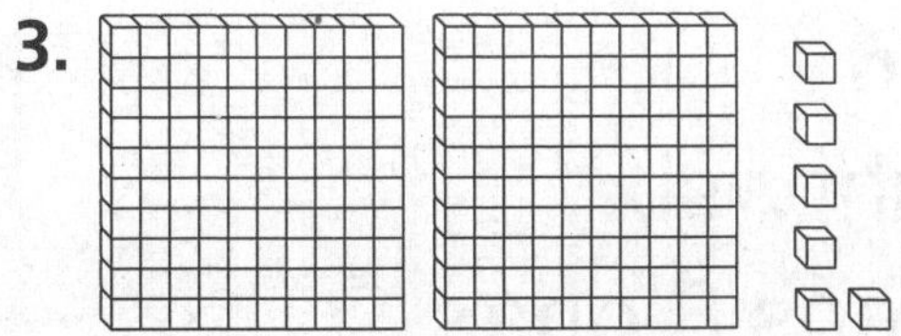

Hundreds	Tens	Ones

______

______ + ______ + ______

PROBLEM SOLVING

4. Write the number that answers the riddle. Use the chart.
A model for my number has 6 ones blocks, 2 hundreds blocks, and 3 tens blocks.
What number am I?

Hundreds	Tens	Ones

______

Lesson Check (CC.2.NBT.1)

1. Which is a way to write the number 254?

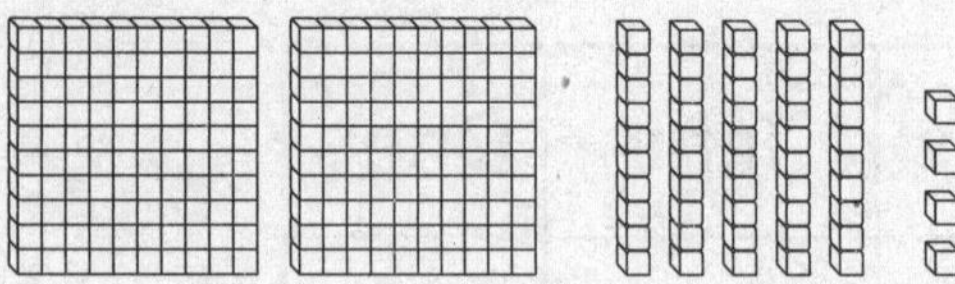

○ 200 + 50 + 4
○ 400 + 20 + 5
○ 400 + 50 + 2
○ 500 + 40 + 3

2. Which is a way to write the number 307?

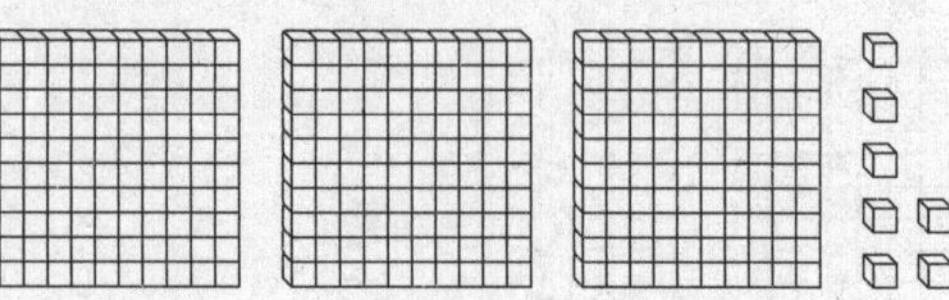

○ 700 + 30 + 0
○ 300 + 0 + 7
○ 30 + 70 + 0
○ 0 + 3 + 7

Spiral Review (CC.2.OA.3, CC.2.NBT.1a, CC.2.NBT.1b, CC.2.NBT.3)

3. Which of these is another way to describe 83? (Lesson 1.4)

○ 8 + 3
○ 8 + 30
○ 80 + 3
○ 80 + 30

4. Which is another way to write 86? (Lesson 1.5)

○ 806
○ eighty-six
○ 6 tens 8 ones
○ 8 + 6

5. Which number has the same value as 32 tens? (Lesson 2.1)

○ 32
○ 320
○ 3200
○ 3210

6. Which of these is an odd number? (Lesson 1.1)

○ 2
○ 6
○ 10
○ 17

Name ______________________________

Place Value to 1,000

COMMON CORE STANDARD CC.2.NBT.1
Understand place value.

Circle the value or the meaning of the underlined digit.

1. 3<u>3</u>7	3	30	300
2. 46<u>2</u>	200	20	2
3. <u>5</u>72	5	50	500
4. 56<u>7</u>	7 ones	7 tens	7 hundreds
5. <u>4</u>62	4 hundreds	4 ones	4 tens
6. <u>1</u>,000	1 ten	1 hundred	1 thousand

PROBLEM SOLVING

7. Write the 3-digit number that answers the riddle.
   - I have the same hundreds digit as ones digit.
   - The value of my tens digit is 50.
   - The value of my ones digit is 4. The number is ________.

Lesson Check (CC.2.NBT.1)

1. What is the value of the underlined digit?

   3̲15

   ○ 3
   ○ 30
   ○ 33
   ○ 300

2. What is the meaning of the underlined digit?

   64̲8

   ○ 4 ones
   ○ 4 tens
   ○ 4 hundreds
   ○ 4 thousands

Spiral Review (CC.2.OA.3, CC.2.NBT.1, CC.2.NBT.3)

3. Which number can be written as 40 + 5? (Lesson 1.4)

   ○ 4
   ○ 9
   ○ 45
   ○ 54

4. Which number has the same value as 14 tens? (Lesson 2.2)

   ○ 140
   ○ 104
   ○ 40
   ○ 14

5. Which of these is a way to show the number 26? (Lesson 1.6)

   ○ 6 tens 2 ones
   ○ 2 tens 2 ones
   ○ 1 ten 16 ones
   ○ 1 ten 6 ones

6. Which of these is an even number? (Lesson 1.1)

   ○ 7
   ○ 16
   ○ 21
   ○ 25

Name ______________________

Lesson 2.6

Number Names

COMMON CORE STANDARD CC.2.NBT.3
Understand place value.

Write the number.

1. two hundred thirty-two

____

2. five hundred forty-four

____

3. one hundred fifty-eight

____

4. nine hundred fifty

____

5. four hundred twenty

____

6. six hundred seventy-eight

____

Write the number using words.

7. 317

____

8. 457

____

PROBLEM SOLVING REAL WORLD

Circle the answer.

9. Six hundred twenty-six children attend Elm Street School. Which is another way to write this number?

266 626 662

Lesson Check (CC.2.NBT.3)

1. Which is another way to write the number 851?
   - ○ one hundred fifty-eight
   - ○ five hundred eighteen
   - ○ five hundred eighty-one
   - ○ eight hundred fifty-one

2. Which is another way to write the number two hundred sixty?
   - ○ 206
   - ○ 216
   - ○ 260
   - ○ 266

Spiral Review (CC.2.NBT.1, CC.2.NBT.2)

3. Which of these numbers has the digit 8 in the tens place? (Lesson 2.5)
   - ○ 280
   - ○ 468
   - ○ 508
   - ○ 819

4. What number is shown with these blocks? (Lesson 2.3)

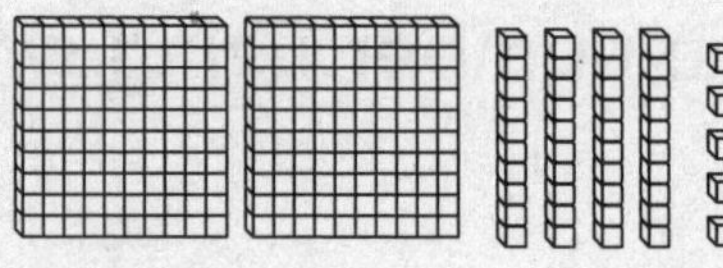

   - ○ 209
   - ○ 425
   - ○ 245
   - ○ 542

5. Which group of numbers shows counting by fives? (Lesson 1.9)
   - ○ 650, 655, 660, 665
   - ○ 555, 655, 755, 855
   - ○ 550, 560, 570, 580
   - ○ 540, 541, 542, 543

6. Sam has 128 marbles. How many hundreds are in this number? (Lesson 2.4)
   - ○ 110
   - ○ 100
   - ○ 10
   - ○ 1

Name ______________________

Different Forms of Numbers

COMMON CORE STANDARD CC.2.NBT.3
Understand place value.

Read the number and draw a quick picture. Then write the number in different ways.

1. two hundred fifty-one

____ hundreds ____ tens ____ one

______ + ______ + ______

______

2. three hundred twelve

____ hundreds ____ ten ____ ones

______ + ______ + ______

______

3. two hundred seven

____ hundreds ____ tens ____ ones

______ + ______ + ______

______

PROBLEM SOLVING

Write the number another way.

4. 200 + 30 + 7

______

5. 895

______

Lesson Check (CC.2.NBT.3)

1. Which is another way to write the number 392?

○ 300 + 90 + 2
○ 300 + 19 + 2
○ 200 + 90 + 3
○ 200 + 30 + 9

2. Which is another way to write the number 271?

○ 1 hundred 7 tens 2 ones
○ 2 hundreds 1 ten 7 ones
○ 2 hundreds 2 tens 7 ones
○ 2 hundreds 7 tens 1 one

Spiral Review (CC.2.NBT.1, CC.2.NBT.3)

3. What is the value of the underlined digit? (Lesson 1.3)

<u>5</u>6

○ 5
○ 6
○ 50
○ 60

4. What number is shown with these blocks? (Lesson 2.3)

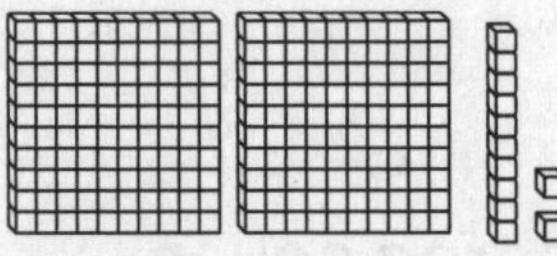

○ 221
○ 212
○ 210
○ 122

5. Which is another way to write the number 75? (Lesson 1.5)

○ 705
○ 70 + 5
○ seventy-one
○ 5 tens 7 ones

6. Which number can be written as 60 + 3? (Lesson 1.4)

○ 6
○ 9
○ 36
○ 63

Name ______________________________

Algebra • Different Ways to Show Numbers

COMMON CORE STANDARD CC.2.NBT.3
Understand place value.

Write how many hundreds, tens, and ones are in the model.

1. 135

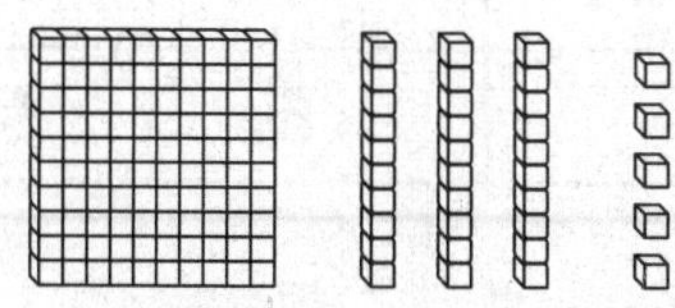

Hundreds	Tens	Ones

Hundreds	Tens	Ones

2. 216

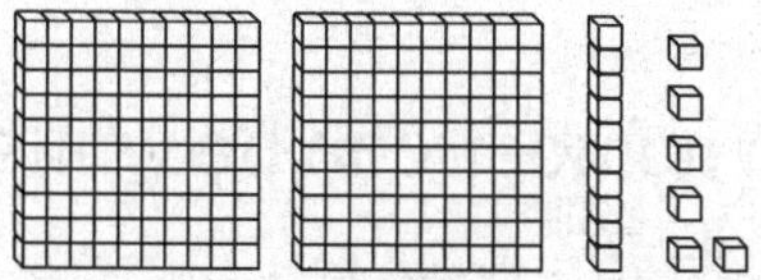

Hundreds	Tens	Ones

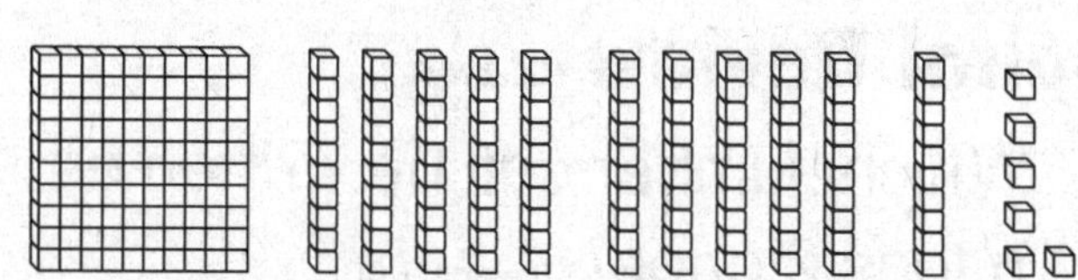

Hundreds	Tens	Ones

PROBLEM SOLVING

Markers are sold in boxes, packs, or as single markers. Each box has 10 packs. Each pack has 10 markers.

3. Draw pictures to show two ways to buy 276 markers.

TEST PREP

Lesson Check (CC.2.NBT.3)

1. Which of the following numbers can be shown with this many hundreds, tens, and ones?

Hundreds	Tens	Ones
1	2	18

- ○ 128
- ○ 129
- ○ 138
- ○ 148

2. Which of the following numbers can be shown with this many hundreds, tens, and ones?

Hundreds	Tens	Ones
2	15	6

- ○ 256
- ○ 266
- ○ 316
- ○ 356

Spiral Review (CC.2.NBT.3)

3. Which number can be written as 6 tens 2 ones? (Lesson 1.6)

- ○ 26
- ○ 62
- ○ 206
- ○ 602

4. Which number can be written as 30 + 2? (Lesson 1.4)

- ○ 302
- ○ 203
- ○ 32
- ○ 23

5. Which is another way to write the number 584? (Lesson 2.7)

- ○ five hundred eighty-four
- ○ 500 + 8 + 4
- ○ five hundred eighteen
- ○ 50 + 80 + 4

6. Which is another way to write the number 29? (Lesson 1.5)

- ○ 209
- ○ 9 tens 2 ones
- ○ 90 + 2
- ○ twenty-nine

Name ______________________

Count On and Count Back by 10 and 100

COMMON CORE STANDARD CC.2.NBT.8
Use place value understanding and properties of operations to add and subtract.

Write the number.

1. 10 more than 451 ______	2. 10 less than 770 ______
3. 100 more than 367 ______	4. 100 less than 895 ______
5. 10 less than 812 ______	6. 100 more than 543 ______
7. 10 more than 218 ______	8. 100 more than 379 ______
9. 100 less than 324 ______	10. 10 less than 829 ______

PROBLEM SOLVING

Solve. Write or draw to explain.

11. Sarah has 128 stickers. Alex has 10 fewer stickers than Sarah. How many stickers does Alex have?

______ stickers

TEST PREP

Lesson Check (CC.2.NBT.8)

1. Which number is 10 less than 526?

   ○ 536
   ○ 516
   ○ 426
   ○ 416

2. Which number is 100 more than 487?

   ○ 387
   ○ 477
   ○ 497
   ○ 587

Spiral Review (CC.2.NBT.1, CC.2.NBT.3)

3. Which has the same value as 14 tens? (Lesson 2.2)

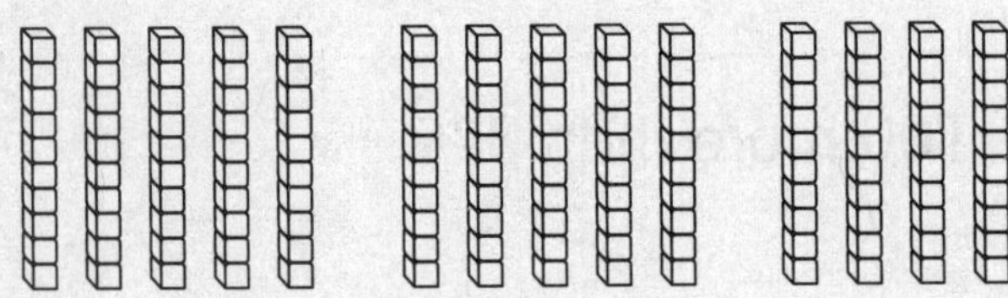

   ○ 1 ten 4 ones
   ○ 1 ten 9 ones
   ○ 1 hundred 4 tens
   ○ 1 hundred 9 tens

4. What is the value of the underlined digit? (Lesson 2.5)

   5<u>8</u>7

   ○ 8
   ○ 80
   ○ 88
   ○ 800

5. Which number can be written as 30 + 5? (Lesson 1.4)

   ○ 93
   ○ 80
   ○ 53
   ○ 35

6. Which number can be written as 9 tens and 1 one? (Lesson 1.6)

   ○ 91
   ○ 90
   ○ 19
   ○ 10

Name ______________________________

Algebra • Number Patterns

COMMON CORE STANDARD CC.2.NBT.8
Use place value understanding and properties of operations to add and subtract.

Look at the digits to find the next two numbers.

1. 232, 242, 252, 262, ☐, ☐

   The next two numbers are ________ and ________.

2. 185, 285, 385, 485, ☐, ☐

   The next two numbers are ________ and ________.

3. 428, 528, 628, 728, ☐, ☐

   The next two numbers are ________ and ________.

4. 654, 664, 674, 684, ☐, ☐

   The next two numbers are ________ and ________.

5. 333, 433, 533, 633, ☐, ☐

   The next two numbers are ________ and ________.

PROBLEM SOLVING

6. What are the missing numbers in the pattern?

   431, 441, 451, 461, ☐, 481, 491, ☐

   The missing numbers are ________ and ________.

TEST PREP

Lesson Check (CC.2.NBT.8)

1. What is the next number in this pattern?

   453, 463, 473, 483, ■

   ○ 484
   ○ 493
   ○ 494
   ○ 583

2. What is the next number in this pattern?

   295, 395, 495, 595, ■

   ○ 395
   ○ 596
   ○ 605
   ○ 695

Spiral Review (CC.2.NBT.1, CC.2.NBT.3)

3. Which is a way to write the number seven hundred fifty-one? (Lesson 2.6)

   ○ 751
   ○ 750
   ○ 715
   ○ 705

4. What is the value of the underlined digit? (Lesson 2.5)

   <u>1</u>95

   ○ 1
   ○ 10
   ○ 100
   ○ 1,000

5. Which is another way to write 56? (Lesson 1.5)

   ○ 506
   ○ sixty-five
   ○ 50 + 6
   ○ 5 tens 5 ones

6. Which of these is a way to show the number 43? (Lesson 1.6)

   ○ 3 tens 4 ones
   ○ 4 tens 3 ones
   ○ 4 tens 13 ones
   ○ 40 tens 3 ones

Name ______________________________

Problem Solving • Compare Numbers

PROBLEM SOLVING
Lesson 2.11

COMMON CORE STANDARD CC.2.NBT.4
Understand place value.

Model the numbers. Draw quick pictures to show how you solved the problem.

1. Lauryn has 128 marbles. Kristin has 118 marbles. Who has more marbles?

____

2. Nick has 189 trading cards. Kyle has 198 trading cards. Who has fewer cards?

____

3. A piano has 36 black keys and 52 white keys. Are there more black keys or white keys on a piano?

____

4. There are 253 cookies in a bag. There are 266 cookies in a box. Are there fewer cookies in the bag or in the box?

____

TEST PREP

Lesson Check (CC.2.NBT.4)

1. Gina has 245 stickers. Which of these numbers is less than 245?
   - ○ 285
   - ○ 254
   - ○ 245
   - ○ 239

2. Carl's book has 176 pages. Which of these numbers is greater than 176?
   - ○ 203
   - ○ 174
   - ○ 168
   - ○ 139

Spiral Review (CC.2.NBT.1, CC.2.NBT.3)

3. Which of these is another way to describe 63? (Lesson 1.4)
   - ○ 60 + 3
   - ○ 6 + 3
   - ○ 30 + 6
   - ○ 30 + 60

4. Which of these is a way to show the number 58? (Lesson 1.6)
   - ○ 80 tens 5 ones
   - ○ 50 tens 8 ones
   - ○ 8 tens 5 ones
   - ○ 5 tens 8 ones

5. Mr. Ford drove 483 miles during his trip. How many hundreds are in this number? (Lesson 2.4)
   - ○ 3
   - ○ 4
   - ○ 8
   - ○ 15

6. Which is another way to write 20? (Lesson 1.5)
   - ○ 202
   - ○ 2 tens 2 ones
   - ○ twenty
   - ○ 2 + 0

Name ____________________

Algebra • Compare Numbers

COMMON CORE STANDARD CC.2.NBT.4
Understand place value.

Compare the numbers. Write >, <, or =.

1. 489
   605

   489 ◯ 605

2. 719
   719

   719 ◯ 719

3. 370
   248

   370 ◯ 248

4. 645
   654

   645 ◯ 654

5. 205
   250

   205 ◯ 250

6. 813
   781

   813 ◯ 781

7. 397
   393

   397 ◯ 393

8. 504
   405

   504 ◯ 405

PROBLEM SOLVING

Solve. Write or draw to explain.

9. Toby has 178 pennies.
   Bella has 190 pennies.
   Who has more pennies?

   ____________ has more pennies.

Lesson Check (CC.2.NBT.4)

1. Which of the following is true?
   - ○ $123 > 456$
   - ○ $135 = 531$
   - ○ $315 < 351$
   - ○ $331 = 313$

2. Which of the following is true?
   - ○ $325 < 254$
   - ○ $401 > 399$
   - ○ $476 > 611$
   - ○ $724 = 742$

Spiral Review (CC.2.OA.3, CC.2.NBT.1, CC.2.NBT.1a, CC.2.NBT.1b, CC.2.NBT.2)

3. Which number has the same value as 50 tens? (Lesson 2.1)
   - ○ 5010
   - ○ 500
   - ○ 50
   - ○ 5

4. Which number has an 8 in the hundreds place? (Lesson 2.5)
   - ○ 44
   - ○ 358
   - ○ 782
   - ○ 816

5. Ned counts by fives. He starts at 80. Which number should he say next? (Lesson 1.8)
   - ○ 805
   - ○ 90
   - ○ 85
   - ○ 75

6. Mr. Dean has an even number of cats and an odd number of dogs. Which of these choices could tell about his pets? (Lesson 1.1)
   - ○ 6 cats and 3 dogs
   - ○ 4 cats and 2 dogs
   - ○ 3 cats and 6 dogs
   - ○ 3 cats and 5 dogs

Name ___________________________

COMMON CORE STANDARDS CC.2.NBT.1, CC.2.NBT.1a, CC.2.NBT.1b, CC.2.NBT.3, CC.2.NBT.4, CC.2.NBT.8

Chapter 2 Extra Practice

Lesson 2.2 (pp. 61 – 64)

Circle tens to make 1 hundred. Write the number in different ways.

1. 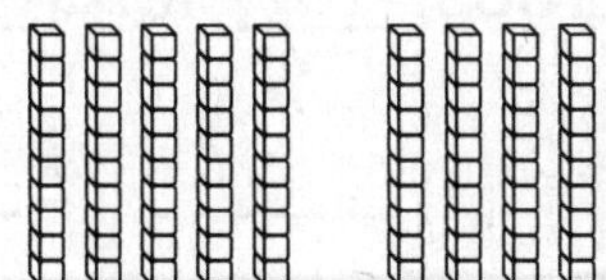

_______ tens

_______ hundred _______ tens

____

Lesson 2.3 (pp. 65 – 68)

Write how many hundreds, tens, and ones. Draw a quick picture.

1. 214

Hundreds	Tens	Ones

2. 125

Hundreds	Tens	Ones

Lesson 2.4 (pp. 69 – 72)

Write how many hundreds, tens, and ones are in the model. Write the number in two ways.

1. 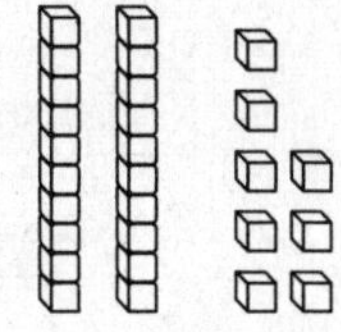

Hundreds	Tens	Ones

____

_______ + _______ + _______

Lesson 2.6 (pp. 77 – 80)

Write the number using words.

1. 643

____

Lesson 2.7 (pp. 81 – 83)

Read the number and draw a quick picture.
Then write the number in different ways.

1. two hundred sixty-nine

_____ hundreds _____ tens _____ ones

_______ + _______ + _______

____

Lesson 2.9 (pp. 89 – 92)

Write the number.

1. 10 more than 543

____

2. 100 less than 256

____

Lesson 2.10 (pp. 93 – 96)

Look at the digits to find the next two numbers.

1. 577, 587, 597, 607, ☐, ☐

The next two numbers are _______ and _______.

2. 494, 594, 694, 794, ☐, ☐

The next two numbers are _______ and _______.

Lesson 2.12 (pp. 101 – 104)

Compare the numbers. Write >, <, or =.

1. 312
321

312 ◯ 321

2. 233
219

233 ◯ 219

Chapter 3

School-Home Letter

Dear Family,

My class started Chapter 3 this week. In this chapter, we will use different ways to practice our basic addition and subtraction facts.

Love, ____________________

Vocabulary

addend 4 + 5 = 9
The addends are **4** and **5**.

sum 4 + 5 = 9
The sum is **9**.

difference 12 − 4 = 8
The difference is **8**.

Home Activity

Write 5 addition problems (with sums through 10) on individual slips of paper. Write their sums on separate slips. Have your child choose a sum and then match it to the correct addition problem. Repeat until all the problems have been matched correctly with sums.

Literature

Reading math stories reinforces ideas. Look for these books at the library.

Cats Add Up
by Marilyn Burns and Dianne Ochiltree. Cartwheel Books, 1998.

Each Orange Had 8 Slices
by Paul Giganti. HarperTrophy, 1999.

Capítulo 3

Carta para la casa

Querida familia:

Mi clase comenzó el Capítulo 3 esta semana. En este capítulo, usaremos diferentes modos de practicar nuestras operaciones básicas de suma y resta.

Con cariño, ______________________________

Vocabulario

sumando 4 + 5 = 9
Los sumandos son **4** y **5**.

suma 4 + 5 = 9
La suma es **9**.

diferencia 12 − 4 = 8
La diferencia es **8**.

Actividad para la casa

Escriba 5 problemas de suma (con sumas hasta 10) en diferentes pedazos de papel. Escriba los totales en papeles diferentes. Pídale a su hijo que elija un total y lo haga coincidir con el problema correcto. Repita los pasos hasta que todos los problemas concuerden con los totales.

Literatura

Leer cuentos de matemáticas refuerza los conceptos. Busque estos libros en la biblioteca.

Cats Add Up
por Marilyn Burns y Dianne Ochiltree.
Cartwheel Books, 1998.

Each Orange Had 8 Slices
por Paul Giganti.
HarperTrophy, 1999.

Name ______________________

Use Doubles Facts

COMMON CORE STANDARD CC.2.OA.2
Add and subtract within 20.

Write a doubles fact you can use to find the sum. Write the sum.

1. 2 + 3 = ____

____ + ____ = ____

2. 7 + 6 = ____

____ + ____ = ____

3. 3 + 4 = ____

____ + ____ = ____

4. 8 + 9 = ____

____ + ____ = ____

5. 6 + 5 = ____

____ + ____ = ____

6. 4 + 5 = ____

____ + ____ = ____

PROBLEM SOLVING

Solve. Write or draw to explain.

7. There are 6 ants on a log. Then 7 ants crawl onto the log. How many ants are on the log now?

______ ants

Lesson Check (CC.2.OA.2)

1. What is the sum?

$4 + 3 = \_\_\_\_$

- ○ 3
- ○ 4
- ○ 6
- ○ 7

2. What is the sum?

$6 + 7 = \_\_\_\_$

- ○ 13
- ○ 12
- ○ 7
- ○ 6

Spiral Review (CC.2.OA.3, CC.2.NBT.1, CC.2.NBT.3, CC.2.NBT.4)

3. There are 451 children in Lia's school. Which of these numbers is greater than 451? (Lesson 2.11)

- ○ 511
- ○ 415
- ○ 399
- ○ 154

4. What number is shown with these blocks? (Lesson 2.8)

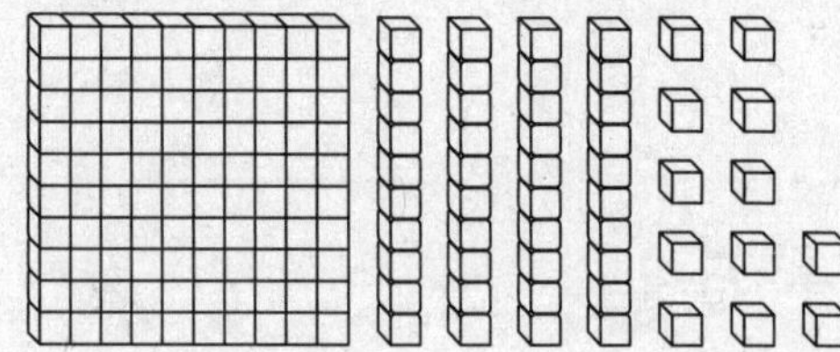

- ○ 112
- ○ 142
- ○ 152
- ○ 162

5. Which of these numbers has the digit 8 in the tens place? (Lesson 2.5)

- ○ 18
- ○ 278
- ○ 483
- ○ 864

6. Which sum is an even number? (Lesson 1.2)

- ○ $2 + 3 = 5$
- ○ $3 + 4 = 7$
- ○ $4 + 5 = 9$
- ○ $6 + 6 = 12$

Name ______________________

Practice Addition Facts

COMMON CORE STANDARD CC.2.OA.2
Add and subtract within 20.

Write the sums.

1. 9 + 1 = ____ 1 + 9 = ____	2. 7 + 6 = ____ 6 + 7 = ____	3. 8 + 0 = ____ 5 + 0 = ____
4. ____ = 7 + 9 ____ = 9 + 7	5. 4 + 4 = ____ 4 + 5 = ____	6. 9 + 9 = ____ 9 + 8 = ____
7. 8 + 8 = ____ 8 + 7 = ____	8. 2 + 2 = ____ 2 + 3 = ____	9. ____ = 6 + 3 ____ = 3 + 6
10. 6 + 6 = ____ 6 + 7 = ____	11. ____ = 0 + 7 ____ = 0 + 9	12. 5 + 5 = ____ 5 + 6 = ____
13. 8 + 5 = ____ 5 + 8 = ____	14. 8 + 2 = ____ 2 + 8 = ____	15. 7 + 4 = ____ 4 + 7 = ____

PROBLEM SOLVING

Solve. Write or draw to explain.

16. Jason has 7 puzzles. Quincy has the same number of puzzles as Jason. How many puzzles do they have altogether?

____ puzzles

Lesson Check (CC.2.OA.2)

1. What is the sum?

   8 + 7 = ____

   ○ 15
   ○ 14
   ○ 12
   ○ 11

2. What is the sum?

   2 + 9 = ____

   ○ 7
   ○ 11
   ○ 12
   ○ 13

Spiral Review (CC.2.NBT.2, CC.2.NBT.3, CC.2.NBT.4, CC.2.NBT.8)

3. Which is another way to describe 43? (Lesson 1.4)

   ○ 40 + 3
   ○ 30 + 4
   ○ 4 + 3
   ○ 40 + 30

4. Which number is 100 more than 276? (Lesson 2.9)

   ○ 176
   ○ 286
   ○ 376
   ○ 672

5. Which group of numbers shows counting by tens? (Lesson 1.8)

   ○ 10, 11, 12, 13, 14
   ○ 15, 20, 25, 30, 35
   ○ 20, 30, 40, 50, 60
   ○ 60, 59, 58, 57, 56

6. Which of the following is true? (Lesson 2.12)

   ○ 127 > 142
   ○ 142 < 127
   ○ 127 = 142
   ○ 127 < 142

Name ______________________________

Algebra • Make a Ten to Add

COMMON CORE STANDARD CC.2.OA.2
Add and subtract within 20.

Show how you can make a ten to find the sum. Write the sum.

1. 9 + 7 = ____
   (7 broken into 1 and 6)
   10 + ____ = ____

2. 8 + 5 = ____
   10 + ____ = ____

3. 8 + 6 = ____
   10 + ____ = ____

4. 3 + 9 = ____
   10 + ____ = ____

5. 8 + 7 = ____
   10 + ____ = ____

6. 6 + 5 = ____
   10 + ____ = ____

7. 7 + 6 = ____
   10 + ____ = ____

8. 5 + 9 = ____
   10 + ____ = ____

PROBLEM SOLVING

Solve. Write or draw to explain.

9. There are 9 children on the bus. Then 8 more children get on the bus. How many children are on the bus now?

____ children

Lesson Check (CC.2.OA.2)

1. Which has the same sum as 8 + 7?

   ○ 10 + 3
   ○ 10 + 4
   ○ 10 + 5
   ○ 10 + 6

2. Which has the same sum as 7 + 5?

   ○ 10 + 1
   ○ 10 + 2
   ○ 10 + 3
   ○ 10 + 4

Spiral Review (CC.2.OA.3, CC.2.NBT.3)

3. Which number can be written as 200 + 10 + 7? (Lesson 2.7)

   ○ 207
   ○ 210
   ○ 217
   ○ 271

4. Which of these is an odd number? (Lesson 1.1)

   ○ 2
   ○ 4
   ○ 6
   ○ 7

5. What is the value of the underlined digit? (Lesson 1.3)

   $\underline{6}5$

   ○ 60
   ○ 50
   ○ 10
   ○ 6

6. Which is another way to write the number 47? (Lesson 1.5)

   ○ 40 + 70
   ○ seventy-four
   ○ 4 tens 7 ones
   ○ 4 + 7

Name ______________________

Algebra • Add 3 Addends

COMMON CORE STANDARD CC.2.OA.2
Add and subtract within 20.

Solve two ways. Circle the two addends you add first.

1. $2 + 3 + 7 =$ ____ $2 + 3 + 7 =$ ____

2. $5 + 3 + 3 =$ ____ $5 + 3 + 3 =$ ____

3. $4 + 5 + 4 =$ ____ $4 + 5 + 4 =$ ____

4. $4 + 4 + 4 =$ ____ $4 + 4 + 4 =$ ____

5.
$$\begin{array}{r} 5 \\ 4 \\ +\ 5 \\ \hline \end{array} \qquad \begin{array}{r} 5 \\ 4 \\ +\ 5 \\ \hline \end{array}$$

6.
$$\begin{array}{r} 6 \\ 3 \\ +\ 4 \\ \hline \end{array} \qquad \begin{array}{r} 6 \\ 3 \\ +\ 4 \\ \hline \end{array}$$

PROBLEM SOLVING

Choose a way to solve. Write or draw to explain.

7. Amber has 2 red crayons, 5 blue crayons, and 4 yellow crayons. How many crayons does she have in all?

____ crayons

Lesson Check (CC.2.OA.2)

1. What is the sum of
   2 + 4 + 6?
   - ○ 6
   - ○ 8
   - ○ 10
   - ○ 12

2. What is the sum of
   5 + 4 + 2?
   - ○ 11
   - ○ 9
   - ○ 7
   - ○ 6

Spiral Review (CC.2.NBT.1a, CC.2.NBT.1b, CC.2.NBT.3, CC.2.NBT.4, CC.2.NBT.8)

3. Which of the following is true? (Lesson 2.12)
   - ○ 264 < 246
   - ○ 688 > 648
   - ○ 234 = 233
   - ○ 825 < 725

4. Which number can be written as 4 tens 2 ones? (Lesson 1.6)
   - ○ 12
   - ○ 14
   - ○ 24
   - ○ 42

5. Which number has the same value as 50 tens? (Lesson 2.1)
   - ○ 5
   - ○ 50
   - ○ 500
   - ○ 505

6. What is the next number in the pattern? (Lesson 2.10)

   420, 520, 620, 720, 
   - ○ 820
   - ○ 850
   - ○ 920
   - ○ 980

Name ___

Algebra • Relate Addition and Subtraction

COMMON CORE STANDARD CC.2.OA.2
Add and subtract within 20.

Write the sum and the difference for the related facts.

1. $9 + 6 =$ ___ $15 - 6 =$ ___	2. $8 + 5 =$ ___ $13 - 5 =$ ___	3. $9 + 9 =$ ___ $18 - 9 =$ ___
4. $7 + 3 =$ ___ $10 - 3 =$ ___	5. $7 + 5 =$ ___ $12 - 5 =$ ___	6. $6 + 8 =$ ___ $14 - 6 =$ ___
7. $6 + 7 =$ ___ $13 - 6 =$ ___	8. $8 + 8 =$ ___ $16 - 8 =$ ___	9. $6 + 4 =$ ___ $10 - 4 =$ ___
10. $7 + 9 =$ ___ $16 - 9 =$ ___	11. $9 + 4 =$ ___ $13 - 9 =$ ___	12. $8 + 7 =$ ___ $15 - 7 =$ ___

PROBLEM SOLVING

Solve. Write or draw to explain.

13. There are 13 children on the bus. Then 5 children get off the bus. How many children are on the bus now?

___ children

Lesson Check (CC.2.OA.2)

1. Which is a related addition fact for 15 − 6 = 9?

   ○ 9 + 6 = 15
   ○ 3 + 3 = 6
   ○ 6 + 6 = 12
   ○ 3 + 6 = 9

2. Which is a related subtraction fact for 5 + 7 = 12?

   ○ 5 − 2 = 3
   ○ 15 − 5 = 10
   ○ 7 − 5 = 2
   ○ 12 − 7 = 5

Spiral Review (CC.2.NBT.1, CC.2.NBT.3, CC.2.NBT.8)

3. Which is another way to write 4 hundreds? (Lesson 2.3)

   ○ 4
   ○ 40
   ○ 400
   ○ 440

4. What is the next number in the pattern? (Lesson 2.10)

   515, 615, 715, 815, 

   ○ 820
   ○ 905
   ○ 915
   ○ 920

5. What number is 10 more than 237? (Lesson 2.9)

   ○ 227
   ○ 247
   ○ 337
   ○ 347

6. Which is another way to write the number 110? (Lesson 2.7)

   ○ 100 + 10 + 1
   ○ 1 hundred 1 ten 1 one
   ○ one hundred eleven
   ○ 100 + 10

Name ______________________

Practice Subtraction Facts

COMMON CORE STANDARD CC.2.OA.2
Add and subtract within 20.

Write the difference.

1. 15 − 9 = ____	2. 10 − 2 = ____	3. ____ = 13 − 5
4. 14 − 7 = ____	5. 10 − 8 = ____	6. 12 − 7 = ____
7. ____ = 10 − 3	8. 16 − 7 = ____	9. 8 − 4 = ____
10. 11 − 5 = ____	11. 13 − 6 = ____	12. ____ = 12 − 9
13. 16 − 9 = ____	14. ____ = 11 − 9	15. 12 − 8 = ____
16. 14 − 8 = ____	17. 10 − 5 = ____	18. 12 − 5 = ____
19. 15 − 7 = ____	20. 14 − 9 = ____	21. 17 − 9 = ____

PROBLEM SOLVING

Solve. Write or draw to explain.

22. Mr. Li has 16 pencils. He gives 9 pencils to some students. How many pencils does Mr. Li have now?

____ pencils

Lesson Check (CC.2.OA.2)

1. What is the difference?

   13 − 6 = ____

   - ○ 6
   - ○ 7
   - ○ 8
   - ○ 9

2. What is the difference?

   12 − 3 = ____

   - ○ 5
   - ○ 6
   - ○ 7
   - ○ 9

Spiral Review (CC.2.NBT.1, CC.2.NBT.1a, CC.2.NBT.1b, CC.2.NBT.2, CC.2.NBT.3)

3. What is the value of the underlined digit? (Lesson 2.5)

   6<u>2</u>5

   - ○ 2
   - ○ 10
   - ○ 20
   - ○ 200

4. Which group of numbers shows counting by fives? (Lesson 1.9)

   - ○ 400, 401, 402, 403
   - ○ 415, 425, 435, 445
   - ○ 405, 410, 415, 420
   - ○ 460, 459, 458, 457

5. Devin has 39 toy blocks. What is the value of the digit 9 in this number? (Lesson 1.3)

   - ○ 9
   - ○ 12
   - ○ 30
   - ○ 90

6. Which number has the same value as 20 tens? (Lesson 2.1)

   - ○ 220
   - ○ 200
   - ○ 20
   - ○ 2

TEST PREP

Lesson Check (CC.2.OA.2)

1. Which has the same difference as 12 − 6?

   ○ 10 − 6
   ○ 10 − 4
   ○ 10 − 2
   ○ 10 − 0

2. Which has the same difference as 13 − 8?

   ○ 10 − 8
   ○ 10 − 3
   ○ 10 − 5
   ○ 10 − 1

Spiral Review (CC.2.OA.2, CC.2.NBT.4)

3. Which is a related subtraction fact for 7 + 3 = 10? (Lesson 3.5)

   ○ 10 − 3 = 7
   ○ 10 − 10 = 0
   ○ 7 − 4 = 3
   ○ 7 − 3 = 4

4. Joe has 8 trucks. Carmen has 1 more truck than Joe. How many trucks do they have in all? (Lesson 3.2)

   ○ 7
   ○ 9
   ○ 15
   ○ 17

5. There were 276 people on an airplane. Which of these numbers is greater than 276? (Lesson 2.11)

   ○ 177 ○ 267
   ○ 189 ○ 279

6. Which of the following is true? (Lesson 2.12)

   ○ 537 > 375
   ○ 495 > 504
   ○ 475 < 429
   ○ 201 = 189

Name ________________________________

Use Ten to Subtract

COMMON CORE STANDARD CC.2.OA.2
Add and subtract within 20.

Show the tens fact you used. Write the difference.

1. 14 − 6 = ____

   10 − ____ = ____

2. 12 − 7 = ____

   10 − ____ = ____

3. 13 − 7 = ____

   10 − ____ = ____

4. 15 − 8 = ____

   10 − ____ = ____

5. 11 − 7 = ____

   10 − ____ = ____

6. 14 − 5 = ____

   10 − ____ = ____

PROBLEM SOLVING

Solve. Write or draw to explain.

7. Carl read 15 pages on Monday night and 9 pages on Tuesday night. How many more pages did he read on Monday night than on Tuesday night?

   ____ more p

Name ______________________

Algebra • Use Drawings to Represent Problems

COMMON CORE STANDARD CC.2.OA.1

Represent and solve problems involving addition and subtraction.

Complete the bar model. Then write a number sentence to solve.

1. Sara has 4 yellow beads and 3 green beads. How many beads does Sara have?

4	3

____

____

____ beads

2. Adam had 12 trucks. He gave 4 trucks to Ed. How many trucks does Adam have now?

____	4

12

____

____ trucks

3. Grandma has 14 red roses and 7 pink roses. How many more red roses than pink roses does she have?

14

7

____

____

____ more red roses

Lesson Check (CC.2.OA.1)

1. Abby has 16 grapes. Jason has 9 grapes. How many more grapes does Abby have than Jason?

16

9 | ____

○ 7
○ 8
○ 15
○ 25

Spiral Review (CC.2.OA.2, CC.2.NBT.3)

2. Which has the same difference as 16 − 7? (Lesson 3.7)

○ 10 − 10
○ 10 − 6
○ 10 − 7
○ 10 − 1

3. What is the difference? (Lesson 3.6)

$18 - 9 = \underline{\quad\quad}$

○ 6
○ 9
○ 10
○ 27

4. Which is another way to write 300 + 20 + 5? (Lesson 2.7)

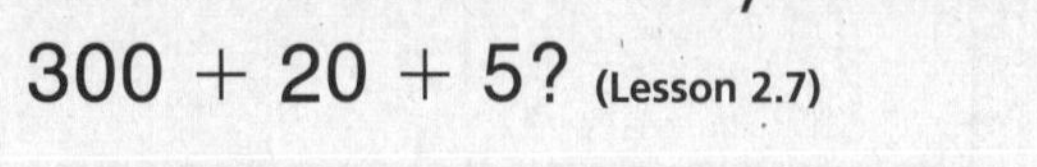

○ 55
○ 235
○ 325
○ 523

5. What is the value of the underlined digit? (Lesson 1.3)

$\underline{2}8$

○ 80
○ 20
○ 10
○ 2

Name ______________________________

Algebra • Use Equations to Represent Problems

COMMON CORE STANDARD CC.2.OA.1
Represent and solve problems involving addition and subtraction.

Write a number sentence for the problem.
Use a ■ for the missing number. Then solve.

1. There were 15 apples in a bowl. Dan used some apples to make a pie. Now there are 7 apples in the bowl. How many apples did Dan use?

    ____

    _____ apples

2. Amy has 16 gift bags. She fills 8 gift bags with whistles. How many gift bags are not filled with whistles?

    ____

    _____ gift bags

3. There were 5 dogs at the park. Then 9 more dogs joined them. How many dogs are at the park now?

    ____

    _____ dogs

PROBLEM SOLVING

Write or draw to show how you solved the problem.

4. Tony has 7 blue cubes and 6 red cubes. How many cubes does he have in all?

    _____ cubes

Lesson Check (CC.2.OA.1)

1. Fred peeled 9 carrots. Nancy peeled 6 carrots. How many fewer carrots did Nancy peel than Fred?

   ○ 15
   ○ 6
   ○ 3
   ○ 2

2. Omar has 8 marbles. Joy has 7 marbles. How many marbles do they have in all?

   ○ 1
   ○ 5
   ○ 8
   ○ 15

Spiral Review (CC.2.OA.2, CC.2.NBT.1)

3. What is the sum? (Lesson 3.1)

   $7 + 8 = ?$

   ○ 2
   ○ 7
   ○ 15
   ○ 17

4. What is the sum? (Lesson 3.4)

   $5 + 4 + 3 =$ ______

   ○ 12
   ○ 15
   ○ 18
   ○ 19

5. Which has the same value as 1 hundred 7 tens? (Lesson 2.2)

   ○ 70 tens
   ○ 17 tens
   ○ 10 tens
   ○ 7 tens

6. Which of the following is a way to describe the number 358? (Lesson 2.4)

   ○ 8 hundreds 5 tens 3 ones
   ○ 5 hundreds 3 tens 8 ones
   ○ 3 hundreds 8 tens 5 ones
   ○ 3 hundreds 5 tens 8 ones

Name ______________________________

Problem Solving • Equal Groups

PROBLEM SOLVING
Lesson 3.10

COMMON CORE STANDARD CC.2.OA.4
Work with equal groups of objects to gain foundations for multiplication.

Act out the problem.
Draw to show what you did.

1. Mr. Anderson has 4 plates of cookies. There are 5 cookies on each plate. How many cookies are there in all?

   _____ cookies

2. Ms. Trane puts some stickers in 3 rows. There are 2 stickers in each row. How many stickers does Ms. Trane have?

   _____ stickers

3. There are 5 books in each box. How many books are in 5 boxes?

   _____ books

TEST PREP

Lesson Check (CC.2.OA.4)

1. Jaime puts 3 oranges on each tray. How many oranges are on 5 trays?

- ○ 8
- ○ 15
- ○ 35
- ○ 53

2. Maurice has 4 rows of toys with 4 toys in each row. How many toys does he have in all?

- ○ 4
- ○ 8
- ○ 16
- ○ 20

Spiral Review (CC.2.OA.1, CC.2.OA.2, CC.2.OA.3)

3. Jack has 12 pencils and 7 pens. How many more pencils than pens does he have? (Lesson 3.8)

- ○ 19
- ○ 9
- ○ 6
- ○ 5

4. Laura has 9 apples. Jon has 6 apples. How many apples do they have in all? (Lesson 3.9)

- ○ 3
- ○ 12
- ○ 15
- ○ 16

5. Which of these is an even number? (Lesson 1.1)

- ○ 1
- ○ 3
- ○ 5
- ○ 8

6. What is the sum? (Lesson 3.2)

$7 + 9 = \_\_\_\_$

- ○ 16
- ○ 17
- ○ 18
- ○ 19

Name ________________________________

Algebra • Repeated Addition

COMMON CORE STANDARD CC.2.OA.4
Work with equal groups of objects to gain foundations for multiplication.

Find the number of shapes in each row.
Complete the addition sentence to find the total.

1. 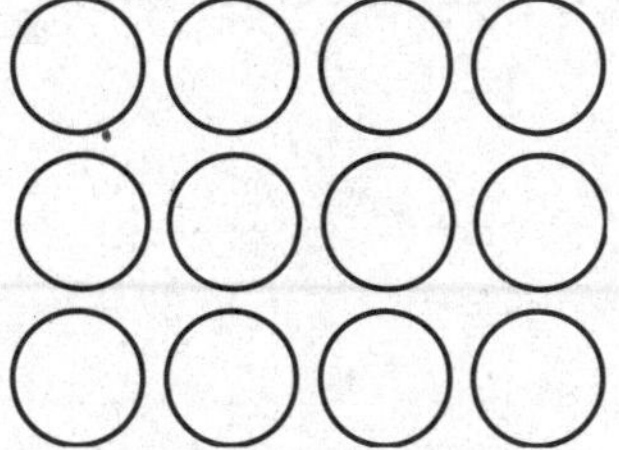

3 rows of ____

____ + ____ + ____ = ____

2. 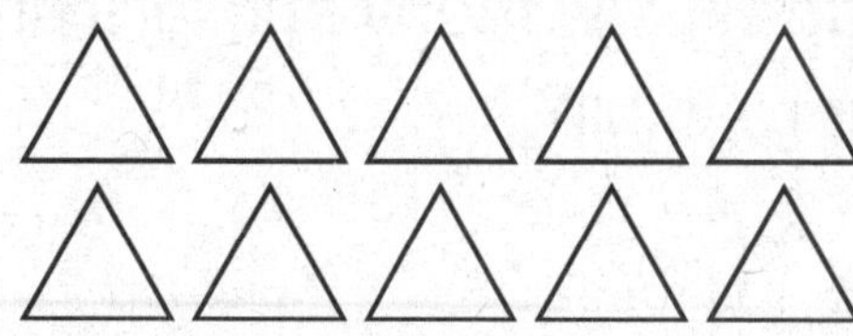

2 rows of ____

____ + ____ = ____

3. 

4 rows of ____

____ + ____ + ____ + ____ = ____

4. 

4 rows of ____

____ + ____ + ____ + ____ = ____

PROBLEM SOLVING

Solve. Write or draw to explain.

5. A classroom has 3 rows of desks. There are 5 desks in each row. How many desks are there altogether?

____ desks

TEST PREP

Lesson Check (CC.2.OA.4)

1. A scrapbook has 4 pages. There are 2 stickers on each page. How many stickers are there in all?

   ○ 4
   ○ 6
   ○ 8
   ○ 10

2. Ben makes 5 rows of coins. He puts 3 coins in each row. How many coins are there in all?

   ○ 9
   ○ 12
   ○ 15
   ○ 18

Spiral Review (CC.2.OA.2, CC.2.NBT.2, CC.2.NBT.3)

3. There are 5 apples and 4 oranges. How many pieces of fruit are there? (Lesson 3.1)

   ○ 10
   ○ 9
   ○ 8
   ○ 1

4. Which group of numbers shows counting by tens? (Lesson 1.8)

   ○ 35, 40, 45, 50, 55
   ○ 40, 50, 60, 70, 80
   ○ 65, 64, 63, 62, 61
   ○ 70, 71, 72, 73, 74

5. Which is a way to write the number 260? (Lesson 2.6)

   ○ twenty-six
   ○ two hundred six
   ○ two hundred sixteen
   ○ two hundred sixty

6. Which has the same sum as 7 + 5? (Lesson 3.3)

   ○ 10 + 4
   ○ 10 + 3
   ○ 10 + 2
   ○ 10 + 1

Name ______________________

COMMON CORE STANDARDS CC.2.OA.1, CC.2.OA.2, CC.2.OA.4

Chapter 3 Extra Practice

Lessons 3.1 – 3.4 (pp. 121 – 136)

Write the sums.

1. 6 + 6 = ____ 6 + 7 = ____	2. ____ = 7 + 4 ____ = 4 + 7	3. 0 + 2 = ____ 0 + 8 = ____

4. 6 + 9 = ____ 10 + ____ = ____	5. 7 + 5 = ____ 10 + ____ = ____
6. 4 + 6 + 4 = ____	7. 4 + 5 + 3 = ____
8. 2 + 7 + 3 = ____	9. 2 + 2 + 8 = ____

Lesson 3.6 (pp. 141 – 143)

Write the difference.

1. 9 − 3 = ____	2. ____ = 12 − 5	3. 16 − 8 = ____
4. ____ = 14 − 6	5. 11 − 8 = ____	6. 12 − 6 = ____
7. 5 − 3 = ____	8. ____ = 15 − 9	9. 7 − 3 = ____
10. 12 − 7 = ____	11. 14 − 7 = ____	12. ____ = 10 − 7

Lesson 3.7 (pp. 145 – 148)

Show the tens fact you used. Write the difference.

1. 16 − 9 = ____

10 − ____ = ____

2. 14 − 6 = ____

10 − ____ = ____

3. 11 − 8 = ____

10 − ____ = ____

4. 12 − 7 = ____

10 − ____ = ____

Lesson 3.9 (pp. 153 – 156)

Write a number sentence for the problem.

Use a ■ for the missing number.
Then solve.

1. There were 14 birds in the tree.
Some birds flew away. Then
there were 5 birds in the tree.
How many birds flew away?

____

____ birds

Lesson 3.11 (pp. 161 – 164)

Find the number of shapes in each row.
Complete the addition sentence to find the total.

1.

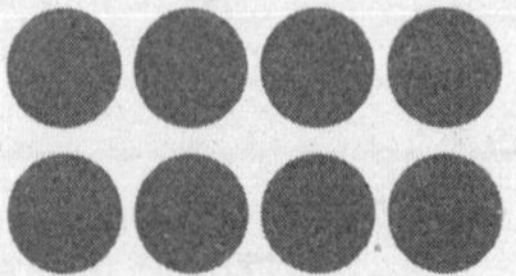

2 rows of ____

____ + ____ = ____

2.

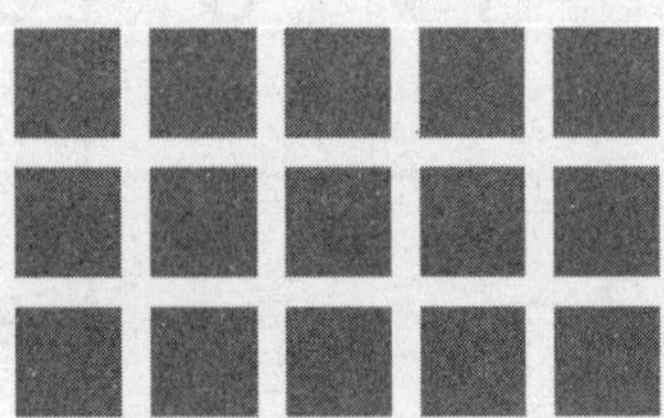

3 rows of ____

____ + ____ + ____ = ____

Chapter 4

School-Home Letter

Dear Family,

My class started Chapter 4 this week. In this chapter, I will learn how to solve addition problems with 2-digit addends using different strategies.

Love, ____________________

Vocabulary

regroup To make a group of 10 ones and trade it for a ten

Home Activity

Pretend you are going on a treasure hunt. Using small pieces of paper, make a path in a small area. Each piece of paper should have an addition problem on it for your child to solve. At the end of the path, place a treasure of some kind.

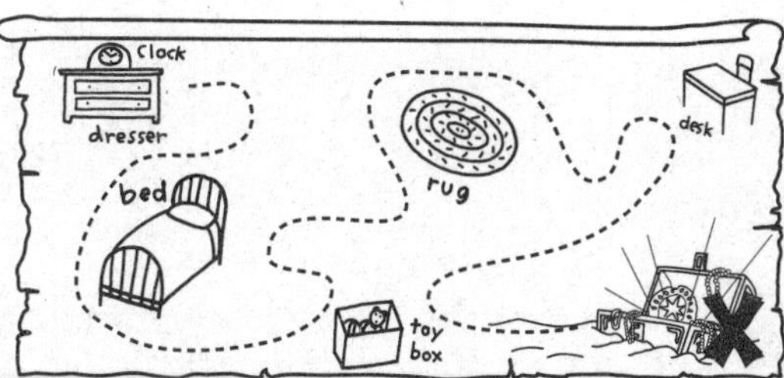

Literature

Reading math stories reinforces ideas. Look for these books at the library.

A Collection for Kate by Barbara deRubertis. Kane Press, 1999.

Mission: Addition by Loreen Leedy. Holiday House, 1997.

Capítulo 4 Carta para la casa

Querida familia:

Mi clase comenzó el Capítulo 4 esta semana. En este capítulo, aprenderé a resolver problemas con sumandos de dos dígitos usando diferentes estrategias.

Con cariño, ______________________________

Vocabulario

reagrupar formar un grupo de 10 unidades y cambiarlo por en una decena

Actividad para la casa

Jueguen a buscar un tesoro. Con pequeños trozos de papel, haga un camino en un espacio pequeño. Cada trozo de papel deberá tener un problema para que su hijo lo resuelva. Al final del camino, coloque algún tipo de tesoro.

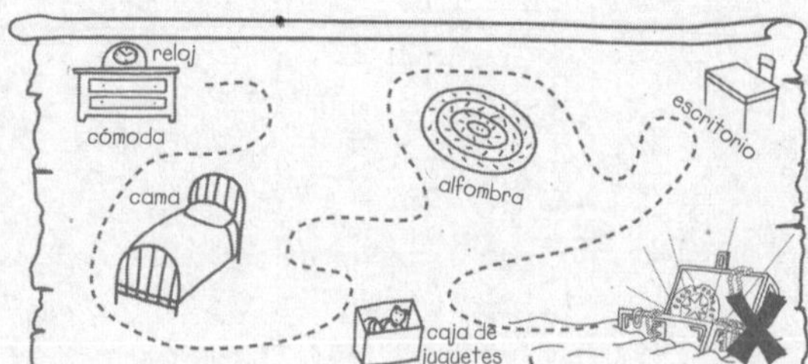

Literatura

Leer cuentos de matemáticas refuerza los conceptos. Busque estos libros en la biblioteca.

A Collection for Kate por Barbara deRubertis. Kane Press, 1999.

Mission: Addition por Loreen Leedy. Holiday House, 1997.

Name ______________________________

Break Apart Ones to Add

COMMON CORE STANDARD CC.2.NBT.6

Use place value understanding and properties of operations to add and subtract.

Break apart ones to make a ten. Then add and write the sum.

1. 62 + 9 = ____	2. 27 + 7 = ____
3. 28 + 5 = ____	4. 17 + 8 = ____
5. 57 + 6 = ____	6. 23 + 9 = ____
7. 39 + 7 = ____	8. 26 + 5 = ____
9. 13 + 8 = ____	10. 18 + 7 = ____
11. 49 + 8 = ____	12. 27 + 5 = ____
13. 39 + 4 = ____	14. 18 + 8 = ____

PROBLEM SOLVING

Solve. Write or draw to explain.

15. Jimmy had 18 toy airplanes. His mother bought him 7 more toy airplanes. How many toy airplanes does he have now?

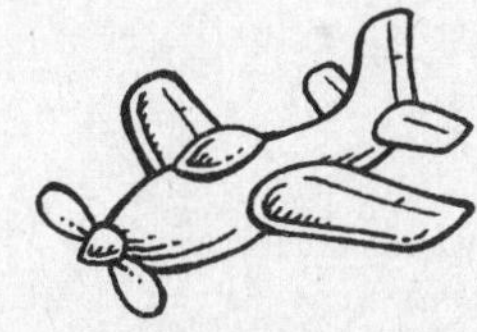

____ toy airplanes

Lesson Check (CC.2.NBT.6)

1. What is the sum?

$26 + 7 =$ ____

○ 96
○ 78
○ 33
○ 19

2. What is the sum?

$15 + 8 =$ ____

○ 7
○ 10
○ 13
○ 23

Spiral Review (CC.2.OA.1, CC.2.OA.2, CC.2.NBT.3)

3. Hannah has 4 blue beads and 8 red beads. How many beads does Hannah have? (Lesson 3.8)

○ 4
○ 7
○ 10
○ 12

4. Rick had 4 stickers. Then he earned 2 more. How many stickers does he have now? (Lesson 3.3)

○ 4
○ 6
○ 7
○ 9

5. What is the sum? (Lesson 3.4)

$4 + 5 + 4 =$

○ 13
○ 12
○ 11
○ 10

6. Which of the following is another way to write 281? (Lesson 2.7)

○ 1 hundred 2 tens 8 ones
○ 1 hundred 8 tens 2 ones
○ 2 hundreds 1 ten 8 ones
○ 2 hundreds 8 tens 1 one

Name ______________________________

Use Compensation

COMMON CORE STANDARD CC.2.NBT.6
Use place value understanding and properties of operations to add and subtract.

Show how to make one addend the next tens number. Complete the new addition sentence.

1. 15 + 37 = ?

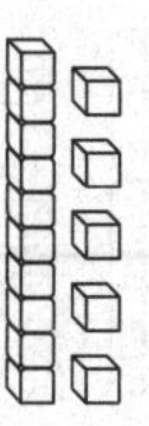

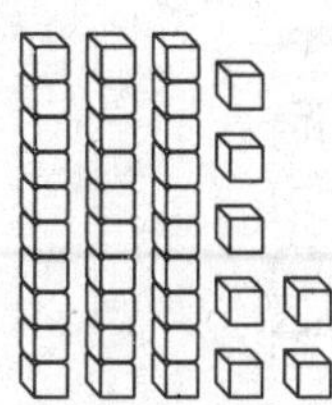

____ + ____ = ____

2. 22 + 49 = ?

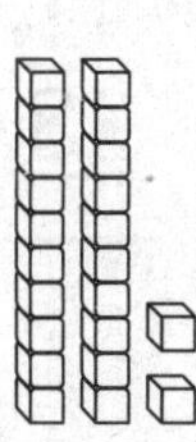

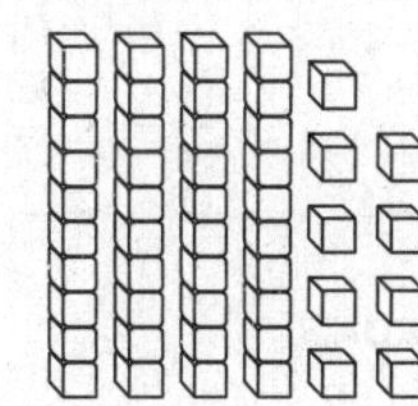

____ + ____ = ____

3. 38 + 26 = ?

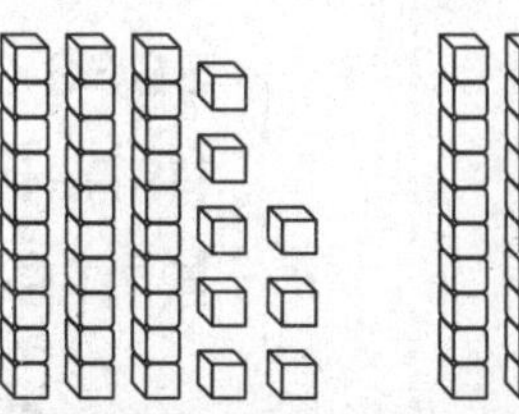

____ + ____ = ____

4. 27 + 47 = ?

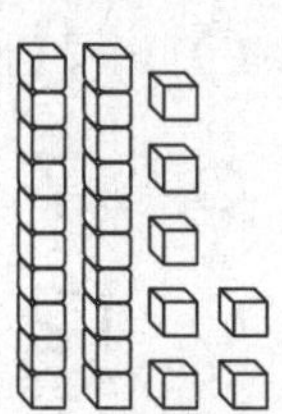

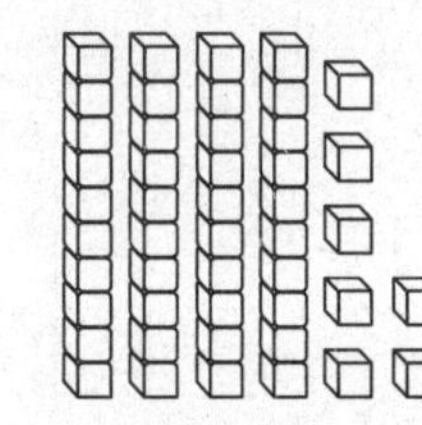

____ + ____ = ____

PROBLEM SOLVING

Solve. Write or draw to explain.

5. The oak tree at the school was 34 feet tall.
Then it grew 18 feet taller.
How tall is the oak tree now?

____ feet tall

Lesson Check (CC.2.NBT.6)

1. What is the sum?

$18 + 25 = ?$

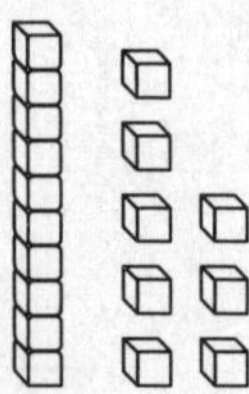 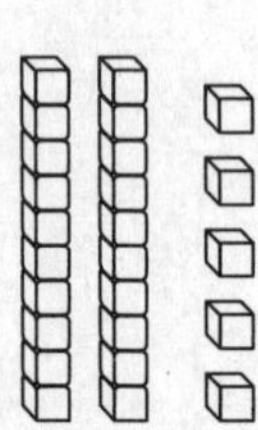

- ○ 43
- ○ 33
- ○ 31
- ○ 17

2. What is the sum?

$27 + 24 = ?$

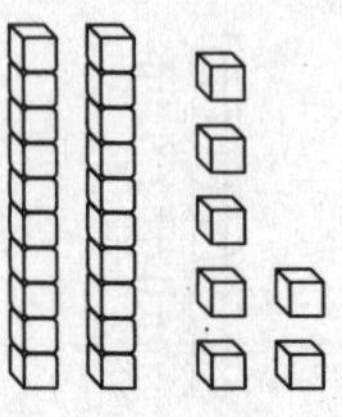 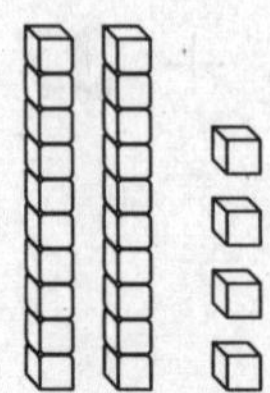

- ○ 41
- ○ 43
- ○ 51
- ○ 59

Spiral Review (CC.2.OA.2, CC.2.OA.3)

3. Which of the following numbers is an even number? (Lesson 1.1)

- ○ 27
- ○ 14
- ○ 11
- ○ 5

4. Andrew sees 4 fish. Kim sees double that number of fish. How many fish does Kim see? (Lesson 3.1)

- ○ 2
- ○ 8
- ○ 7
- ○ 12

5. Which is a related subtraction fact for $7 + 6 = 13$? (Lesson 3.5)

- ○ $13 - 6 = 7$
- ○ $7 - 1 = 6$
- ○ $7 - 6 = 1$
- ○ $13 + 6 = 19$

6. What is the sum? (Lesson 3.2)

$2 + 8 =$ ____

- ○ 0
- ○ 6
- ○ 8
- ○ 10

Name ______________________________

Break Apart Addends as Tens and Ones

COMMON CORE STANDARD CC.2.NBT.6
Use place value understanding and properties of operations to add and subtract.

Break apart the addends to find the sum.

1.
```
   18  →  ___ + ___
 + 21  →  ___ + ___
 ____    __________
          ___ + ___ = ___
```

2.
```
   33  →  ___ + ___
 + 49  →  ___ + ___
 ____    __________
          ___ + ___ = ___
```

3.
```
   72  →  ___ + ___
 + 18  →  ___ + ___
 ____    __________
          ___ + ___ = ___
```

PROBLEM SOLVING

Choose a way to solve.
Write or draw to explain.

4. Christopher has 28 baseball cards. Justin has 18 baseball cards. How many baseball cards do they have in all?

_____ baseball cards

Lesson Check (CC.2.NBT.6)

1. What is the sum?

$$\begin{array}{r} 27 \\ +\ 12 \\ \hline \end{array}$$

- ○ 15
- ○ 19
- ○ 29
- ○ 39

2. What is the sum?

$$\begin{array}{r} 17 \\ +\ 35 \\ \hline \end{array}$$

- ○ 40
- ○ 42
- ○ 52
- ○ 59

Spiral Review (CC.2.OA.2, CC.2.NBT.1, CC.2.NBT.3, CC.2.NBT.6)

3. What is the value of the underlined digit? (Lesson 1.3)

2<u>5</u>

- ○ 5
- ○ 7
- ○ 50
- ○ 55

4. Which has the same value as 12 tens? (Lesson 2.2)

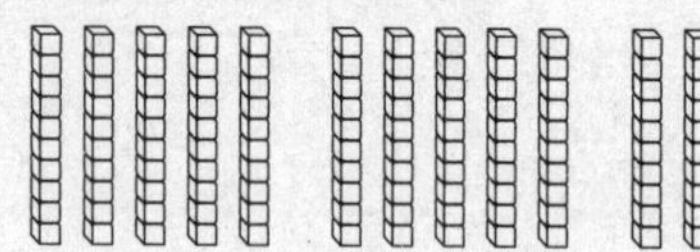

- ○ 10
- ○ 12
- ○ 100
- ○ 120

5. Ally has 7 connecting cubes. Greg has 4 connecting cubes. How many connecting cubes do they have in all? (Lesson 3.2)

- ○ 3
- ○ 8
- ○ 11
- ○ 25

6. Juan painted a picture of a tree. First he painted 15 leaves. Then he painted 23 more leaves. How many leaves did he paint in all? (Lesson 4.2)

- ○ 8
- ○ 25
- ○ 33
- ○ 38

Name ______________________________

Model Regrouping for Addition

COMMON CORE STANDARDS CC.2.NBT.6, CC.2.NBT.9
Use place value understanding and properties of operations to add and subtract.

Draw to show the regrouping. Write how many tens and ones in the sum. Write the sum.

1. Add 63 and 9.

Tens	Ones

_____ tens _____ ones

_____

2. Add 25 and 58.

Tens	Ones

_____ tens _____ ones

_____

3. Add 58 and 18.

Tens	Ones

_____ tens _____ ones

_____

4. Add 64 and 26.

Tens	Ones

_____ tens _____ ones

_____

5. Add 17 and 77.

Tens	Ones

_____ tens _____ ones

_____

6. Add 16 and 39.

Tens	Ones

_____ tens _____ ones

_____

PROBLEM SOLVING

Choose a way to solve.
Write or draw to explain.

7. Cathy has 43 leaves in her collection. Jane has 38 leaves. How many leaves do the two children have?

_____ leaves

TEST PREP

Lesson Check (CC.2.NBT.6)

1. Add 27 and 48. What is the sum?

Tens	Ones
2 tens	7 ones
4 tens	8 ones

- ○ 27
- ○ 48
- ○ 65
- ○ 75

Spiral Review (CC.2.OA.2, CC.2.OA.3, CC.2.NBT.6)

2. What is the sum? (Lesson 3.2)

$7 + 7 =$ ____

- ○ 14
- ○ 13
- ○ 12
- ○ 11

3. Which of these is an odd number? (Lesson 1.1)

- ○ 6
- ○ 12
- ○ 21
- ○ 22

4. What is the sum? (Lesson 4.2)

$39 + 46 = ?$

- ○ 37
- ○ 58
- ○ 75
- ○ 85

5. What is the sum? (Lesson 3.4)

$5 + 3 + 4 =$ ____

- ○ 9
- ○ 12
- ○ 14
- ○ 16

Name ____________________

Model and Record 2-Digit Addition

COMMON CORE STANDARD CC.2.NBT.6
Use place value understanding and properties of operations to add and subtract.

Draw quick pictures to help you solve. Write the sum.

1.

	Tens	Ones
	☐	
	3	8
+	1	7

Tens	Ones

2.

	Tens	Ones
	☐	
	5	8
+	2	6

Tens	Ones

3.

	Tens	Ones
	☐	
	4	2
+	3	7

Tens	Ones

4.

	Tens	Ones
	☐	
	5	3
+	3	8

Tens	Ones

PROBLEM SOLVING

Choose a way to solve.
Write or draw to explain.

5. There were 37 children at the park on Saturday and 25 children at the park on Sunday. How many children were at the park on those two days?

_____ children

Lesson Check (CC.2.NBT.6)

1. What is the sum?

	Tens	Ones
	□	
	3	4
+	2	8

○ 44 ○ 52
○ 54 ○ 62

2. What is the sum?

	Tens	Ones
	□	
	4	3
+	2	7

○ 64 ○ 65
○ 70 ○ 74

Spiral Review (CC.2.OA.2)

3. Adam collected 14 pennies in the first week and 9 pennies in the second week. How many more pennies did he collect in the first week than in the second week? (Lesson 3.5)

○ 25 ○ 14
○ 5 ○ 3

4. What is the sum? (Lesson 3.4)

$3 + 7 + 9 =$ ____

○ 7 ○ 10
○ 13 ○ 19

5. Janet has 5 marbles. She finds double that number of marbles in her art box. How many marbles does Janet have now? (Lesson 3.1)

○ 5 ○ 15
○ 10 ○ 20

6. What is the difference? (Lesson 3.6)

$13 - 5 =$ ____

○ 7 ○ 8
○ 9 ○ 18

Name ______________________________

2-Digit Addition

COMMON CORE STANDARD CC.2.NBT.5
Use place value understanding and properties of operations to add and subtract.

Regroup if you need to. Write the sum.

1.
	tens	ones
	4	7
+	2	5

2.
	tens	ones
	3	3
+	1	8

3.
	tens	ones
	2	8
+	6	4

4.
	tens	ones
	1	3
+	6	5

5.
	tens	ones
	1	7
+	2	6

6.
	tens	ones
	3	6
+	5	3

7.
	tens	ones
	5	8
+	2	5

8.
	tens	ones
	3	7
+	4	9

9.
	tens	ones
	5	2
+	2	9

10.
	tens	ones
	6	6
+	2	4

11.
	tens	ones
	7	4
+	1	4

12.
	tens	ones
	3	7
+	3	7

PROBLEM SOLVING

Solve. Write or draw to explain.

13. Angela drew 16 flowers on her paper in the morning. She drew 25 more flowers in the afternoon. How many flowers did she draw in all?

_____ flowers

Lesson Check (CC.2.NBT.5)

1. What is the sum?

	Tens	Ones
	2	1
+	3	7

○ 16
○ 18
○ 56
○ 58

2. What is the sum?

	Tens	Ones
	3	8
+	5	2

○ 90
○ 86
○ 80
○ 76

Spiral Review (CC.2.OA.1, CC.2.NBT.3, CC.2.NBT.8)

3. What is the next number in the counting pattern? (Lesson 2.10)

103, 203, 303, 403, ____

○ 433
○ 500
○ 503
○ 613

4. Rita counted 13 bubbles. Ben counted 5 bubbles. How many fewer bubbles did Ben count than Rita? (Lesson 3.9)

○ 8
○ 10
○ 13
○ 18

5. Which number is 100 more than 265? (Lesson 2.9)

○ 165
○ 275
○ 305
○ 365

6. Which of the following is another way to write 42? (Lesson 1.5)

○ 402
○ 40 + 2
○ 400 + 2
○ 40 tens 2 ones

Name ___________________________

Lesson 4.7

Practice 2-Digit Addition

COMMON CORE STANDARD CC.2.NBT.5
Use place value understanding and properties of operations to add and subtract.

Write the sum.

1.
  58
+ 17

2.
  44
+ 86

3.
  36
+ 13

4.
  49
+ 72

5.
  58
+ 87

6.
  32
+ 59

7.
  77
+ 58

8.
  45
+ 45

9.
  54
+ 28

PROBLEM SOLVING

Solve. Write or draw to explain.

10. There are 45 books on the shelf. There are 37 books on the table. How many books in all are on the shelf and the table?

_____ books

Lesson Check (CC.2.NBT.5)

1. What is the sum?

$$\begin{array}{r} 56 \\ +\ 35 \\ \hline \end{array}$$

- ○ 91
- ○ 81
- ○ 51
- ○ 21

2. What is the sum?

$$\begin{array}{r} 74 \\ +\ 15 \\ \hline \end{array}$$

- ○ 61
- ○ 69
- ○ 89
- ○ 91

Spiral Review (CC.2.OA.1, CC.2.OA.2, CC.2.NBT.1, CC.2.NBT.3)

3. What is the value of the underlined digit? (Lesson 2.5)

$\underline{5}26$

- ○ 600
- ○ 500
- ○ 50
- ○ 5

4. Mr. Stevens wants to put 17 books on the shelf. He put 8 books on the shelf. How many more books does he need to put on the shelf? (Lesson 3.8)

- ○ 3
- ○ 7
- ○ 9
- ○ 12

5. What is the difference? (Lesson 3.6)

$11 - 6 =$ ____

- ○ 17
- ○ 15
- ○ 7
- ○ 5

6. Which of these is another way to describe 83? (Lesson 1.4)

- ○ $80 + 3$
- ○ $80 + 30$
- ○ $30 + 8$
- ○ $8 + 3$

Name ______________________________

Rewrite 2-Digit Addition

COMMON CORE STANDARD CC.2.NBT.5
Use place value understanding and properties of operations to add and subtract.

Rewrite the numbers. Then add.

1. 27 + 19	2. 36 + 23	3. 31 + 29	4. 48 + 23
+ ______	+ ______	+ ______	+ ______
5. 53 + 12	6. 69 + 13	7. 24 + 38	8. 46 + 37
+ ______	+ ______	+ ______	+ ______

PROBLEM SOLVING

Use the table. Show how you solved the problem.

9. How many pages in all did Sasha and Kara read?

_____ pages

Pages Read This Week	
Child	**Number of Pages**
Sasha	62
Kara	29
Juan	50

Lesson Check (CC.2.NBT.5)

1. What is the sum of 39 + 17?

   +

   ○ 66
   ○ 56
   ○ 50
   ○ 22

2. What is the sum of 28 + 16?

   +

   ○ 44
   ○ 42
   ○ 34
   ○ 18

Spiral Review (CC.2.OA.4, CC.2.NBT.1, CC.2.NBT.3, CC.2.NBT.6)

3. Which of the following is another way to write 60 + 4? (Lesson 1.5)

   ○ 46
   ○ 64
   ○ 100
   ○ 604

4. The classroom has 4 desks in each row. There are 5 rows. How many desks are there in the classroom? (Lesson 3.10)

   ○ 9
   ○ 15
   ○ 20
   ○ 35

5. A squirrel collected 17 acorns. Then the squirrel collected 31 acorns. How many acorns did the squirrel collect in all? (Lesson 4.2)

   ○ 14　　○ 21
   ○ 33　　○ 48

6. What number can be written as 3 hundreds 7 tens 5 ones? (Lesson 2.4)

   ○ 753
   ○ 573
   ○ 375
   ○ 357

Name ______________________________

Problem Solving • Addition

COMMON CORE STANDARD CC.2.OA.1
Represent and solve problems involving addition and subtraction.

Label the bar model. Write a number sentence with a ■ for the missing number. Solve.

1. Jacob counts 37 ants on the sidewalk and 11 ants on the grass. How many ants does Jacob count?

____ ants

2. There are 14 bees in the hive and 17 bees in the garden. How many bees are there in all?

____ bees

3. There are 28 flowers in Sasha's garden. 16 flowers are yellow and the rest are white. How many white flowers are in Sasha's garden?

____ white flowers

Lesson Check (CC.2.OA.1)

1. Sean and Abby have 23 markers altogether. Abby has 14 markers. How many markers does Sean have?

____ ____

____

- ○ 9
- ○ 7
- ○ 8
- ○ 6

2. Mrs. James has 22 students in her class. Mr. Williams has 24 students in his class. How many students are in the two classes?

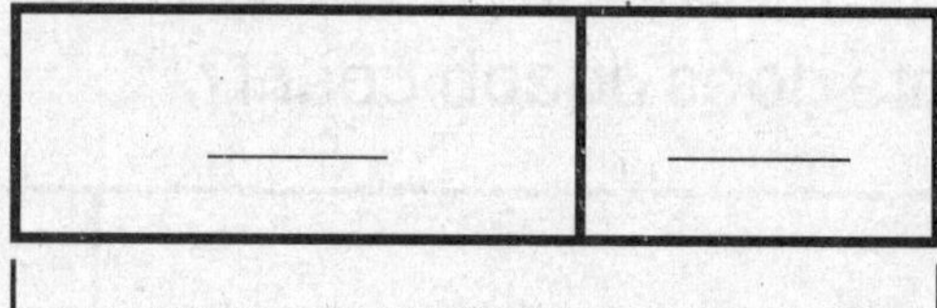

____

- ○ 42
- ○ 51
- ○ 46
- ○ 56

Spiral Review (CC.2.OA.2, CC.2.NBT.8)

3. What is the difference? (Lesson 3.6)

$15 - 9 = $ ____

- ○ 24
- ○ 14
- ○ 7
- ○ 6

4. What is the sum? (Lesson 3.3)

$7 + 5 = $ ____

- ○ 12
- ○ 11
- ○ 10
- ○ 9

5. Jan has 14 blocks. She gives 9 blocks to Tim. How many blocks does Jan have now? (Lesson 3.5)

- ○ 3
- ○ 5
- ○ 18
- ○ 23

6. What is the next number in the counting pattern? (Lesson 2.10)

29, 39, 49, 59, ____

- ○ 49
- ○ 69
- ○ 75
- ○ 79

Name ______________________________

Algebra • Write Equations to Represent Addition

COMMON CORE STANDARD CC.2.OA.1
Represent and solve problems involving addition and subtraction.

Write a number sentence for the problem. Use a ■ for the missing number. Then solve.

1. Emily and her friends went to the park. They saw 15 robins and 9 blue jays. How many birds did they see?

____

____ birds

2. Joe has 13 fish in one tank. He has 8 fish in another tank. How many fish does Joe have?

____

____ fish

PROBLEM SOLVING

Solve.

3. There are 21 children in Kathleen's class. 12 of the children are girls. How many children in her class are boys?

____ boys

Lesson Check (CC.2.OA.1)

1. Clare has 14 blocks. Jasmine has 6 blocks. How many blocks do they have in all?

   ○ 8
   ○ 19
   ○ 20
   ○ 22

2. Matt finds 16 acorns at the park. Trevor finds 18 acorns. How many acorns do they find?

   ○ 38
   ○ 34
   ○ 32
   ○ 22

Spiral Review (CC.2.OA.1, CC.2.OA.2, CC.2.OA.3, CC.2.OA.4)

3. Leanne counted 19 ants. Gregory counted 6 ants. How many more ants did Leanne count than Gregory? (Lesson 3.8)

   ○ 3
   ○ 8
   ○ 13
   ○ 25

4. What is the sum? (Lesson 3.4)

   $4 + 3 + 6 = \_\_\_\_$

   ○ 13
   ○ 10
   ○ 9
   ○ 7

5. Ms. Santos puts seashells into 4 rows. She puts 6 seashells in each row. How many seashells are there altogether? (Lesson 3.11)

   ○ 12
   ○ 24
   ○ 36
   ○ 42

6. Which of these is an even number? (Lesson 1.1)

   ○ 9
   ○ 14
   ○ 17
   ○ 21

Name ______________________________

Algebra • Find Sums for 3 Addends

COMMON CORE STANDARD CC.2.NBT.6
Use place value understanding and properties of operations to add and subtract.

Add.

1.
$$\begin{array}{r} 23 \\ 20 \\ +25 \\ \hline \end{array}$$

2.
$$\begin{array}{r} 15 \\ 22 \\ +38 \\ \hline \end{array}$$

3.
$$\begin{array}{r} 13 \\ 52 \\ +34 \\ \hline \end{array}$$

4.
$$\begin{array}{r} 27 \\ 40 \\ +19 \\ \hline \end{array}$$

5.
$$\begin{array}{r} 31 \\ 45 \\ +24 \\ \hline \end{array}$$

6.
$$\begin{array}{r} 34 \\ 11 \\ +28 \\ \hline \end{array}$$

7.
$$\begin{array}{r} 42 \\ 36 \\ +11 \\ \hline \end{array}$$

8.
$$\begin{array}{r} 18 \\ 22 \\ +34 \\ \hline \end{array}$$

9.
$$\begin{array}{r} 53 \\ 19 \\ +25 \\ \hline \end{array}$$

PROBLEM SOLVING

Solve. Write or draw to explain.

10. Liam has 24 yellow pencils, 15 red pencils, and 9 blue pencils. How many pencils does he have altogether?

_____ pencils

Lesson Check (CC.2.NBT.6)

1. What is the sum?

$$\begin{array}{r} 22 \\ 31 \\ +\ 16 \\ \hline \end{array}$$

- ○ 69
- ○ 79
- ○ 83
- ○ 96

2. What is the sum?

$$\begin{array}{r} 17 \\ 26 \\ +\ 30 \\ \hline \end{array}$$

- ○ 47
- ○ 56
- ○ 63
- ○ 73

Spiral Review (CC.2.OA.1, CC.2.OA.4, CC.2.NBT.3, CC.2.NBT.8)

3. What number is 10 more than 127? (Lesson 2.9)

- ○ 117
- ○ 137
- ○ 227
- ○ 277

4. Mr. Howard's phone has 4 rows of buttons. There are 3 buttons in each row. How many buttons are on Mr. Howard's phone? (Lesson 3.11)

- ○ 7
- ○ 8
- ○ 12
- ○ 16

5. Bob tosses 8 horseshoes. Liz tosses 9 horseshoes. How many horseshoes do they toss in all? (Lesson 3.9)

- ○ 15
- ○ 17
- ○ 18
- ○ 27

6. Which of the following is another way to write 315? (Lesson 2.7)

- ○ 1 hundred 3 tens 5 ones
- ○ 3 hundreds 1 ten 5 ones
- ○ 3 hundreds 5 tens 1 one
- ○ 5 hundreds 1 ten 3 ones

Name ____________________

Algebra • Find Sums for 4 Addends

COMMON CORE STANDARD CC.2.NBT.6
Use place value understanding and properties of operations to add and subtract.

Add.

1.
```
  18
  32
  23
+  3
----
```

2.
```
  45
  31
  29
+ 72
----
```

3.
```
  24
  62
  70
+ 33
----
```

4.
```
  83
  32
  61
+ 22
----
```

5.
```
  37
  15
  31
+ 12
----
```

6.
```
  21
  13
  96
+ 18
----
```

PROBLEM SOLVING

Solve. Show how you solved the problem.

7. Kinza jogs 16 minutes on Monday, 13 minutes on Tuesday, 9 minutes on Wednesday, and 20 minutes on Thursday. What is the total number of minutes she jogged?

_____ minutes

Lesson Check (CC.2.NBT.6)

1. What is the sum?

$$\begin{array}{r} 12 \\ 33 \\ 56 \\ +\ 32 \\ \hline \end{array}$$

- ○ 123
- ○ 133
- ○ 131
- ○ 151

2. What is the sum?

$$\begin{array}{r} 41 \\ 74 \\ 43 \\ +\ 20 \\ \hline \end{array}$$

- ○ 175
- ○ 188
- ○ 178
- ○ 195

Spiral Review (CC.2.OA.1, CC.2.NBT.5)

3. Laura had 6 daisies. Then she found 7 more daisies. How many daisies does she have now? (Lesson 3.8)

- ○ 6
- ○ 10
- ○ 13
- ○ 15

4. What is the sum? (Lesson 4.7)

$$\begin{array}{r} 52 \\ +\ 27 \\ \hline \end{array}$$

- ○ 89
- ○ 79
- ○ 65
- ○ 16

5. Alan has 25 trading cards. He buys 8 more. How many cards does he have now? (Lesson 4.9)

- ○ 15 ○ 17
- ○ 23 ○ 33

6. Jen saw 13 guinea pigs and 18 gerbils at the pet store. How many pets did she see? (Lesson 4.10)

- ○ 31 ○ 21
- ○ 13 ○ 5

Name ______________________

COMMON CORE STANDARDS CC.2.OA.1, CC.2.NBT.5, CC.2.NBT.6, CC.2.NBT.9

Chapter 4 Extra Practice

Lessons 4.1 - 4.2 (pp. 173 – 180)

Break apart ones to make a ten. Add.

1. 42 + 9 = ____

2. 38 + 7 = ____

Show how to make one addend the next tens number. Complete the new addition sentence.

3. 22 + 49 = ?

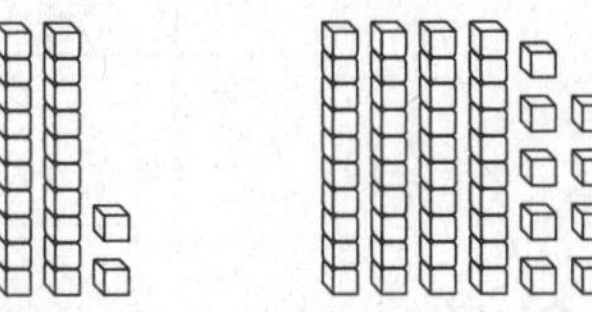

____ + ____ = ____

Lesson 4.3 (pp. 181 – 184)

Break apart the addends to find the sum.

1.
 18 → ____ + ____
+ 26 → ____ + ____

____ + ____ = ____

Lesson 4.4 (pp. 185 – 188)

Write how many tens and ones in the sum.
Write the sum.

1. Add 45 and 29.

Tens	Ones

____ tens ____ ones

____

2. Add 13 and 48.

Tens	Ones

____ tens ____ ones

____

3. Add 38 and 18.

Tens	Ones

____ tens ____ ones

____

Lessons 4.5 - 4.6 (pp. 189 – 196)

Draw quick pictures to help you solve. Write the sum.

1.

	Tens	Ones
	□	
	4	6
+	3	8

Tens	Ones

2.

	Tens	Ones
	□	
	3	2
+	5	7

Tens	Ones

Regroup if you need to. Write the sum.

3.

	5	8
+	1	7

4.

	4	3
+	2	7

5.

	3	3
+	5	8

Lesson 4.10 (pp. 209 – 212)

Write a number sentence for the problem.
Use a ▇ for the missing number. Then solve.

1. Tony has 24 blue marbles and 18 red marbles. How many marbles does he have?

_____ marbles

____

Lesson 4.11 (pp. 213 – 216)

Add.

1.
```
  50
  25
+ 19
```

2.
```
  26
  21
+ 31
```

3.
```
  64
  17
+ 22
```

Chapter 5

School-Home Letter

Dear Family,

My class started Chapter 5 this week. In this chapter, I will learn how to solve 2-digit subtraction problems using different strategies.

Love, ______________________________

Vocabulary

minus sign a symbol used in a subtraction problem

difference the answer to a subtraction problem

7 − 4 = 3
↑
difference

Home Activity

Write 2-digit numbers, such as 56, 67, and 89, each on a separate index card. Use a pencil and a paper clip to make a pointer for the spinner. Have your child choose a card, spin the pointer, and subtract the number on the spinner from the number on the card.

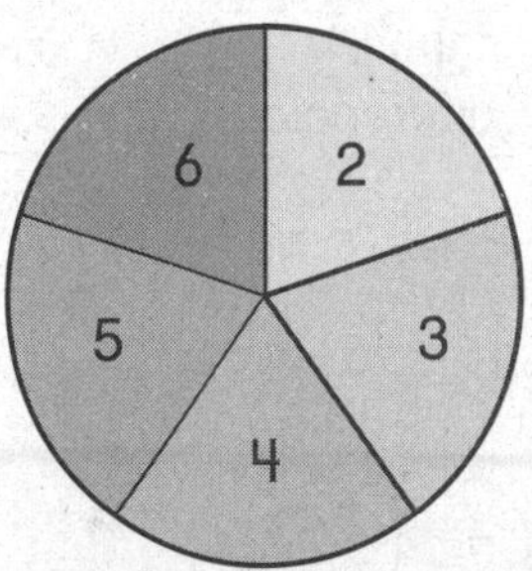

Literature

Look for these books at the library. Read them with your child to reinforce learning.

The Action of Subtraction
by Brian P. Cleary
Millbrook Press, 2006

The Shark Swimathon
by Stuart J. Murphy
HarperCollins, 2001

Capítulo 5

Carta para la casa

Querida familia:

Mi clase comenzó el Capítulo 5 esta semana. En este capítulo, aprenderé a resolver problemas de resta de números de 2 dígitos usando estrategias diferentes.

Con cariño, ______________________________

Vocabulario

signo de menos símbolo que se usa en un problema de resta

diferencia la respuesta a un problema de resta

$7 - 4 = 3$ ↑ diferencia

Actividad para la casa

Escriba números de 2 dígitos, como 56, 67 y 89, cada uno en una tarjeta. Con un lápiz y un clip, haga una flecha giratoria para la rueda. Pida a su hijo que elija una tarjeta, gire la flecha, y reste el número en que se detenga en la rueda del número de la tarjeta.

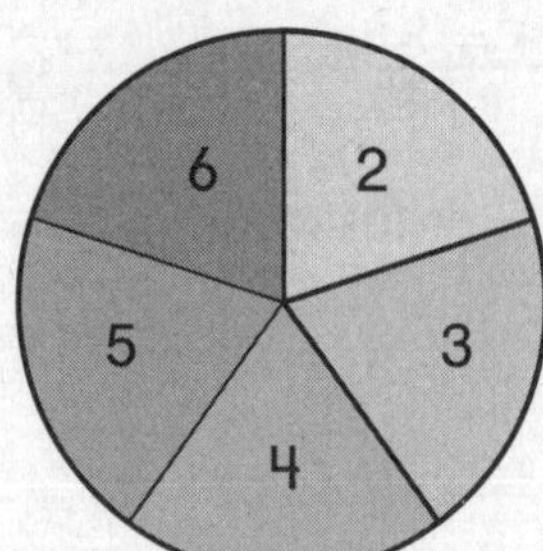

Literatura

Busque estos libros en la biblioteca. Léalos con su hijo para reforzar el aprendizaje.

The Action of Subtraction
por Brian P. Cleary
Millbrook Press, 2006

The Shark Swimathon
por Stuart J. Murphy
HarperCollins, 2001

Name ______________________

Algebra • Break Apart Ones to Subtract

COMMON CORE STANDARD CC.2.NBT.5
Use place value understanding and properties of operations to add and subtract.

Break apart ones to subtract.
Write the difference.

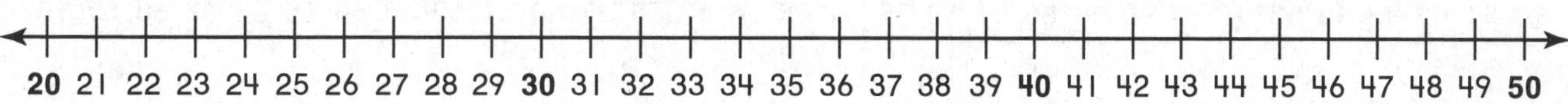

1. 36 − 7 = _____
2. 35 − 8 = _____
3. 37 − 9 = _____
4. 41 − 6 = _____
5. 44 − 5 = _____
6. 33 − 7 = _____
7. 32 − 4 = _____
8. 31 − 6 = _____
9. 46 − 9 = _____
10. 43 − 5 = _____

PROBLEM SOLVING

Choose a way to solve. Write or draw to explain.

11. Beth had 44 marbles. She gave 9 marbles to her brother. How many marbles does Beth have now?

_____ marbles

Lesson Check (CC.2.NBT.5)

1. What is the difference?

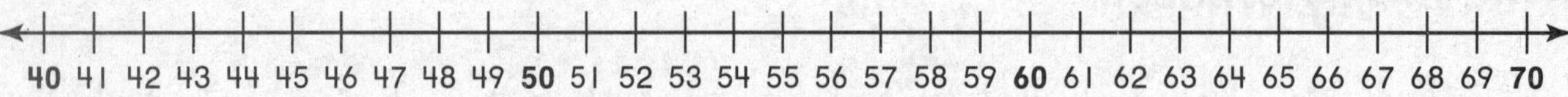

$58 - 9 =$ ____

67	51	49	41
○	○	○	○

Spiral Review (CC.2.OA.2, CC.2.NBT.6)

2. What is the difference? (Lesson 3.6)

$14 - 6 =$ ____

○ 7
○ 8
○ 9
○ 10

3. What is the sum? (Lesson 3.4)

$3 + 6 + 2 =$ ____

○ 11
○ 10
○ 9
○ 5

4. What is the sum? (Lesson 4.1)

$64 + 7 =$ ____

○ 81
○ 73
○ 71
○ 68

5. What is the sum? (Lesson 4.2)

$56 + 18 =$ ____

○ 74
○ 72
○ 64
○ 62

Name ______________________________

Algebra • Break Apart Numbers to Subtract

COMMON CORE STANDARD CC.2.NBT.5
Use place value understanding and properties of operations to add and subtract.

Break apart the number you are subtracting. Write the difference.

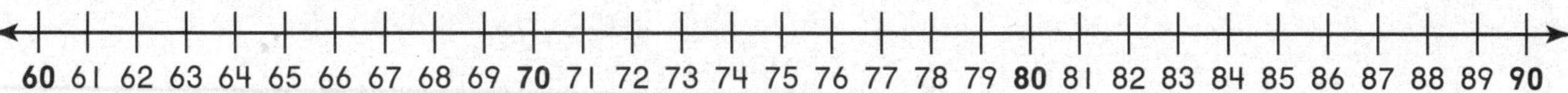

1. 81 − 14 = _____
2. 84 − 16 = _____
3. 77 − 14 = _____
4. 83 − 19 = _____
5. 81 − 17 = _____
6. 88 − 13 = _____
7. 84 − 19 = _____
8. 86 − 18 = _____
9. 84 − 17 = _____
10. 76 − 15 = _____
11. 86 − 12 = _____
12. 82 − 19 = _____

PROBLEM SOLVING

Solve. Write or draw to explain.

13. Mr. Pearce bought 43 plants. He gave 14 plants to his sister. How many plants does Mr. Pearce have now?

_____ plants

Lesson Check (CC.2.NBT.5)

1. What is the difference?

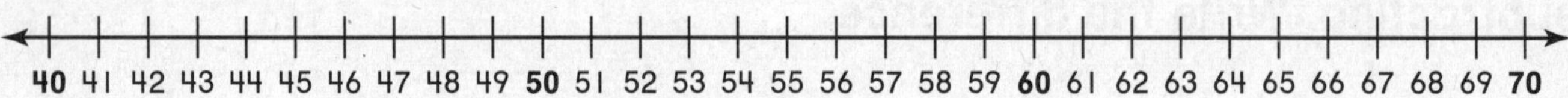

$63 - 19 =$ ____

82	56	44	36
○	○	○	○

Spiral Review (CC.2.OA.1, CC.2.OA.2, CC.2.NBT.6)

2. What is the sum? (Lesson 4.3)

$$\begin{array}{r} 14 \\ +\ 23 \\ \hline \end{array}$$

○ 11 ○ 37
○ 31 ○ 47

3. What is the sum? (Lesson 3.1)

$8 + 7 =$ ____

○ 1
○ 14
○ 15
○ 16

4. Which is a related subtraction fact for $6 + 8 = 14$? (Lesson 3.5)

○ $18 - 6 = 12$
○ $16 - 8 = 8$
○ $14 - 8 = 6$
○ $8 - 2 = 6$

5. John has 7 kites. Annie has 4 kites. How many kites do they have altogether? (Lesson 3.9)

○ 12
○ 11
○ 7
○ 3

Name ______________________

Model Regrouping for Subtraction

COMMON CORE STANDARDS CC.2.NBT.9, CC.2.NBT.5
Use place value understanding and properties of operations to add and subtract.

Draw to show the regrouping. Write the difference two ways. Write the tens and ones. Write the number.

1. Subtract 9 from 35.

Tens	Ones
3 tens	5 ones

_____ tens _____ ones

_____

2. Subtract 14 from 52.

Tens	Ones
5 tens	2 ones

_____ tens _____ ones

_____

3. Subtract 17 from 46.

Tens	Ones
4 tens	6 ones

_____ tens _____ ones

_____

4. Subtract 28 from 63.

Tens	Ones
6 tens	3 ones

_____ tens _____ ones

_____

PROBLEM SOLVING

Choose a way to solve. Write or draw to explain.

5. Mr. Ortega made 51 cookies. He gave 14 cookies away. How many cookies does he have now?

_____ cookies

Lesson Check (CC.2.NBT.9, CC.2.NBT.5)

1. Subtract 9 from 36.
   What is the difference?

Tens	Ones

○ 45 ○ 26
○ 27 ○ 7

2. Subtract 28 from 45.
   What is the difference?

Tens	Ones

○ 73 ○ 23
○ 37 ○ 17

Spiral Review (CC.2NBT.5, CC.2.NBT.6)

3. What is the difference? (Lesson 5.1)

$51 - 8 =$ ____

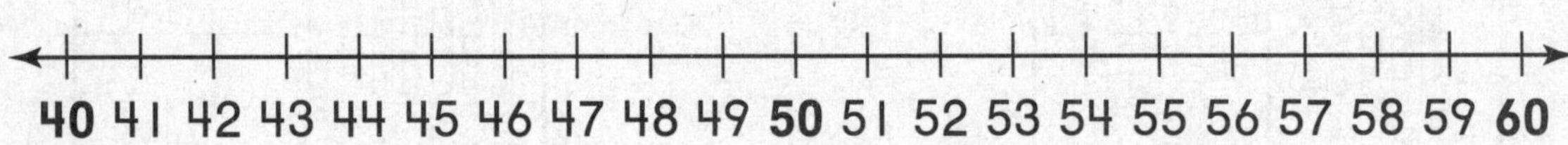

○ 41 ○ 43 ○ 57 ○ 59

4. What is the sum? (Lesson 4.2)

$38 + 35 =$ ____

○ 63
○ 67
○ 73
○ 76

5. What is the sum? (Lesson 4.11)

$$\begin{array}{r} 63 \\ 18 \\ +\ 9 \\ \hline \end{array}$$

○ 62 ○ 87
○ 80 ○ 90

Name ______________________________

Model and Record 2-Digit Subtraction

COMMON CORE STANDARD CC.2.NBT.5
Use place value understanding and properties of operations to add and subtract.

Draw a quick picture to solve.
Write the difference.

1.

	Tens	Ones
	☐	☐
	4	3
−	1	7

Tens	Ones

2.

	Tens	Ones
	☐	☐
	3	8
−	2	9

Tens	Ones

3.

	Tens	Ones
	☐	☐
	5	2
−	3	7

Tens	Ones

4.

	Tens	Ones
	☐	☐
	3	5
−	1	9

Tens	Ones

PROBLEM SOLVING

Solve. Write or draw to explain.

5. Kendall has 63 stickers.
Her sister has 57 stickers.
How many more stickers does
Kendall have than her sister?

_______ more stickers

TEST PREP

Lesson Check (CC.2.NBT.5)

1. What is the difference?

	Tens	Ones
	☐	☐
	4	7
−	1	8

○ 55 ○ 29

○ 31 ○ 19

2. What is the difference?

	Tens	Ones
	☐	☐
	3	3
−	2	9

○ 16 ○ 8

○ 12 ○ 4

Spiral Review (CC.2.OA.2, CC.2.NBT.5, CC.2.NBT.6)

3. What is the difference? (Lesson 3.6)

$10 - 6 =$ ____

○ 5 ○ 3

○ 4 ○ 2

4. What is the sum? (Lesson 4.2)

$16 + 49 =$ ____

○ 33 ○ 67

○ 65 ○ 75

5. What is the sum? (Lesson 4.1)

$28 + 8 =$ ____

○ 36

○ 20

○ 18

○ 10

6. What is the difference? (Lesson 5.1)

$52 - 6 =$ ____

○ 58

○ 50

○ 48

○ 46

Name ___________________________

2-Digit Subtraction

COMMON CORE STANDARD CC.2.NBT.5
Use place value understanding and properties of operations to add and subtract.

Regroup if you need to.
Write the difference.

1.

Tens	Ones
☐	☐
4	7
− 2	8

2.

Tens	Ones
☐	☐
3	3
− 1	8

3.

Tens	Ones
☐	☐
2	8
− 1	4

4.

Tens	Ones
☐	☐
6	6
− 1	9

5.

7	7
− 2	6

6.

5	8
− 3	4

7.

5	2
− 2	5

8.

8	7
− 4	9

PROBLEM SOLVING

Solve. Write or draw to explain.

9. Mrs. Paul bought 32 erasers. She gave 19 erasers to students. How many erasers does she still have?

_____ erasers

Lesson Check (CC.2.NBT.5)

1. What is the difference?

	4	8
−	3	9

○ 9 ○ 11
○ 10 ○ 19

2. What is the difference?

	8	4
−	6	6

○ 48 ○ 28
○ 38 ○ 18

Spiral Review (CC.2.OA.1, CC.2.OA.2, CC.2.NBT.5)

3. What is the difference? (Lesson 5.4)

	Tens	Ones
	□	□
	3	2
−	1	9

○ 11
○ 13
○ 23
○ 51

4. Which of the following has the same sum as 8 + 7? (Lesson 3.3)

○ 10 + 2
○ 10 + 3
○ 10 + 5
○ 10 + 6

5. 27 boys and 23 girls go on a field trip to the museum. How many children go to the museum in all? (Lesson 4.9)

○ 40 ○ 50
○ 44 ○ 54

6. There were 17 berries in the basket. Then 9 berries are eaten. How many berries are there now? (Lesson 3.9)

○ 6 ○ 12
○ 8 ○ 26

Name ________________

Practice 2-Digit Subtraction

COMMON CORE STANDARD CC.2.NBT.5
Use place value understanding and properties of operations to add and subtract.

Write the difference.

1.

$$\begin{array}{r} 50 \\ -18 \\ \hline \end{array}$$

2.

$$\begin{array}{r} 43 \\ -17 \\ \hline \end{array}$$

3.

$$\begin{array}{r} 75 \\ -18 \\ \hline \end{array}$$

4.

$$\begin{array}{r} 22 \\ -\ 6 \\ \hline \end{array}$$

5.

$$\begin{array}{r} 60 \\ -35 \\ \hline \end{array}$$

6.

$$\begin{array}{r} 42 \\ -34 \\ \hline \end{array}$$

7.

$$\begin{array}{r} 21 \\ -\ 8 \\ \hline \end{array}$$

8.

$$\begin{array}{r} 39 \\ -27 \\ \hline \end{array}$$

9.

$$\begin{array}{r} 61 \\ -37 \\ \hline \end{array}$$

PROBLEM SOLVING

Solve. Write or draw to explain.

10. Julie has 42 sheets of paper. She gives 17 sheets to Kari. How many sheets of paper does Julie have now?

_______ sheets of paper

Lesson Check (CC.2.NBT.5)

1. What is the difference?

$$\begin{array}{r} 73 \\ -\ 47 \\ \hline \end{array}$$

- ○ 24
- ○ 26
- ○ 34
- ○ 36

2. What is the difference?

$$\begin{array}{r} 54 \\ -\ 13 \\ \hline \end{array}$$

- ○ 31
- ○ 37
- ○ 39
- ○ 41

Spiral Review (CC.2.OA.2, CC.2.NBT.6)

3. What is the sum? (Lesson 3.2)

9 + 9 = _____

- ○ 20
- ○ 18
- ○ 9
- ○ 0

4. What is the difference? (Lesson 3.6)

14 − 7 = _____

- ○ 21
- ○ 13
- ○ 7
- ○ 6

5. What is the sum? (Lesson 4.2)

36 + 25 = _____

- ○ 61
- ○ 54
- ○ 51
- ○ 11

6. What is the sum? (Lesson 3.4)

7 + 2 + 3 = _____

- ○ 6
- ○ 11
- ○ 12
- ○ 14

Name ______________________

Rewrite 2-Digit Subtraction

COMMON CORE STANDARD CC.2.NBT.5
Use place value understanding and properties of operations to add and subtract.

Rewrite the subtraction problem. Then find the difference.

1. 35 − 19	2. 47 − 23	3. 55 − 28
− ____	− ____	− ____
4. 22 − 15	5. 61 − 32	6. 70 − 37
− ____	− ____	− ____

PROBLEM SOLVING

Solve. Write or draw to explain.

7. Jimmy went to the toy store. He saw 23 wooden trains and 41 plastic trains. How many more plastic trains than wooden trains did he see?

____ more plastic trains

Lesson Check (CC.2.NBT.5)

1. What is the difference for 43 − 17?

   −

   ○ 16　○ 36
   ○ 26　○ 60

2. What is the difference for 50 − 16?

   −

   ○ 66　○ 34
   ○ 46　○ 24

Spiral Review (CC.2.OA.2, CC.2.NBT.5, CC.2.NBT.6, CC.2.NBT.9)

3. What is the sum? (Lesson 4.12)

$$\begin{array}{r} 29 \\ 4 \\ 25 \\ +\ 16 \\ \hline \end{array}$$

   ○ 100　○ 70
   ○ 74　○ 65

4. What is the sum of 41 + 19? (Lesson 4.7)

   ○ 60
   ○ 50
   ○ 38
   ○ 30

5. Which of the following has the same sum as 5 + 9? (Lesson 3.3)

   ○ 10 + 6
   ○ 10 + 5
   ○ 10 + 4
   ○ 10 + 3

6. What is the difference? (Lesson 5.2)

   45 − 13 = ____

   ○ 28
   ○ 32
   ○ 52
   ○ 58

Name ______________________________

Add to Find Differences

COMMON CORE STANDARD CC.2.NBT.5
Use place value understanding and properties of operations to add and subtract.

Use the number line. Count up to find the difference.

1. 36 − 29 = ____

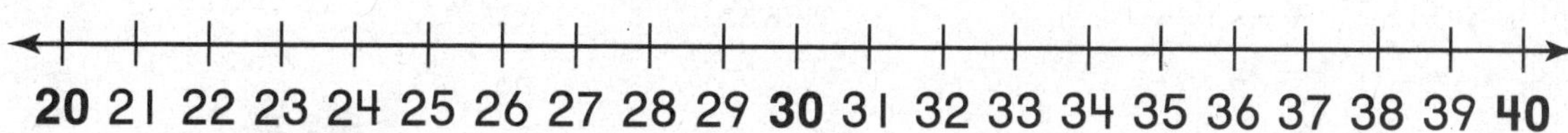

2. 43 − 38 = ____

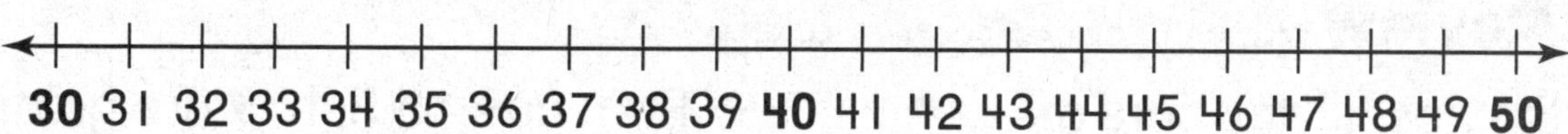

3. 76 − 68 = ____

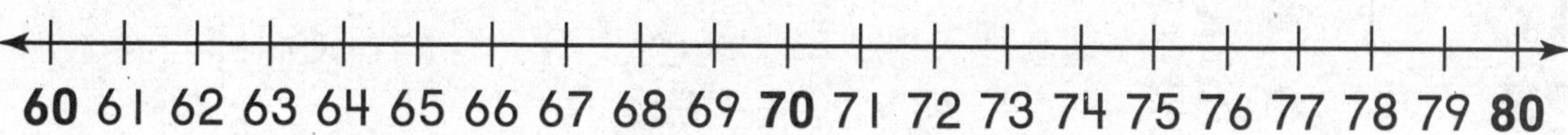

PROBLEM SOLVING

Solve. You may wish to use the number line.

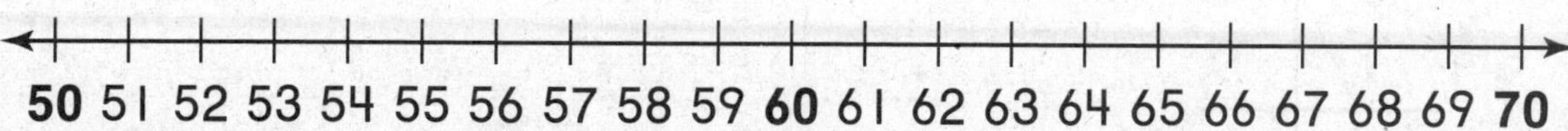

4. Jill has 63 index cards. She uses 57 of them for a project. How many index cards does Jill have now?

____ index cards

Lesson Check (CC.2.NBT.5)

Use the number line. Count up to find the difference.

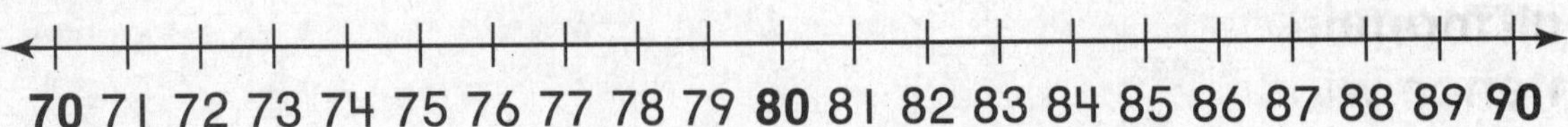

1. 82 − 75 = _____

○ 2　○ 6
○ 5　○ 7

2. 90 − 82 = _____

○ 2　○ 8
○ 4　○ 9

Spiral Review (CC.2.OA.1, CC.2.OA.4, CC.2.NBT.5, CC.NBT.9)

3. Jordan has 41 toy cars at home. He brings 24 cars to school. How many cars are at home? (Lesson 5.3)

○ 17　○ 25
○ 23　○ 57

4. Pam has 15 fish. 9 are goldfish and the rest are guppies. How many fish are guppies? (Lesson 3.9)

○ 24　○ 6
○ 9　○ 4

5. What is the sum? (Lesson 4.6)

	Tens	Ones
	3	5
+	1	9

○ 16　○ 44
○ 24　○ 54

6. Each table has 5 pencils. There are 3 tables. How many pencils are there altogether? (Lesson 3.11)

○ 20
○ 15
○ 8
○ 2

Name ______________________

PROBLEM SOLVING
Lesson 5.9

Problem Solving • Subtraction

COMMON CORE STANDARD CC.2.OA.1
Represent and solve problems involving addition and subtraction.

Label the bar model. Write a number sentence with a ■ for the missing number. Solve.

1. Megan picked 34 flowers. Some of the flowers are yellow and 18 flowers are pink. How many of the flowers are yellow?

   ____ yellow flowers

2. Alex had 45 toy cars. He put 26 toy cars in a box. How many toy cars are not in the box?

   ____ toy cars

3. Mr. Kane makes 43 pizzas. 28 of the pizzas are small. The rest are large. How many pizzas are large?

   ____ large pizzas

Lesson Check (CC.2.OA.1)

1. There were 39 pumpkins at the store. Then 17 of the pumpkins were sold. How many pumpkins are still at the store?

   ○ 22 ○ 42
   ○ 26 ○ 56

2. There were 48 ants on a hill. Then 13 of the ants marched away. How many ants are still on the hill?

   ○ 21 ○ 55
   ○ 35 ○ 61

Spiral Review (CC.2.OA.1, CC.2.OA.2, CC.2.NBT.5, CC.2.NBT.6)

3. Ashley had 26 markers. Her friend gave her 17 more markers. How many markers does Ashley have now? (Lesson 4.10)

   ○ 17 ○ 33
   ○ 26 ○ 43

4. What is the sum? (Lesson 4.7)

$$\begin{array}{r} 46 \\ +\ 24 \\ \hline \end{array}$$

   ○ 22 ○ 70
   ○ 60 ○ 72

5. Which of the following has the same difference as $15 - 7$? (Lesson 3.7)

   ○ $10 - 8$
   ○ $10 - 7$
   ○ $10 - 3$
   ○ $10 - 2$

6. What is the sum? (Lesson 4.1)

$$34 + 5 = \_\_\_\_$$

   ○ 39
   ○ 41
   ○ 49
   ○ 51

Name ______________________________

Algebra • Write Equations to Represent Subtraction

COMMON CORE STANDARD CC.2.OA.1
Represent and solve problems involving addition and subtraction.

Write a number sentence for the problem. Use a ■ for the missing number. Then solve.

1. 29 children rode their bikes to school. After some of the children rode home, there were 8 children with bikes still at school. How many children rode their bikes home?

____

_____ children

2. 32 children were on the school bus. Then 24 children got off the bus. How many children were still on the bus?

____

_____ children

PROBLEM SOLVING

Solve. Write or draw to explain.

3. There were 21 children in the library. After 7 children left the library, how many children were still in the library?

_____ children

Lesson Check (CC.2.OA.1)

1. Cindy had 42 beads. She used some beads for a bracelet. She has 14 beads left. How many beads did she use for the bracelet?

○ 22
○ 28
○ 32
○ 56

2. Jake had 36 baseball cards. He gave 17 cards to his sister. How many baseball cards does Jake have now?

○ 19
○ 21
○ 23
○ 41

Spiral Review (CC.2.OA.2, CC.2.NBT.5)

3. What is the sum? (Lesson 3.2)

$6 + 7 = \_\_\_\_$

○ 11
○ 12
○ 13
○ 15

4. What is the difference? (Lesson 3.6)

$16 - 9 = \_\_\_\_$

○ 11
○ 9
○ 8
○ 7

5. What is the difference? (Lesson 5.5)

$$\begin{array}{r|l} 4 & 6 \\ -\ 3 & 9 \\ \hline & \end{array}$$

○ 7 ○ 13
○ 15 ○ 26

6. Which of the following has the same sum as 6 + 8? (Lesson 3.3)

○ 10 + 2
○ 10 + 3
○ 10 + 4
○ 10 + 5

Name ______________________

Solve Multistep Problems

COMMON CORE STANDARD CC.2.OA.1
Represent and solve problems involving addition and subtraction.

Complete the bar models for the steps you do to solve the problem.

1. Greg has 60 building blocks. His sister gives him 17 more blocks. He uses 38 blocks to make a tower. How many blocks are not used in the tower?

______ blocks

2. Jenna has a train of 26 connecting cubes and a train of 37 connecting cubes. She gives 15 cubes to a friend. How many cubes does Jenna have now?

______ cubes

PROBLEM SOLVING

Solve. Write or draw to explain.

3. Ava has 25 books. She gives away 7 books. Then Tom gives her 12 books. How many books does Ava have now?

______ books

Lesson Check (CC.2.OA.1)

1. Sara has 18 crayons. Max has 19 crayons. How many more crayons do they need to get to have 50 crayons altogether?

○ 13
○ 23
○ 31
○ 37

2. Jon has 12 pennies. Lucy has 17 pennies. How many more pennies do they need to have 75 pennies altogether?

○ 21
○ 35
○ 46
○ 61

Spiral Review (CC.2.OA.1, CC.2.NBT.5, CC.2.NBT.6)

3. What is the difference? (Lesson 5.2)

58 − 13 = ____

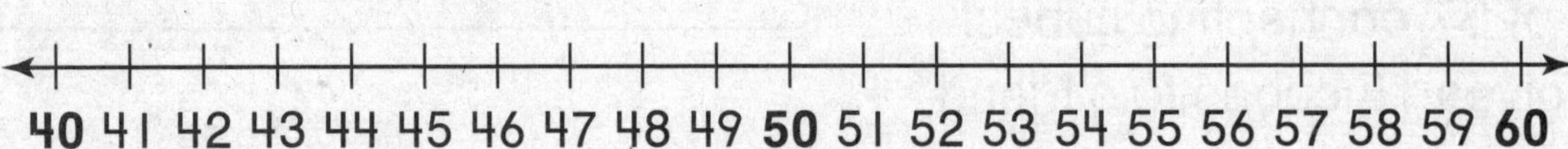

○ 71 ○ 65 ○ 45 ○ 22

4. What is the sum? (Lesson 4.6)

4	7
+ 1	5

○ 62 ○ 43
○ 52 ○ 32

5. There are 26 cards in a box. Bryan takes 12 cards. How many cards are still in the box? (Lesson 5.9)

○ 34
○ 22
○ 18
○ 14

Name ______________________________ COMMON CORE STANDARDS CC.2.OA.1, CC.2.NBT.5, CC.2.NBT.9

Chapter 5 Extra Practice

Lessons 5.1 - 5.2 (pp. 229–236)

Break apart the number you are subtracting.
Write the difference.

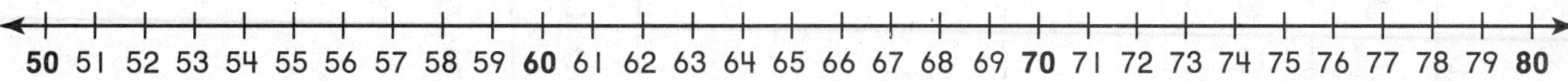

1. 73 − 7 = _____
2. 65 − 7 = _____
3. 64 − 8 = _____
4. 75 − 18 = _____
5. 72 − 12 = _____
6. 74 − 19 = _____

Lesson 5.3 (pp. 237–240)

Draw to show the regrouping. Write the difference two ways.
Write the tens and ones. Write the number.

1. Subtract 7 from 52.

Tens	Ones

_____ tens _____ ones

_____

2. Subtract 28 from 41.

Tens	Ones

_____ tens _____ ones

_____

3. Subtract 16 from 34.

Tens	Ones

_____ tens _____ ones

_____

Lesson 5.4 (pp. 241–244)

Draw a quick picture to solve.
Write the difference.

1.

Tens	Ones
□	□
4	5
− 1	9

Tens	Ones

2.

Tens	Ones
□	□
5	3
− 2	6

Tens	Ones

Lessons 5.5 - 5.6 (pp. 245–251)

Write the difference.

1.

7	3
− 2	8

2.

9	5
− 4	7

3.

$$\begin{array}{r} 60 \\ -\,48 \\ \hline \end{array}$$

4.

$$\begin{array}{r} 49 \\ -\,24 \\ \hline \end{array}$$

Lesson 5.11 (pp. 269–272)

Complete the bar models for the steps you do to solve the problem.

1. Ryan buys a pack of 30 stickers. His mom gives him 14 stickers. How many more stickers does he need to have 62 stickers in all?

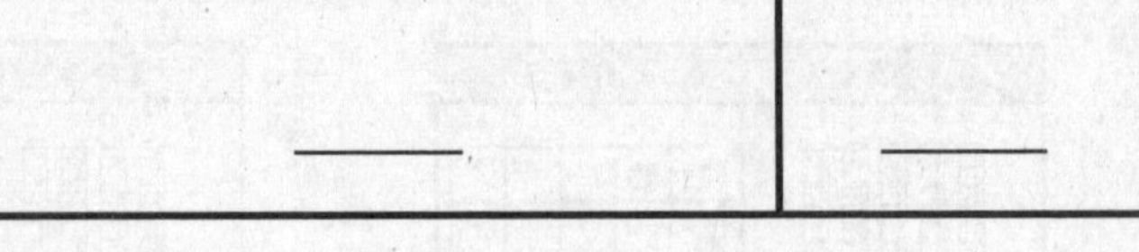

____ more stickers

Chapter 6

School-Home Letter

Dear Family,

My class started Chapter 6 this week. In this chapter, I will learn how to add and subtract 3-digit numbers, including regrouping ones, tens, and hundreds.

Love, ____________________

Vocabulary

addends Numbers added together in addition problems

$7 + 2 = 9$ (7 and 2 are the addends)

sum Answer to an addition problem

$7 + 2 = 9$ (9 is the sum)

difference Answer to a subtraction problem

Home Activity

Write addition and subtraction problems with two 3-digit numbers for your child. Write some problems where regrouping is needed and other problems where regrouping is not needed.

$$\begin{array}{r} 462 \\ +341 \\ \hline \end{array} \qquad \begin{array}{r} 796 \\ -578 \\ \hline \end{array}$$

Literature

Reading math stories reinforces learning. Look for these books at the library.

A Collection for Kate
by Barbara deRubertis.
Kane Press, 1999.

The Action of Subtraction
by Brian P. Cleary.
Millbrook Press, 2006.

Capítulo 6

Carta para la casa

Querida familia:

Mi clase comenzó el Capítulo 6 esta semana. En este capítulo, aprenderé a sumar y restar números de 3 dígitos, incluyendo la reagrupación de unidades, decenas y centenas.

Con cariño, ______________________________

Vocabulario

sumandos números que se suman unos a otros en problemas de suma

$7 + 2 = 9$

(7 y 2: sumandos)

suma resultado de un problema de suma

$7 + 2 = 9$

(9: suma)

diferencia resultado de un problema de resta

Actividad para la casa

Escríbale a su hijo problemas de suma y resta con dos números de 3 dígitos. Escriba algunos problemas que necesiten reagrupación y otros que no la necesiten.

$$\begin{array}{r} 462 \\ +341 \\ \hline \end{array} \qquad \begin{array}{r} 796 \\ -578 \\ \hline \end{array}$$

Literatura

Leer cuentos de matemáticas refuerza el aprendizaje. Busque estos libros en la biblioteca.

A Collection for Kate
por Barbara Derubertis.
Kane Press, 1999.

The Action of Subtraction
por Brian P. Cleary.
Millbrook Press, 2006.

Name ______________________________

Draw to Represent 3-Digit Addition

COMMON CORE STANDARD CC.2.NBT.7
Use place value understanding and properties of operations to add and subtract.

Draw quick pictures. Write how many hundreds, tens, and ones in all. Write the number.

1. Add 142 and 215.

Hundreds	Tens	Ones

_____ hundreds _____ tens _____ ones

____

2. Add 263 and 206.

Hundreds	Tens	Ones

_____ hundreds _____ tens _____ ones

____

PROBLEM SOLVING

Solve. Write or draw to explain.

3. A farmer sold 324 lemons and 255 limes. How many pieces of fruit did the farmer sell altogether?

_________ pieces of fruit

Lesson Check (CC.2.NBT.7)

1. Ms. Carol sold 346 child tickets and 253 adult tickets. How many tickets did Ms. Carol sell in all?

○ 113

○ 569

○ 599

○ 699

2. Mr. Harris counted 227 gray pebbles and 341 white pebbles. How many pebbles did Mr. Harris count?

○ 658

○ 568

○ 526

○ 468

Spiral Review (CC.2.OA.4, CC.2.NBT.5, CC.2.NBT.6)

3. Pat has 3 rows of shells. There are 4 shells in each row. How many shells does Pat have in all? (Lesson 3.11)

○ 7 ○ 10

○ 9 ○ 12

4. Kara counted 32 red pens, 25 blue pens, 7 black pens, and 24 green pens. How many pens did Kara count in all? (Lesson 4.12)

○ 88 ○ 81

○ 87 ○ 78

5. Kai had 46 blocks. He gave 39 blocks to his sister. How many blocks does Kai have left? (Lesson 5.8)

○ 8

○ 7

○ 6

○ 3

6. A shop has 55 posters for sale. 34 posters show sports. The rest of the posters show animals. How many posters show animals? (Lesson 5.5)

○ 89

○ 29

○ 21

○ 11

Name ____________________

Break Apart 3-Digit Addends

COMMON CORE STANDARD CC.2.NBT.7
Use place value understanding and properties of operations to add and subtract.

Break apart the addends to find the sum.

1. 518 → _____ + _____ + _____
+ 221 → _____ + _____ + _____

_____ + _____ + _____ = _____

2. 438 → _____ + _____ + _____
+ 142 → _____ + _____ + _____

_____ + _____ + _____ = _____

3. 324 → _____ + _____ + _____
+ 239 → _____ + _____ + _____

_____ + _____ + _____ = _____

PROBLEM SOLVING REAL WORLD

Solve. Write or draw to explain.

4. There are 126 crayons in a bucket. A teacher puts 144 more crayons in the bucket. How many crayons are in the bucket now?

_____ crayons

Lesson Check (CC.2.NBT.7)

1. What is the sum?

$$\begin{array}{r} 218 \\ +\ 145 \\ \hline \end{array}$$

○ 263
○ 363
○ 463
○ 541

2. What is the sum?

$$\begin{array}{r} 664 \\ +\ 223 \\ \hline \end{array}$$

○ 441
○ 881
○ 887
○ 888

Spiral Review (CC.2.OA.2, CC.2.NBT.5, CC.2.NBT.6, CC.2.NBT.9)

3. What is the sum? (Lesson 4.2)

$19 + 21 = ?$

○ 41
○ 40
○ 39
○ 38

4. Which is a related subtraction fact for $9 + 6 = 15$? (Lesson 3.5)

○ $15 - 9 = 6$
○ $9 - 6 = 3$
○ $6 + 9 = 15$
○ $9 - 3 = 6$

5. There are 25 goldfish and 33 betta fish. How many fish are there in all? (Lesson 4.7)

○ 8
○ 48
○ 58
○ 68

6. Subtract 16 from 41. What is the difference? (Lesson 5.3)

○ 57
○ 35
○ 25
○ 16

Tens	Ones

Name ___________________________

3-Digit Addition: Regroup Ones

COMMON CORE STANDARD CC.2.NBT.7
Use place value understanding and properties of operations to add and subtract.

Write the sum.

1.

	Hundreds	Tens	Ones
		□	
	1	4	8
+	2	3	4

2.

	Hundreds	Tens	Ones
		□	
	3	2	1
+	3	1	8

3.

	Hundreds	Tens	Ones
		□	
	4	1	4
+	1	7	9

4.

	Hundreds	Tens	Ones
		□	
	6	0	2
+	2	5	8

PROBLEM SOLVING

Solve. Write or draw to explain.

5. In the garden, there are 258 yellow daisies and 135 white daisies. How many daisies are in the garden altogether?

__________ daisies

TEST PREP

Lesson Check (CC.2.NBT.7)

1. What is the sum?

Hundreds	Tens	Ones
	□	
4	3	5
+ 1	4	6

○ 311 ○ 571
○ 371 ○ 581

2. What is the sum?

Hundreds	Tens	Ones
	□	
4	3	6
+ 3	0	6

○ 712 ○ 742
○ 730 ○ 832

Spiral Review (CC.2.OA.2, CC.2.NBT.5, CC.2.NBT.6, CC.2.NBT.7)

3. What is the difference? (Lesson 3.6)

$9 - 4 =$ ____

○ 13
○ 9
○ 5
○ 3

4. What is the sum? (Lesson 4.7)

$$\begin{array}{r} 82 \\ +\ 59 \\ \hline \end{array}$$

○ 141
○ 64
○ 37
○ 23

5. What is the sum? (Lesson 3.6)

$26 + 7 =$ ____

○ 19
○ 32
○ 33
○ 34

6. Add 243 and 132. How many hundreds, tens, and ones are there in all? (Lesson 6.1)

○ 3 hundreds 7 tens 5 ones
○ 2 hundreds 7 tens 5 ones
○ 2 hundreds 3 tens 2 ones
○ 1 hundred 1 ten 1 one

Name ___________________________

3-Digit Addition: Regroup Tens

COMMON CORE STANDARD CC.2.NBT.7
Use place value understanding and properties of operations to add and subtract.

Write the sum.

1.

Hundreds	Tens	Ones
□	□	
1	8	7
+ 2	3	2

2.

Hundreds	Tens	Ones
□	□	
3	2	2
+ 3	5	6

3.

Hundreds	Tens	Ones
□	□	
2	8	5
+ 5	3	1

4.

$$\begin{array}{r} 445 \\ +\ \ 34 \\ \hline \end{array}$$

5.

$$\begin{array}{r} 620 \\ +\ 288 \\ \hline \end{array}$$

6.

$$\begin{array}{r} 557 \\ +\ 180 \\ \hline \end{array}$$

7.

$$\begin{array}{r} 671 \\ +\ 154 \\ \hline \end{array}$$

8.

$$\begin{array}{r} 463 \\ +\ 481 \\ \hline \end{array}$$

9.

$$\begin{array}{r} 746 \\ +\ 133 \\ \hline \end{array}$$

PROBLEM SOLVING

Solve. Write or draw to explain.

10. There are 142 blue toy cars and 293 red toy cars at the toy store. How many toy cars are there in all?

_________ toy cars

Lesson Check (CC.2.NBT.7)

1. What is the sum?

$$\begin{array}{r} 472 \\ +\ 255 \\ \hline \end{array}$$

○ 623
○ 627
○ 727
○ 728

2. What is the sum?

$$\begin{array}{r} 144 \\ +\ 284 \\ \hline \end{array}$$

○ 328
○ 418
○ 428
○ 518

Spiral Review (CC.2.OA.2, CC.2.NBT.5, CC.2.NBT.7)

3. What is the sum? (Lesson 4.6)

$$\begin{array}{r} 56 \\ +\ 38 \\ \hline \end{array}$$

○ 82
○ 84
○ 92
○ 94

4. What is the sum? (Lesson 6.3)

$$\begin{array}{r} 326 \\ +\ 139 \\ \hline \end{array}$$

○ 465
○ 351
○ 259
○ 187

5. What is the sum? (Lesson 3.1)

$8 + 9 =$ ____

○ 19
○ 17
○ 9
○ 1

6. What is the difference? (Lesson 5.5)

$$\begin{array}{r} 82 \\ -\ 34 \\ \hline \end{array}$$

○ 25
○ 48
○ 52
○ 56

Name ______________________________

Addition: Regroup Ones and Tens

COMMON CORE STANDARD CC.2.NBT.7
Use place value understanding and properties of operations to add and subtract.

Write the sum.

1. $547 + 435$

2. $367 + 284$

3. $485 + 456$

4. $187 + 306$

5. $647 + 128$

6. $523 + 174$

7. $255 + 231$

8. $294 + 176$

9. $375 + 364$

PROBLEM SOLVING

Solve. Write or draw to explain.

10. Saul and Luisa each scored 167 points on a computer game. How many points did they score in all?

_________ points

Lesson Check (CC.2.NBT.7)

1. What is the sum?

$$\begin{array}{r} 348 \\ +\ 272 \\ \hline \end{array}$$

○ 136 ○ 520

○ 510 ○ 620

2. What is the sum?

$$\begin{array}{r} 123 \\ +\ 217 \\ \hline \end{array}$$

○ 314 ○ 340

○ 330 ○ 417

Spiral Review (CC.2.OA.1, CC.2.OA.2, CC.2.NBT.6, CC.2.NBT.9)

3. Which has the same sum as 9 + 4? (Lesson 3.3)

○ 10 + 3

○ 10 + 4

○ 10 + 5

○ 10 + 6

4. What is the sum? (Lesson 4.11)

$$\begin{array}{r} 32 \\ 15 \\ +\ 46 \\ \hline \end{array}$$

○ 47 ○ 83

○ 78 ○ 93

5. Add 29 and 35. What is the sum? (Lesson 4.4)

Tens	Ones

○ 16 ○ 64

○ 36 ○ 95

6. Tom had 25 pretzels. He gave away 12 pretzels. How many pretzels does Tom have left? (Lesson 5.10)

○ 4

○ 13

○ 37

○ 46

Name ______________________

Problem Solving • 3-Digit Subtraction

COMMON CORE STANDARD CC.2.NBT.7
Use place value understanding and properties of operations to add and subtract.

Make a model to solve. Then draw a quick picture of your model.

1. On Saturday, 770 people went to the snack shop. On Sunday, 628 people went. How many more people went to the snack shop on Saturday than on Sunday?

   _______ more people

2. There were 395 lemon ice cups at the snack shop. People bought 177 lemon ice cups. How many lemon ice cups are still at the snack shop?

   _______ cups

3. There were 576 bottles of water at the snack shop. People bought 469 bottles of water. How many bottles of water are at the snack shop now?

   _______ bottles

4. There were 279 bags of apple chips at the snack shop. Then 134 bags of apple chips were bought. How many bags of apple chips are at the snack shop now?

   _______ bags

Lesson Check (CC.2.NBT.7)

1. There are 278 math and science books. 128 of them are math books. How many science books are there?

   - ○ 50
   - ○ 140
   - ○ 150
   - ○ 406

2. A book has 176 pages. Mr. Roberts has read 119 pages. How many pages does he have left to read?

   - ○ 55
   - ○ 57
   - ○ 67
   - ○ 295

Spiral Review (CC.2.OA.2, CC.2.NBT.5, CC.2.NBT.6, CC.2.NBT.7)

3. What is the sum? (Lesson 3.4)

   $1 + 6 + 2 = \_\_\_\_$

   - ○ 9
   - ○ 8
   - ○ 7
   - ○ 4

4. What is the difference? (Lesson 5.1)

   $54 - 8 = \_\_\_\_$

   - ○ 62
   - ○ 46
   - ○ 44
   - ○ 34

5. What is the sum? (Lesson 6.5)

   $$\begin{array}{r} 356 \\ +\ 174 \\ \hline \end{array}$$

   - ○ 182
   - ○ 220
   - ○ 451
   - ○ 530

6. What is the sum? (Lesson 4.3)

   $$\begin{array}{r} 22 \\ +\ 16 \\ \hline \end{array}$$

   - ○ 47
   - ○ 38
   - ○ 18
   - ○ 6

Name ______________________

3-Digit Subtraction: Regroup Tens

COMMON CORE STANDARD CC.2.NBT.7
Use place value understanding and properties of operations to add and subtract.

Solve. Write the difference.

1.

	Hundreds	Tens	Ones
		☐	☐
	7	7	4
−	2	3	6

2.

	Hundreds	Tens	Ones
		☐	☐
	5	5	1
−	1	1	3

3.

	Hundreds	Tens	Ones
		☐	☐
	4	8	9
−	2	7	3

4.

	Hundreds	Tens	Ones
		☐	☐
	7	7	2
−	2	5	4

PROBLEM SOLVING

Solve. Write or draw to explain.

5. There were 985 pencils. Some pencils were sold. Then there were 559 pencils left. How many pencils were sold?

_______ pencils

Lesson Check (CC.2.NBT.7)

1. What is the difference?

$$\begin{array}{r} 346 \\ -\ 127 \\ \hline \end{array}$$

○ 119
○ 219
○ 229
○ 473

2. What is the difference?

$$\begin{array}{r} 568 \\ -\ 226 \\ \hline \end{array}$$

○ 342
○ 344
○ 742
○ 794

Spiral Review (CC.2.OA.1, CC.2.OA.4, CC.2.NBT.5, CC.2.NBT.7)

3. What is the difference? (Lesson 5.1)

$45 - 7 = \_\_\_$

○ 32
○ 36
○ 38
○ 42

4. Leroy has 11 cubes. Jane has 15 cubes. How many cubes do they have altogether? (Lesson 4.10)

○ 4
○ 15
○ 19
○ 26

5. Mina puts 5 flowers in each vase. How many flowers will she put in 3 vases? (Lesson 3.10)

○ 5
○ 10
○ 15
○ 20

6. Mr. Hill had 428 pencils. He gave away 150 pencils. How many pencils did he keep? (Lesson 6.6)

○ 278
○ 338
○ 350
○ 578

Name ______________________________

3-Digit Subtraction: Regroup Hundreds

COMMON CORE STANDARD CC.2.NBT.7
Use place value understanding and properties of operations to add and subtract.

Solve. Write the difference.

1.

	Hundreds	Tens	Ones
	☐	☐	☐
	7	2	7
−	2	5	6

2.

	Hundreds	Tens	Ones
	☐	☐	☐
	9	6	7
−	1	5	3

3.

	6	3	9
−	4	7	2

4.

	4	4	8
−	3	6	3

PROBLEM SOLVING REAL WORLD

Solve. Write or draw to explain.

5. There were 537 people in the parade. 254 of these people were playing an instrument. How many people were not playing an instrument?

_______ people

Lesson Check (CC.2.NBT.7)

1. What is the difference?

$$\begin{array}{r} 538 \\ -\ 135 \\ \hline \end{array}$$

- ○ 403
- ○ 463
- ○ 663
- ○ 673

2. What is the difference?

$$\begin{array}{r} 218 \\ -\ 126 \\ \hline \end{array}$$

- ○ 82
- ○ 92
- ○ 132
- ○ 192

Spiral Review (CC.2.OA.2, CC.2.NBT.5, CC.2.NBT.6, CC.2.NBT.7)

3. What is the difference? (Lesson 5.2)

$52 - 15 =$ ____

- ○ 63
- ○ 43
- ○ 37
- ○ 33

4. What is the sum? (Lesson 3.2)

$8 + 7 =$ ____

- ○ 1
- ○ 9
- ○ 14
- ○ 15

5. What is the sum? (Lesson 4.5)

$$\begin{array}{r} 47 \\ +\ 26 \\ \hline \end{array}$$

- ○ 73
- ○ 65
- ○ 46
- ○ 21

6. What is the difference? (Lesson 6.7)

$$\begin{array}{r} 392 \\ -\ 173 \\ \hline \end{array}$$

- ○ 565
- ○ 361
- ○ 246
- ○ 219

Name ____________________

Subtraction: Regroup Hundreds and Tens

COMMON CORE STANDARD CC.2.NBT.7
Use place value understanding and properties of operations to add and subtract.

Solve. Write the difference.

1.
$$\begin{array}{r} 816 \\ -\ 345 \\ \hline \end{array}$$

2.
$$\begin{array}{r} 942 \\ -\ 163 \\ \hline \end{array}$$

3.
$$\begin{array}{r} 796 \\ -\ 468 \\ \hline \end{array}$$

4.
$$\begin{array}{r} 723 \\ -\ 543 \\ \hline \end{array}$$

5.
$$\begin{array}{r} 986 \\ -\ 712 \\ \hline \end{array}$$

6.
$$\begin{array}{r} 547 \\ -\ 289 \\ \hline \end{array}$$

PROBLEM SOLVING

Solve.

7. Mia's coloring book has 432 pages. She has already colored 178 pages. How many pages in the book are left to color?

_______ pages

Lesson Check (CC.2.NBT.7)

1. What is the difference?

$$\begin{array}{r} 349 \\ -\ 187 \\ \hline \end{array}$$

○ 162
○ 242
○ 462
○ 536

2. What is the difference?

$$\begin{array}{r} 336 \\ -\ 178 \\ \hline \end{array}$$

○ 242
○ 188
○ 168
○ 158

Spiral Review (CC.2.OA.1, CC.2.OA.2, CC.2.NBT.5, CC.2.NBT.7)

3. What is the sum? (Lesson 6.2)

$$\begin{array}{r} 246 \\ +\ 533 \\ \hline \end{array}$$

○ 313
○ 719
○ 773
○ 779

4. What is the difference? (Lesson 5.6)

$$\begin{array}{r} 38 \\ -\ 14 \\ \hline \end{array}$$

○ 52
○ 24
○ 18
○ 12

5. What is the difference? (Lesson 3.7)

$17 - 9 =$ ____

○ 8
○ 9
○ 10
○ 12

6. Lisa had 15 daisies. She gave away 7 daisies. Then she found 3 more daisies. How many daisies does Lisa have now? (Lesson 5.11)

○ 25
○ 13
○ 19
○ 11

Name ____________________

Regrouping with Zeros

COMMON CORE STANDARD CC.2.NBT.7
Use place value understanding and properties of operations to add and subtract.

Solve. Write the difference.

1.
$$\begin{array}{r} 806 \\ -\ 345 \\ \hline \end{array}$$

2.
$$\begin{array}{r} 902 \\ -\ 783 \\ \hline \end{array}$$

3.
$$\begin{array}{r} 794 \\ -\ 268 \\ \hline \end{array}$$

4.
$$\begin{array}{r} 687 \\ -\ 144 \\ \hline \end{array}$$

5.
$$\begin{array}{r} 505 \\ -\ 167 \\ \hline \end{array}$$

6.
$$\begin{array}{r} 307 \\ -\ 154 \\ \hline \end{array}$$

PROBLEM SOLVING

Solve.

7. There are 303 students.
There are 147 girls.
How many boys are there?

________ boys

Lesson Check (CC.2.NBT.7)

1. What is the difference?

$$\begin{array}{r} 301 \\ -\ 187 \\ \hline \end{array}$$

- ○ 114
- ○ 116
- ○ 186
- ○ 286

2. What is the difference?

$$\begin{array}{r} 406 \\ -\ 268 \\ \hline \end{array}$$

- ○ 128
- ○ 138
- ○ 162
- ○ 262

Spiral Review (CC.2.OA.2, CC.2.NBT.5, CC.2.NBT.7, CC.2.NBT.9)

3. What is the sum? (Lesson 4.7)

$$\begin{array}{r} 35 \\ +\ 79 \\ \hline \end{array}$$

- ○ 44
- ○ 62
- ○ 104
- ○ 114

4. What is the sum? (Lesson 6.4)

$$\begin{array}{r} 555 \\ +\ 282 \\ \hline \end{array}$$

- ○ 847
- ○ 837
- ○ 737
- ○ 273

5. What is the difference? (Lesson 3.6)

$10 - 2 =$ ____

- ○ 12
- ○ 9
- ○ 8
- ○ 7

6. Subtract 11 from 43. What is the difference? (Lesson 5.3)

- ○ 32
- ○ 34
- ○ 42
- ○ 52

Name ______________________________

Chapter 6 Extra Practice

Lesson 6.2 (pp. 285–288)

Break apart the addends to find the sum.

1. 121 → ______ + ______ + ______

+ 269 → ______ + ______ + ______

______ + ______ + ______ = ______

Lesson 6.3 (pp. 289–292)

Write the sum.

1.

	Hundreds	Tens	Ones
		☐	
	6	5	8
+	2	1	6

2.

	Hundreds	Tens	Ones
		☐	
	4	0	3
+	3	2	9

Lessons 6.4 – 6.5 (pp. 293–299)

Write the sum.

1.

	2	9	3
+	5	8	5

2.

$$\begin{array}{r} 368 \\ +\,464 \\ \hline \end{array}$$

3.

$$\begin{array}{r} 176 \\ +\,348 \\ \hline \end{array}$$

Lesson 6.6 (pp. 301–304)

Make a model to solve. Then draw a quick picture of your model.

1. There are 485 books on the shelves and 114 books on the tables. How many more books are on the shelves than on the tables?

_____ more books

Lesson 6.7 (pp. 305–308)

Solve. Write the difference.

1.

	Hundreds	Tens	Ones
		☐	☐
	6	8	1
−	3	1	2

2.

	Hundreds	Tens	Ones
		☐	☐
	7	3	4
−	5	2	6

Lesson 6.8 (pp. 309–312)

Solve. Write the difference.

1.

	6	1	3
−	2	8	3

2.

	8	7	5
−	2	8	3

Chapter 7

School-Home Letter

Dear Family,

My class started Chapter 7 this week. In this chapter, I will learn about the values of coins and how to find the total value of a group of money. I will also learn how to tell time on analog clocks and digital clocks.

Love, ____________________

Vocabulary

penny a coin with a value of 1 cent

nickel a coin with a value of 5 cents

dime a coin with a value of 10 cents

quarter a coin with a value of 25 cents

dollar an amount equal to 100 cents

minute a unit of time

Home Activity

With your child, set up a play store together. Use objects such as food items or small toys. Put price tags on each object, using amounts less than one dollar. On a sheet of paper, have your child write the price of an object and then draw a group of coins that has that as its total value. Take turns doing this for several objects.

Literature

Reading math stories reinforces ideas. Look for these books at the library.

A Dollar for Penny
by Julie Glass
Random House Books for Young Readers, 2000

What Time Is It, Mr. Crocodile?
by Judy Sierra
Gulliver Books, 2004

Capítulo 7

Carta para la casa

Querida familia:

Mi clase comenzó el Capítulo 7 esta semana. En este capítulo, aprenderé sobre el valor de las monedas y cómo hallar el valor total de una cantidad de dinero. También aprenderé a decir la hora usando relojes analógicos y relojes digitales.

Con cariño, ____________________

Vocabulario

moneda de 1¢ una moneda con un valor de 1 centavo

moneda de 5¢ una moneda con un valor de 5 centavos

moneda de 10¢ una moneda con valor de 10 centavos

moneda de 25¢ una moneda con valor de 25 centavos

dólar una cantidad igual a 100 centavos

minuto una unidad de tiempo

Actividad para la casa

Junto a su hijo, jueguen a que están en una tienda. Use objetos tales como artículos de comida o juguetes pequeños. Coloque etiquetas en cada artículo con un precio menor a un dólar. En una hoja de papel, pida su hijo que escriba el precio de un objeto y que dibuje un grupo de monedas que muestren ese valor. Túrnense para repetir la actividad con diferentes objetos.

Literatura

Leer cuentos de matemáticas refuerza los conceptos. Busque estos libros en la biblioteca.

A Dollar for Penny
por Julie Glass.
Random House Books for Young Readers, 2000.

What Time Is It, Mr. Crocodile?
por Judy Sierra.
Gulliver Books, 2004.

Name ______________________

Dimes, Nickels, and Pennies

COMMON CORE STANDARD CC.2.MD.8
Work with time and money.

Count on to find the total value.

1. 

______________________ total value

2. 

______________________ total value

3. 

total value

4. 

total value

PROBLEM SOLVING

Solve. Write or draw to explain.

5. Aaron has 5 dimes and 2 nickels.
   How much money does Aaron have?

______

Lesson Check (CC.2.MD.8)

1. What is the total value of this group of coins?

○ 21¢ ○ 26¢ ○ 31¢ ○ 36¢

Spiral Review (CC.2.OA.2, CC.2.OA.4, CC.2.NBT.1, CC.2.NBT.2)

2. Hayden is building toy cars. Each car needs 4 wheels. How many wheels will Hayden use to build 3 toy cars? (Lesson 3.10)

○ 7

○ 8

○ 12

○ 16

3. What is the value of the underlined digit? (Lesson 2.5)

<u>4</u>29

○ 4

○ 40

○ 44

○ 400

4. Which group of numbers shows counting by fives? (Lesson 1.8)

○ 76, 75, 74, 73, 72

○ 55, 56, 57, 58, 59

○ 40, 45, 50, 55, 60

○ 10, 20, 30, 40, 50

5. What is the difference? (Lesson 3.7)

$12 - 7 =$ ______

○ 5

○ 9

○ 10

○ 19

Name ______________________

Quarters

COMMON CORE STANDARD CC.2.MD.8
Work with time and money.

Count on to find the total value.

1.

____

total value

2.

____

total value

3.

total value

PROBLEM SOLVING

Read the clue. Choose the name of a coin from the box to answer the question.

nickel	dime
quarter	penny

4. I have the same value as a group of 2 dimes and 1 nickel.
   What coin am I?

____

TEST PREP

Lesson Check (CC.2.MD.8)

1. What is the total value of this group of coins?

○ 61¢ ○ 63¢ ○ 65¢ ○ 70¢

Spiral Review (CC.2.OA.1, CC.2.OA.3, CC.2NBT.3, CC.2NBT.4)

2. Which of these is an odd number? (Lesson 1.1)

○ 8
○ 14
○ 17
○ 22

3. Kai scored 4 points and Gail scored 7 points. How many points did they score altogether? (Lesson 3.9)

○ 15
○ 11
○ 10
○ 3

4. There were 382 chairs in the music hall. Which number is greater than 382? (Lesson 2.11)

○ 423
○ 328
○ 283
○ 182

5. Which is another way to write the number 61? (Lesson 1.5)

○ 16
○ sixty-one
○ 60 + 10
○ 6 tens 6 ones

Name ______________________________

Count Collections

COMMON CORE STANDARD CC.2.MD.8
Work with time and money.

Draw and label the coins from greatest to least value. Find the total value.

1.

______

2.

______

3.

______

PROBLEM SOLVING

Solve. Write or draw to explain.

4. Rebecca has these coins. She spends 1 quarter. How much money does she have left?

______

Lesson Check (CC.2.MD.8)

1. What is the total value of this group of coins?

○ 22¢ ○ 47¢ ○ 51¢ ○ 65¢

Spiral Review (CC.2.OA.2, CC.2.NBT.1, CC.2.NBT.3, CC.2.NBT.8)

2. Which number is 100 more than 562? (Lesson 2.9)

○ 662
○ 572
○ 552
○ 462

3. Which of these is another way to describe 58? (Lesson 1.4)

○ $8 + 5$
○ $50 + 8$
○ $80 + 5$
○ $50 + 80$

4. What is the sum? (Lesson 3.2)

$6 + 3 =$ ______

○ 3
○ 6
○ 9
○ 18

5. What number do the blocks show? (Lesson 2.4)

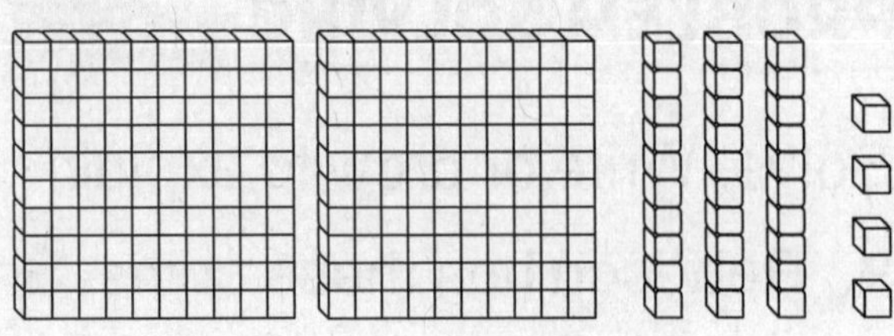

○ 134 ○ 243
○ 234 ○ 423

Name ____________________

Show Amounts in Two Ways

HANDS ON
Lesson 7.4

COMMON CORE STANDARD CC.2.MD.8
Work with time and money.

Use coins. Show the amounts in two ways. Draw and label the coins.

1. 39¢		
2. 70¢		
3. 57¢		

PROBLEM SOLVING

4. Madeline uses fewer than 5 coins to pay 60¢. Draw coins to show one way she could pay 60¢.

Lesson Check (CC.2.MD.8)

1. Which group of coins has the same total value?

○ 

○ 

○ 

○ 

Spiral Review (CC.2.OA.2, CC.2NBT.1, CC.2NBT.3)

2. Which of these is another way to show the number 31? (Lesson 1.6)

○ 1 ten 3 ones
○ 1 ten 13 ones
○ 2 tens 3 ones
○ 2 tens 11 ones

3. Which has the same value as 13 tens? (Lesson 2.2)

○ 1 hundred 3 tens
○ 3 hundreds 3 tens
○ 3 tens 1 one
○ 1 ten 3 ones

4. What is the value of the underlined digit? (Lesson 1.3)

2<u>8</u>

○ 2
○ 8
○ 18
○ 80

5. What is the sum? (Lesson 3.1)

5 + 6 = ______

○ 1
○ 10
○ 11
○ 13

Name ______________________________

One Dollar

COMMON CORE STANDARD CC.2.MD.8
Work with time and money.

Circle coins to make $1.00.
Cross out the coins you do not use.

1.

2.

3.

PROBLEM SOLVING

4. Draw more coins to show $1.00 in all.

Lesson Check (CC.2.MD.8)

1. Which group of coins has a value of $1.00?

○ ○ ○

Spiral Review (CC.2.OA.3, CC.2.NBT.2, CC.2.NBT.3, CC.2.MD.8)

2. Which is another way to write 692? (Lesson 2.7)

○ six hundred ninety-two
○ 600 + 9 + 2
○ six hundred nineteen
○ 60 + 90 + 2

3. Which sum is an even number? (Lesson 1.2)

○ 5 + 4 = 9
○ 6 + 5 = 11
○ 7 + 7 = 14
○ 8 + 9 = 17

4. Which group of coins has a total value of 40¢? (Lesson 7.4)

○ 4 quarters
○ 4 dimes and 1 nickel
○ 1 quarter and 3 nickels
○ 2 dimes and 2 pennies

5. Which group of numbers shows counting by tens? (Lesson 1.9)

○ 110, 109, 108, 107
○ 115, 116, 117, 118
○ 220, 225, 230, 235
○ 230, 240, 250, 260

Name ______________________

Amounts Greater Than $1

COMMON CORE STANDARD CC.2.MD.8
Work with time and money.

Circle the money that makes $1.00. Then write the total value of the money shown.

1.

______

2.

______

3.

______

PROBLEM SOLVING

Solve. Write or draw to explain.

4. Grace found 3 quarters, 3 dimes, and 1 nickel in her pocket. How much money did she find?

______

TEST PREP

Lesson Check (CC.2.MD.8)

1. Julie has this money in her bank. What is the total value of this money?

○ $1.10
○ $1.25
○ $1.30
○ $1.35

Spiral Review (CC.2.OA.2, CC.2.NBT.5, CC.2.NBT.8)

2. What is the sum? (Lesson 4.7)

$$\begin{array}{r} 79 \\ +42 \\ \hline \end{array}$$

○ 37
○ 111
○ 121
○ 127

3. What is the difference? (Lesson 5.5)

$$\begin{array}{r} 61 \\ -27 \\ \hline \end{array}$$

○ 28
○ 34
○ 48
○ 88

4. Which number is 100 less than 694? (Lesson 2.9)

○ 594
○ 684
○ 704
○ 794

5. Which of the following has the same sum as 6 + 5? (Lesson 3.3)

○ 10 + 6
○ 10 + 5
○ 10 + 3
○ 10 + 1

Name ____________________

Problem Solving • Money

COMMON CORE STANDARD CC.2.MD.8
Work with time and money.

Use play coins and bills to solve.
Draw to show what you did.

1. Sara has 2 quarters, 1 nickel, and two $1 bills. How much money does Sara have?

____

2. Brad has one $1 bill, 4 dimes, and 2 nickels in his bank. How much money does Brad have in his bank?

____

3. Mr. Morgan gives 1 quarter, 3 nickels, 4 pennies, and one $1 bill to the clerk. How much money does Mr. Morgan give the clerk?

____

Lesson Check (CC.2.MD.8)

1. Lee has two $1 bills and 4 dimes. How much money does Lee have?

   ○ $1.40

   ○ $2.40

   ○ $2.50

   ○ $2.90

2. Dawn has 2 quarters, 1 nickel, and one $1 bill. How much money does Dawn have?

   ○ $1.05

   ○ $1.25

   ○ $1.55

   ○ $2.55

Spiral Review (CC.2.OA.2, CC.2.NBT.3, CC.2.NBT.4, CC.2.NBT.8)

3. What is the value of the underlined digit? (Lesson 1.3)

   $5\underline{6}$

   ○ 5

   ○ 6

   ○ 16

   ○ 60

4. Which of the following is true? (Lesson 2.12)

   ○ 342 > 243

   ○ 142 > 162

   ○ 280 > 306

   ○ 417 < 380

5. What is the difference? (Lesson 3.6)

   15 − 8 = ____

   ○ 7

   ○ 9

   ○ 15

   ○ 23

6. What is the next number in this pattern? (Lesson 2.10)

   225, 325, 425, 525, 

   ○ 445

   ○ 535

   ○ 625

   ○ 645

Name ______________________________

Time to the Hour and Half Hour

COMMON CORE STANDARD CC.2.MD.7
Work with time and money.

Look at the clock hands. Write the time.

1.

2.

3.

4.

5.

6.

PROBLEM SOLVING

7. Amy's music lesson begins at 4:00. Draw hands on the clock to show this time.

TEST PREP

Lesson Check (CC.2.MD.7)

1. What is the time on this clock?

○ 3:00
○ 3:30
○ 4:00
○ 4:30

2. What is the time on this clock?

○ 12:00
○ 12:30
○ 6:00
○ 6:30

Spiral Review (CC.2.OA.3, CC.2.NBT.1, CC.2.NBT.4, CC.2.MD.8)

3. Rachel has one $1 bill, 3 quarters, and 2 pennies. How much money does Rachel have? (Lesson 7.7)

○ $1.32　○ $1.53
○ $1.77　○ $3.21

4. Which of the following is true? (Lesson 2.12)

○ 185 = 581
○ 167 = 176
○ 273 > 304
○ 260 < 362

5. What number is shown with these blocks? (Lesson 2.3)

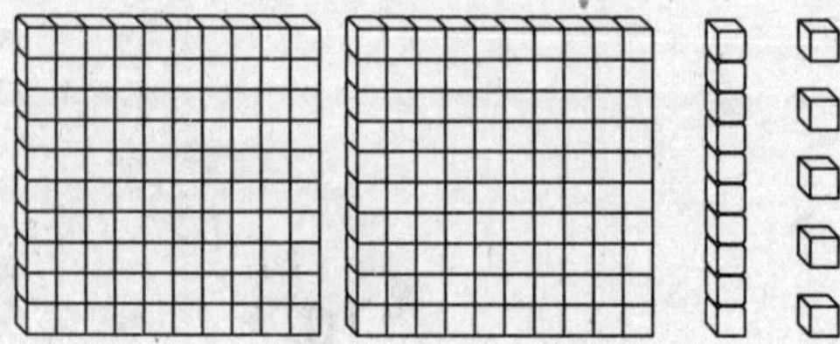

○ 215　○ 251
○ 512　○ 521

6. Which of these numbers is an even number? (Lesson 1.1)

○ 1
○ 3
○ 4
○ 5

Name ______________________________

Time to 5 Minutes

COMMON CORE STANDARD CC.2.MD.7
Work with time and money.

Look at the clock hands. Write the time.

1.

2.

3.

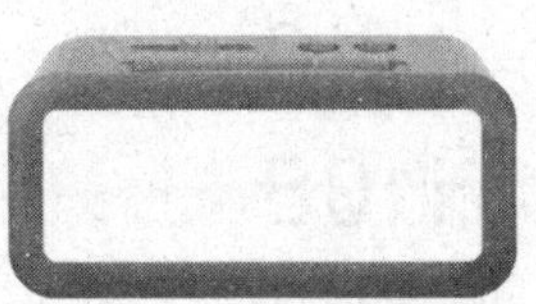

4.

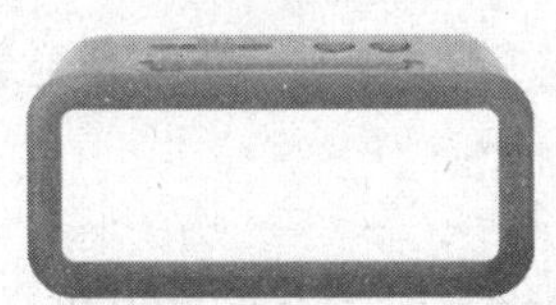

5.

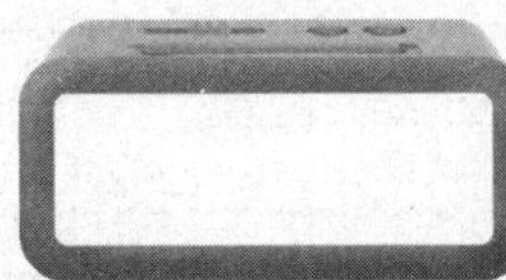

6.

PROBLEM SOLVING

Draw the minute hand to show the time. Then write the time.

7. My hour hand points between the 4 and the 5. My minute hand points to the 9. What time do I show?

TEST PREP

Lesson Check (CC.2.MD.7)

1. What is the time on this clock?

- ○ 8:05
- ○ 8:01
- ○ 1:40
- ○ 1:08

2. What is the time on this clock?

- ○ 4:07
- ○ 4:35
- ○ 7:20
- ○ 7:30

Spiral Review (CC.2.OA.1, CC.2.OA.2, CC.2.OA.4, CC.2.NBT.1a, CC.2.NBT.1b)

3. What is the sum of 1 + 6 + 8? (Lesson 3.4)

- ○ 16
- ○ 15
- ○ 13
- ○ 11

4. Which number has the same value as 30 tens? (Lesson 2.1)

- ○ 3
- ○ 30
- ○ 300
- ○ 3010

5. Steven has 3 rows of toys. There are 4 toys in each row. How many toys are there in all? (Lesson 3.11)

- ○ 4
- ○ 7
- ○ 8
- ○ 12

6. Jill has 14 buttons. She buys 8 more buttons. How many buttons does Jill have in all? (Lesson 3.8)

- ○ 22
- ○ 20
- ○ 12
- ○ 6

Name ______________________________

Practice Telling Time

COMMON CORE STANDARD CC.2.MD.7
Work with time and money.

Draw the minute hand to show the time. Write the time.

1. quarter past 7

2. half past 3

3. 50 minutes after 1

4. quarter past 11

5. 15 minutes after 8

6. 5 minutes after 6

PROBLEM SOLVING

Draw a minute hand on the clock to solve.

7. Josh got to school at half past 8.
Show this time on the clock.

TEST PREP

Lesson Check (CC.2.MD.7)

1. What is the time on this clock?

- ○ quarter past 3
- ○ 6 minutes after 3
- ○ quarter past 6
- ○ half past 6

Spiral Review (CC.2.OA.4, CC.2.NBT.3, CC.2.MD.7, CC.2.MD.8)

2. What is the value of this group of coins? (Lesson 7.3)

- ○ 21¢
- ○ 26¢
- ○ 31¢
- ○ 46¢

3. What time is shown on this clock? (Lesson 7.9)

- ○ 8:05
- ○ 7:15
- ○ 4:13
- ○ 3:35

4. Which is another way to write 647? (Lesson 2.6)

- ○ six hundred forty-seven
- ○ 60 + 40 + 7
- ○ 4 hundreds 6 tens 7 ones
- ○ 674

Name ______________________________

A.M. and P.M.

COMMON CORE STANDARD CC.2.MD.7
Work with time and money.

Write the time. Then circle A.M. or P.M.

1. walk the dog

A.M.

P.M.

2. finish breakfast

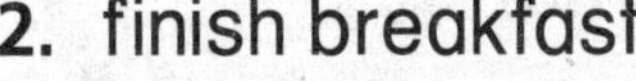

A.M.

P.M.

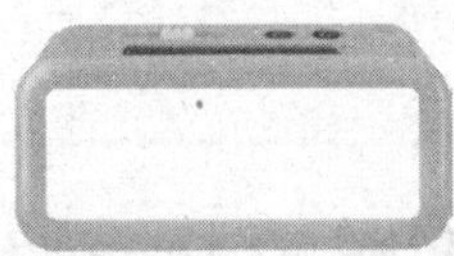

3. put on pajamas

A.M.

P.M.

4. read a bedtime story

A.M.

P.M.

PROBLEM SOLVING

Use the list of times. Complete the story.

5. Jess woke up at ______________. She got on the bus at ______________ and went to school. She left school at ______________.

3:15 P.M.
8:30 A.M.
7:00 A.M.

Lesson Check (CC.2.MD.7)

1. The clock shows when the soccer game ended. What time was it?

- ○ 4:50 A.M.
- ○ 10:20 A.M.
- ○ 4:50 P.M.
- ○ 10:20 P.M.

2. The clock shows when Dad gets up for work. What time is it?

- ○ 2:30 A.M.
- ○ 6:10 A.M.
- ○ 2:30 P.M.
- ○ 6:10 P.M.

Spiral Review (CC.2.NBT.3, CC.2.NBT.7, CC.2.MD.7, CC.2.MD.8)

3. Which coin has the same value as 25 pennies? (Lesson 7.2)

- ○ penny
- ○ nickel
- ○ dime
- ○ quarter

4. Which of these is another way to describe 72? (Lesson 1.4)

- ○ 7 + 2
- ○ 20 + 7
- ○ 70 + 2
- ○ 70 + 20

5. What is the sum? (Lesson 6.3)

$$\begin{array}{r} 437 \\ +\ \ 24 \\ \hline \end{array}$$

- ○ 461
- ○ 451
- ○ 431
- ○ 413

6. Which time is quarter past 3? (Lesson 7.10)

- ○ 3:45
- ○ 3:15
- ○ 3:30
- ○ 2:45

Name ______________________________

Chapter 7 Extra Practice

Lessons 7.1 – 7.2 (pp. 337–344)

Count on to find the total value.

1.     

total value

2.       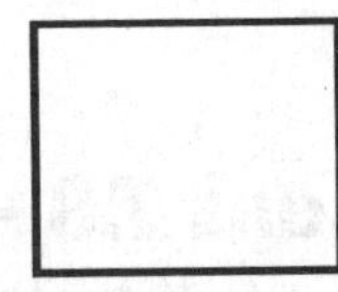

total value

Lesson 7.3 (pp. 345–348)

Draw and label the coins from greatest to least value. Find the total value.

1. 

______

Lesson 7.4 (pp. 349–352)

Use coins. Show the amount in two ways. Draw and label the coins.

1. 

Lesson 7.5 (pp. 353–355)

Circle coins to make $1.00.
Cross out the coins you do not use.

1.

Lessons 7.8 –7.9 (pp. 365–372)

Look at the clock hands. Write the time.

1.

2.

3.

4.

5.

6.

Chapter 8

School-Home Letter

Dear Family,

My class started Chapter 8 this week. In this chapter, I will learn about inches and feet. I will also learn about measuring tools and showing measurement data.

Love, ______________________________

Vocabulary

inch Unit of length

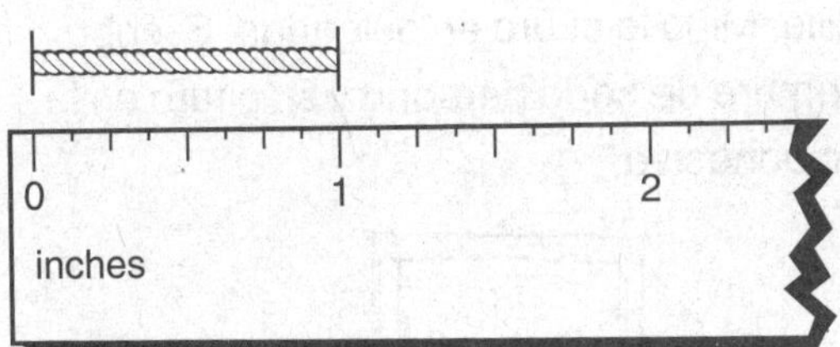

foot 12 inches

yardstick A tool that shows 3 feet

Home Activity

Record each family member's height with masking tape in a doorway of your house. Measure the height in inches. Write each person's name and height on the tape.

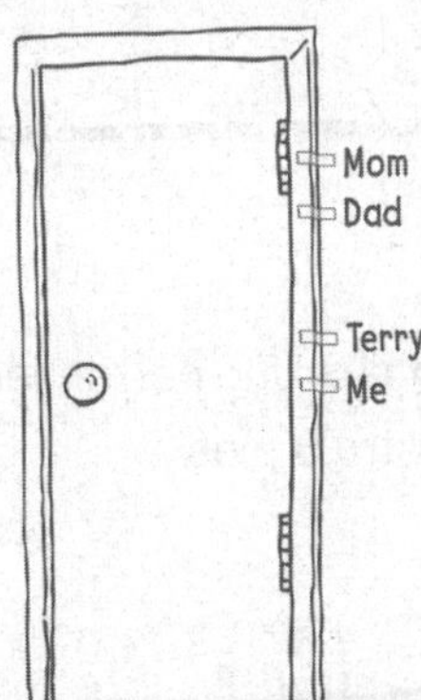

Literature

Reading math stories reinforces ideas. Look for these books at the library.

Measuring Penny
by Loreen Leedy.
Henry Holt and Company, 1998.

Twelve Snails to One Lizard
by Susan Hightower.
Simon & Schuster, 1997.

Capítulo 8

Carta para la casa

Querida familia:

Mi clase comenzó el Capítulo 8 esta semana. En este capítulo, aprenderé acerca de pulgadas y pies. También aprenderé sobre herramientas para medir y mostrar información sobre medidas.

Con cariño, ______________________________

Vocabulario

pulgada Unidad de longitud

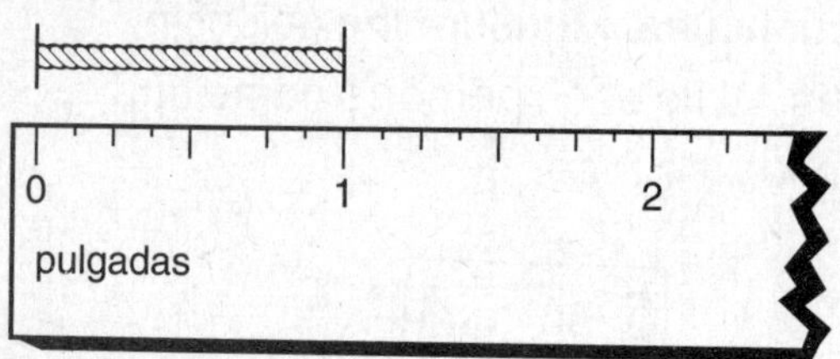

pie 12 pulgadas

regla de 1 yarda Una herramienta con marcas que mostra 3 pies

Actividad para la casa

En el marco de una puerta, marque con cinta adhesiva la altura de cada miembro de la familia. Mida la altura en pulgadas. Escriba el nombre de cada persona y su altura en la cinta adhesiva.

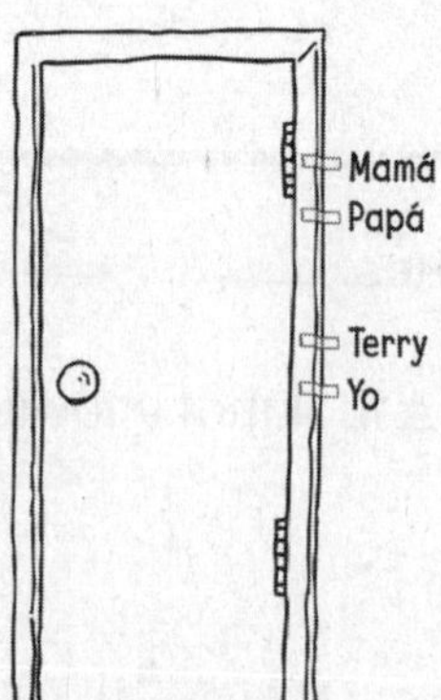

Literatura

La lectura de cuentos matemáticos refuerza las ideas. Busque estos libros en la biblioteca.

Measuring Penny
por Loreen Leedy.
Henry Holt and Company, 1998.

Twelve Snails to One Lizard
por Susan Hightower.
Simon & Schuster, 1997.

Name ______________________________

Measure with Inch Models

COMMON CORE STANDARD CC.2.MD.1
Measure and estimate lengths in standard units.

Use color tiles. Measure the length of the object in inches.

1.

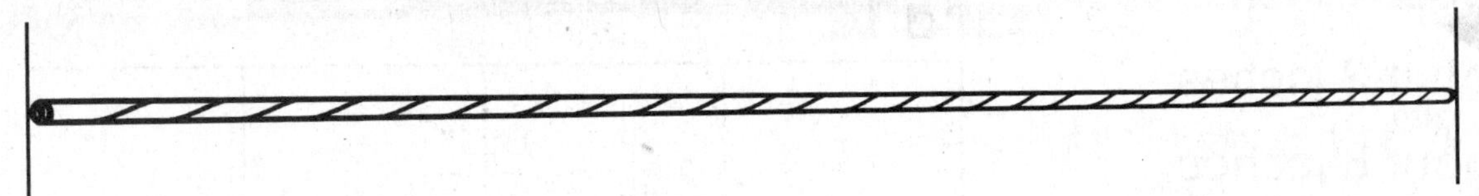

about _____ inches

2.

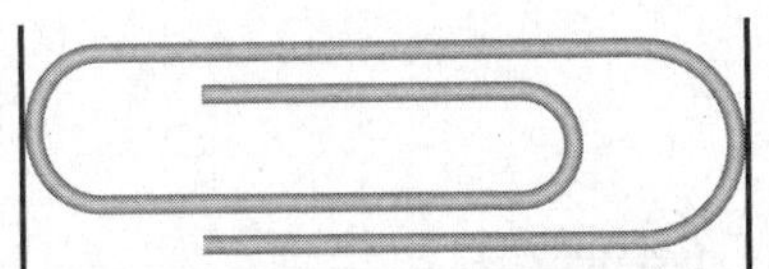

about _____ inches

3.

about _____ inches

4.

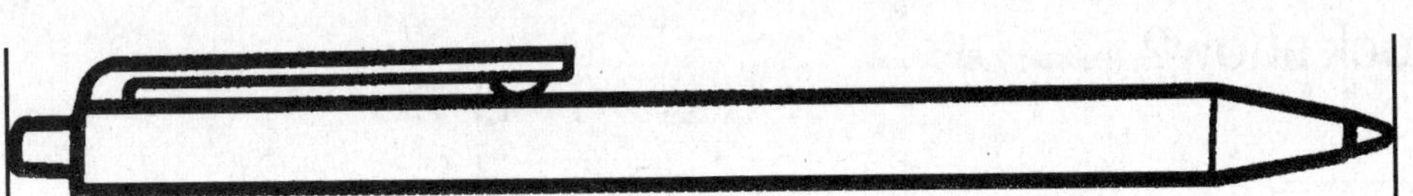

about _____ inches

PROBLEM SOLVING

5. Look around your classroom.
Find an object that is about 4 inches long.
Draw and label the object.

Lesson Check (CC.2.MD.1)

1. Jessie used color tiles to measure the rope. Which is the best choice for the length of the rope?

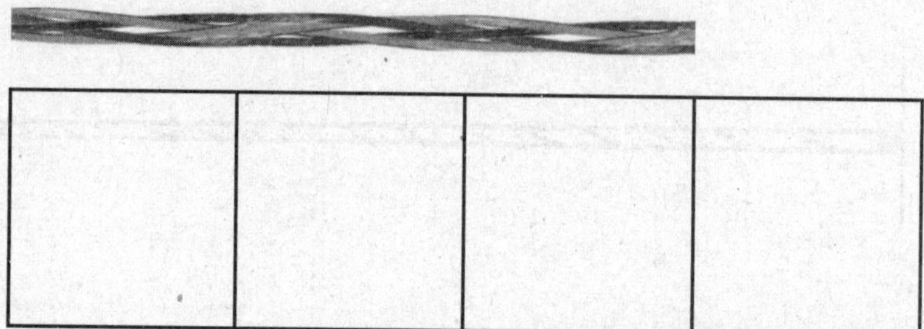

- ○ about 1 inch
- ○ about 2 inches
- ○ about 3 inches
- ○ about 4 inches

Spiral Review (CC.2.NBT.5, CC.2.MD.7, CC.2.MD.8)

2. Adam has these coins. How much money is this? (Lesson 7.1)

- ○ 5¢
- ○ 20¢
- ○ 25¢
- ○ 40¢

3. Look at the clock hands. What time does this clock show? (Lesson 7.8)

- ○ 4:30
- ○ 5:00
- ○ 5:30
- ○ 6:00

4. What is the sum? (Lesson 4.7)

$$\begin{array}{r} 84 \\ +\ 71 \\ \hline \end{array}$$

- ○ 165
- ○ 155
- ○ 53
- ○ 13

Name ________________________________

Make and Use a Ruler

COMMON CORE STANDARD CC.2.MD.1
Measure and estimate lengths in standard units.

Measure the length with your ruler.
Count the inches.

1.

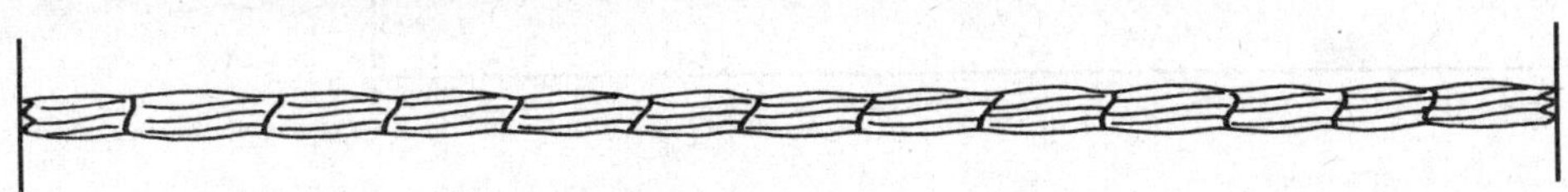

about _____ inches

2.

about _____ inches

3.

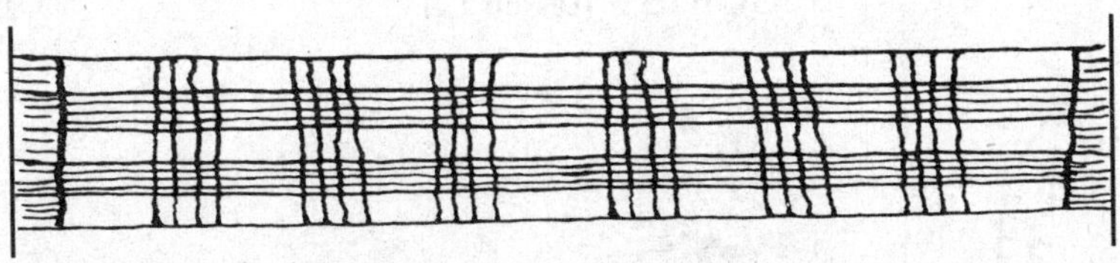

about _____ inches

4.

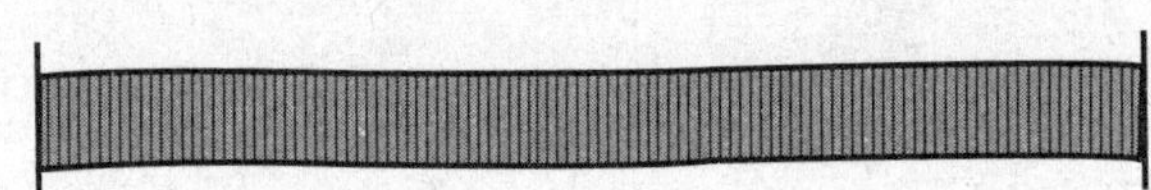

about _____ inches

PROBLEM SOLVING

5. Use your ruler. Measure the width of this page in inches.

about _____ inches

Lesson Check (CC.2.MD.1)

1. Use your ruler. What is the best choice for the length of this ribbon?

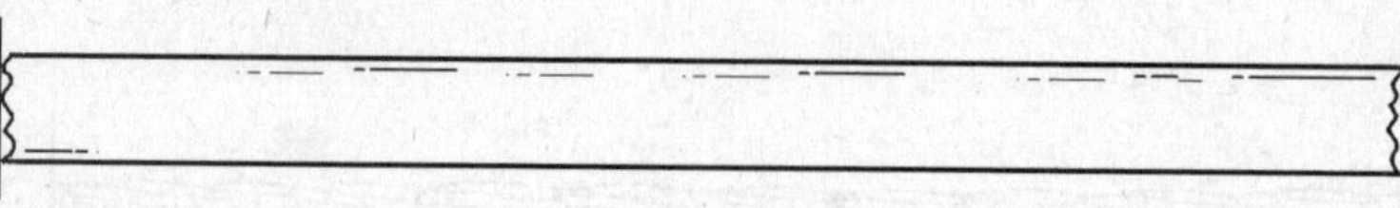

- ○ about 5 inches
- ○ about 4 inches
- ○ about 3 inches
- ○ about 2 inches

Spiral Review (CC.2.OA.4, CC.2.NBT.7, CC.2.MD.7, CC.2.MD.8)

2. What time is shown on this clock? (Lesson 7.9)

- ○ 9:15
- ○ 4:45
- ○ 3:45
- ○ 3:09

3. What is the total value of these coins? (Lesson 7.2)

- ○ 60¢
- ○ 50¢
- ○ 55¢
- ○ 35¢

4. The first group collected 238 cans. The second group collected 345 cans. How many cans did the two groups collect? (Lesson 6.3)

- ○ 107
- ○ 573
- ○ 583
- ○ 585

5. There are 2 children in each row. How many children are in 5 rows? (Lesson 3.10)

- ○ 3
- ○ 5
- ○ 7
- ○ 10

Name ______________________________

Estimate Lengths in Inches

COMMON CORE STANDARD CC.2.MD.3
Measure and estimate lengths in standard units.

**The bead is 1 inch long.
Circle the best estimate for the length of the string.**

1. 

1 inch 4 inches 7 inches

2. 

3 inches 6 inches 9 inches

3. 

2 inches 3 inches 6 inches

4. 

2 inches 5 inches 8 inches

PROBLEM SOLVING

Solve. Write or draw to explain.

5. Ashley has some beads. Each bead is 2 inches long. How many beads will fit on a string that is 8 inches long?

_____ beads

Lesson Check (CC.2.MD.3)

1. The bead is 1 inch long. Which is the best estimate for the length of the string?

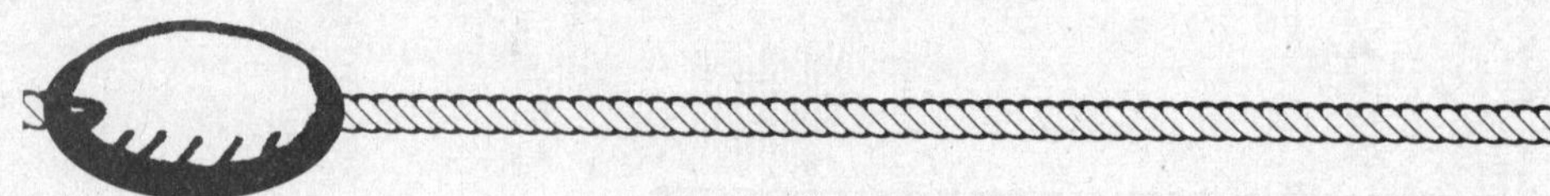

- ○ 1 inch
- ○ 3 inches
- ○ 5 inches
- ○ 7 inches

Spiral Review (CC.2.OA.1, CC.2.NBT.6, CC.2.MD.7)

2. Which clock shows 5 minutes after 6? (Lesson 7.10)

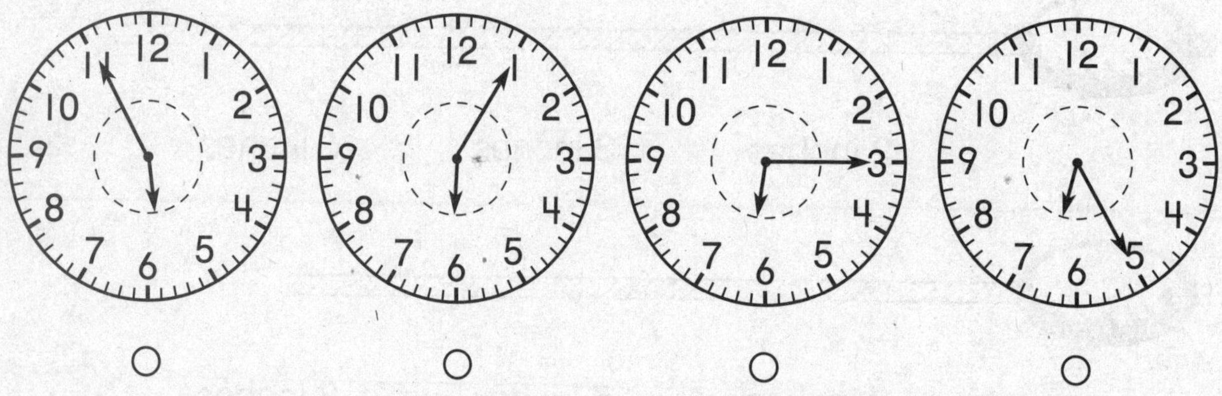

○ ○ ○ ○

3. Ella read 16 pages of her book on Monday and 26 pages on Tuesday. There are 64 pages in the book. How many more pages are left for Ella to read? (Lesson 5.11)

- ○ 106
- ○ 34
- ○ 32
- ○ 22

4. What is the sum? (Lesson 4.2)

$38 + 24 = \_\_\_\_$

- ○ 54
- ○ 60
- ○ 62
- ○ 66

Name ______________________________

Measure with an Inch Ruler

COMMON CORE STANDARD CC.2.MD.1
Measure and estimate lengths in standard units.

Measure the length to the nearest inch.

1.

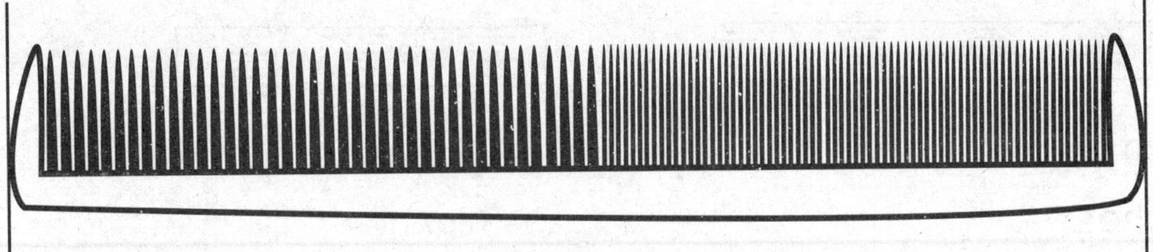

_____ inches

2.

_____ inches

3.

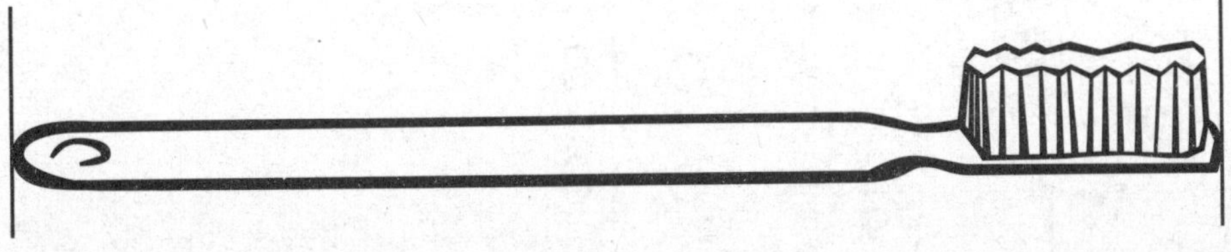

_____ inches

4.

_____ inches

PROBLEM SOLVING REAL WORLD

5. Measure the string. What is its total length?

_____ inches

TEST PREP

Lesson Check (CC.2.MD.1)

1. Use an inch ruler. What is the length to the nearest inch?

- ○ 1 inch
- ○ 2 inches
- ○ 3 inches
- ○ 4 inches

2. Use an inch ruler. What is the length to the nearest inch?

- ○ 2 inches
- ○ 3 inches
- ○ 4 inches
- ○ 5 inches

Spiral Review (CC.2.OA.2, CC.2.MD.1, CC.2.MD.7)

3. The clock shows the time that Jen got to school. What time did Jen get to school? (Lesson 7.11)

- ○ 6:30 A.M.
- ○ 8:30 A.M.
- ○ 6:30 P.M.
- ○ 8:30 P.M.

4. What is the difference? (Lesson 3.7)

$13 - 5 = \_\_\_\_$

- ○ 18
- ○ 10
- ○ 9
- ○ 8

5. Each color tile is about 1 inch long. Which is the best choice for the length of the ribbon? (Lesson 8.1)

- ○ about 1 inch
- ○ about 2 inches
- ○ about 3 inches
- ○ about 4 inches

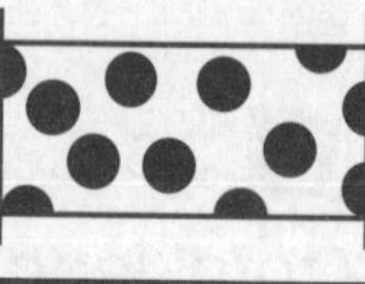

Name ______________________________

Problem Solving • Add and Subtract in Inches

COMMON CORE STANDARDS CC.2.MD.5, CC.2.MD.6

Relate addition and subtraction to length.

Draw a diagram. Write a number sentence using a ■ for the missing number. Solve.

1. Molly had a ribbon that was 23 inches long. She cut 7 inches off the ribbon. How long is her ribbon now?

____

Molly's ribbon is ________ inches long now.

2. Jed has a paper clip chain that is 11 inches long. He adds 7 inches of paper clips to the chain. How long is the paper clip chain now?

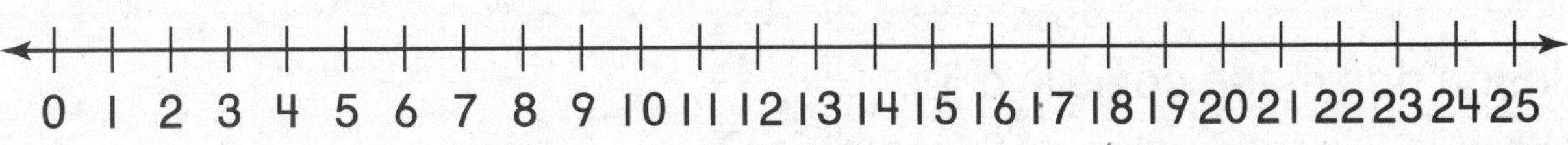

____

The paper clip chain is ________ inches long now.

Lesson Check (CC.2.MD.5, CC.2.MD.6)

1. Allie has two pieces of string. Each one is 8 inches long. How many inches of string does she have altogether?

   ○ 16 inches ○ 14 inches
   ○ 15 inches ○ 12 inches

2. Jeff has a cube train that is 26 inches long. He removes 12 inches of cubes from the train. How long is Jeff's cube train now?

   ○ 38 inches ○ 14 inches
   ○ 18 inches ○ 12 inches

Spiral Review (CC.2.MD.1, CC.2.MD.8)

3. Ann buys a pencil that costs 45¢. Which group of coins has a total value of 45¢? (Lesson 7.4)

   ○ 1 quarter and 1 dime
   ○ 1 quarter and 2 dimes
   ○ 2 quarters
   ○ 6 nickels and 1 dime

4. Use an inch ruler. What is the best choice for the length of this string? (Lesson 8.4)

   ○ about 1 inch
   ○ about 2 inches
   ○ about 3 inches
   ○ about 4 inches

5. Jason has these coins in a jar. What is the total value of these coins? (Lesson 7.3)

   ○ 30¢
   ○ 45¢
   ○ 50¢
   ○ 55¢

Name ____________________

Measure in Inches and Feet

HANDS ON
Lesson 8.6

COMMON CORE STANDARD CC.2.MD.2
Measure and estimate lengths in standard units.

Measure to the nearest inch.
Then measure to the nearest foot.

Find the real object.	Measure.
1. bookcase	_____ inches _____ feet
2. window	_____ inches _____ feet
3. chair	_____ inches _____ feet

PROBLEM SOLVING REAL WORLD

4. Jake has a piece of yarn that is 4 feet long. Blair has a piece of yarn that is 4 inches long. Who has the longer piece of yarn? Explain.

____

____

Lesson Check (CC.2.MD.2)

1. Larry is telling his sister about using a ruler to measure length. Which sentence is true?

   ○ 1 foot is shorter than 1 inch.

   ○ 1 foot is longer than 1 inch.

   ○ 1 inch is longer than 1 foot.

   ○ 1 foot is the same length as 1 inch.

Spiral Review (CC.2.NBT.5, CC.2.NBT.7, CC.2.MD.7, CC.2.MD.8)

2. Matt put this money in his pocket. What is the total value of this money? (Lesson 7.6)

   ○ $1.01

   ○ $1.06

   ○ $1.10

   ○ $1.11

3. What time is shown on this clock? (Lesson 7.9)

   ○ 12:50   ○ 1:50

   ○ 10:05   ○ 1:10

4. Ali had 38 game cards. Her friend gave her 15 more game cards. How many game cards does Ali have now? (Lesson 4.7)

   ○ 53

   ○ 48

   ○ 43

   ○ 23

Name ____________________

Estimate Lengths in Feet

COMMON CORE STANDARD CC.2.MD.3
Measure and estimate lengths in standard units.

Find each object.
Estimate how many 12-inch rulers will be about the same length as the object.

1. door

Estimate: _____ rulers, or _____ feet

2. flag

Estimate: _____ rulers, or _____ feet

3. wall of a small room

Estimate: _____ rulers, or _____ feet

PROBLEM SOLVING

Solve. Write or draw to explain.

4. Mr. and Mrs. Baker place 12-inch rulers along the length of a rug. They each line up 3 rulers along the edge of the rug. What is the length of the rug?

about _____ feet

Lesson Check (CC.2.MD.3)

1. Which is the best estimate for the length of a bike?

   - O 1 foot
   - O 2 feet
   - O 5 feet
   - O 9 feet

2. Which is the best estimate for the length of a football?

   - O 1 foot
   - O 4 feet
   - O 5 feet
   - O 8 feet

Spiral Review (CC.2.NBT.5, CC.2.NBT.7, CC.2.MD.8)

3. Which group of coins has a value of $1.00? (Lesson 7.5)

   - O 2 quarters, 2 dimes, 3 nickels
   - O 2 quarters, 3 dimes, 4 nickels
   - O 2 quarters, 4 dimes, 3 nickels
   - O 3 quarters, 2 dimes, 2 nickels

4. Which group of coins has a total value of 37¢? (Lesson 7.4)

   - O 3 nickels, 7 pennies
   - O 1 quarter, 2 dimes, 1 nickel
   - O 2 dimes, 3 nickels, 2 pennies
   - O 7 quarters, 3 dimes

5. There are 68 children in the school. There are 19 children on the playground. How many more children are in the school than on the playground? (Lesson 5.2)

   - O 87
   - O 79
   - O 49
   - O 47

6. What is the sum? (Lesson 6.3)

$$\begin{array}{r} 548 \\ +\ 436 \\ \hline \end{array}$$

   - O 112
   - O 912
   - O 974
   - O 984

Name ______________________________

Choose a Tool

COMMON CORE STANDARD CC.2.MD.1
Measure and estimate lengths in standard units.

Choose the best tool for measuring the real object. Then measure and record the length or distance.

inch ruler
yardstick
measuring tape

1. the length of your desk

Tool: ______________________________

Length: ______________________________

2. the distance around a basket

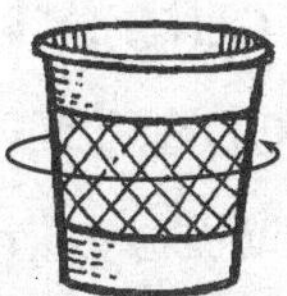

Tool: ______________________________

Length: ______________________________

PROBLEM SOLVING

Choose the better tool for measuring.
Explain your choice.

3. Mark wants to measure the length of his room. Should he use an inch ruler or a yardstick?

Mark should use ______________________ because

____

____

TEST PREP

Lesson Check (CC.2.MD.1)

1. Kim wants to measure the distance around her bike tire. Which is the best tool for her to use?

   ○ cup
   ○ yardstick
   ○ color tiles
   ○ measuring tape

2. Ben wants to measure the length of a seesaw. Which is the best tool for him to use?

   ○ cup
   ○ yardstick
   ○ color tiles
   ○ paper clips

Spiral Review (CC.2.MD.2, CC.2.MD.3, CC.2.MD.5, CC.2.MD.6)

3. Which is the best estimate for the length of a sheet of paper? (Lesson 8.7)

   ○ 1 foot
   ○ 3 feet
   ○ 6 feet
   ○ 10 feet

4. Andy has a rope that is 24 inches long. He cuts off 7 inches from the rope. How long is the rope now? (Lesson 8.5)

   ○ 20 inches
   ○ 17 inches
   ○ 15 inches
   ○ 9 inches

5. Jan is telling her friend about using a ruler to measure length. Which sentence is true? (Lesson 8.6)

   ○ 3 inches is longer than 1 foot.
   ○ 1 foot is shorter than 3 inches.
   ○ 1 foot is longer than 12 inches.
   ○ 12 inches is the same length as 1 foot.

Name ______________________

Display Measurement Data

COMMON CORE STANDARD CC.2.MD.9
Represent and interpret data.

1. Use an inch ruler. Measure and record the lengths of 4 different books in inches.

1st book: ______ inches
2nd book: ______ inches
3rd book: ______ inches
4th book: ______ inches

2. Make a line plot of the information above. Write a title for a line plot. Then write the numbers and draw the ***X***s.

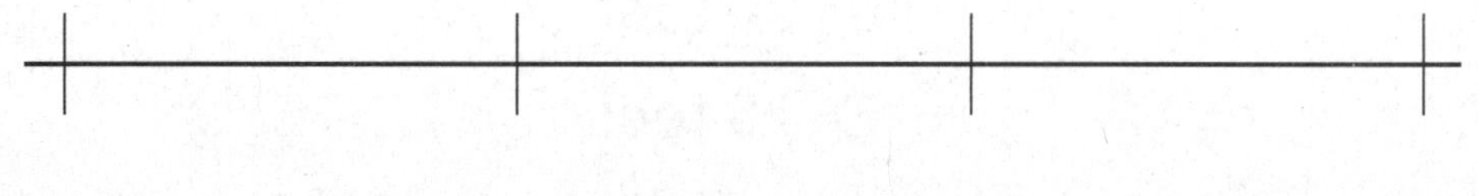

______ ______ ______ ______

____

PROBLEM SOLVING

3. Jesse measured the lengths of some strings. Use his list to complete the line plot.

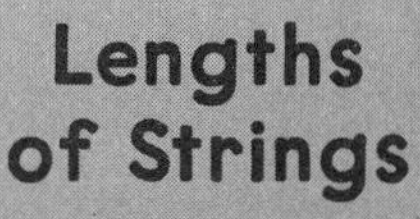

Lengths of Strings
5 inches
7 inches
6 inches
8 inches
5 inches

______ ______ ______ ______

____

Lesson Check (CC.2.MD.9)

1. Use the line plot. How many sticks are 4 inches long?

   ○ 4
   ○ 3
   ○ 2
   ○ 1

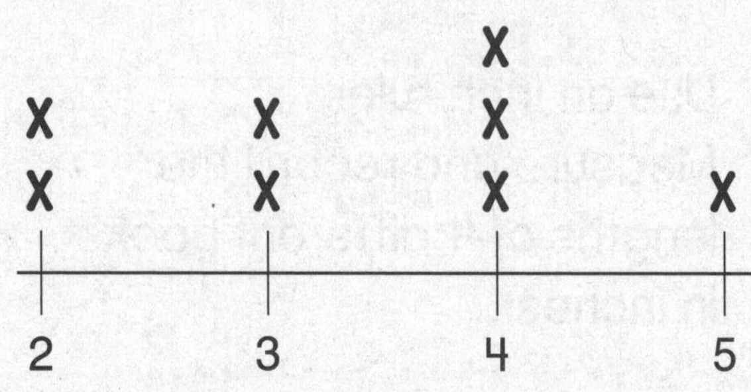

Lengths of Sticks in Inches

Spiral Review (CC.2.NBT.7, CC.2.MD.1, CC.2.MD.3, CC.2.MD.5, CC.2.MD.6)

2. Kim wants to measure a ball. Which is the best tool for Kim to use? (Lesson 8.8)

   ○ counter
   ○ pencil
   ○ paper clip
   ○ measuring tape

3. Which is the best estimate for the length of a teacher's desk? (Lesson 8.7)

   ○ 20 feet
   ○ 15 feet
   ○ 5 feet
   ○ 1 foot

4. Kurt has a string that is 12 inches long and another string that is 5 inches long. How many inches of string does he have altogether? (Lesson 8.5)

   ○ 7 inches
   ○ 12 inches
   ○ 17 inches
   ○ 19 inches

5. One box has 147 books. The other box has 216 books. How many books are there in both boxes? (Lesson 6.3)

   ○ 363
   ○ 361
   ○ 352
   ○ 349

Name ______________________________

COMMON CORE STANDARDS CC.2.MD.1, CC.2.MD.2, CC.2.MD.3, CC.2.MD.9

Chapter 8 Extra Practice

Lesson 8.1 (pp. 389–392)

Use color tiles. Measure the length of the object in inches.

1.

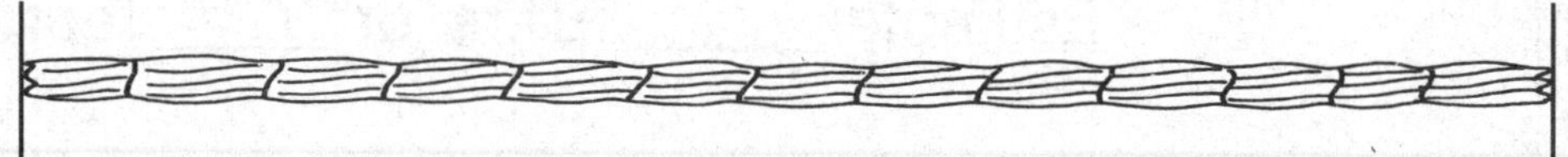

about _____ inches

Lesson 8.3 (pp. 397–400)

The bead is 1 inch long. Circle the best estimate for the length of the string.

1.

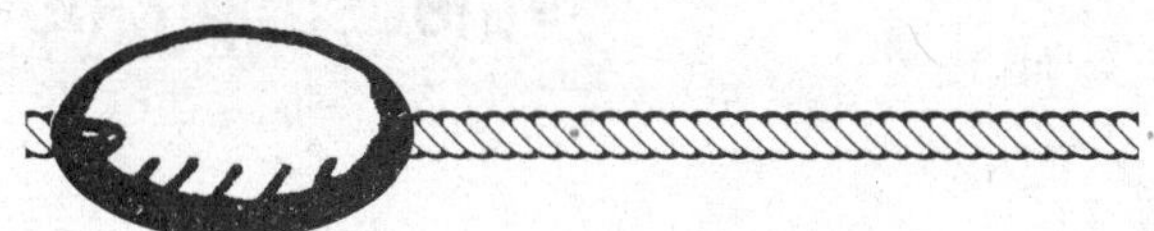

3 inches   5 inches   7 inches

Lesson 8.4 (pp. 401–404)

Measure the length to the nearest inch.

1.

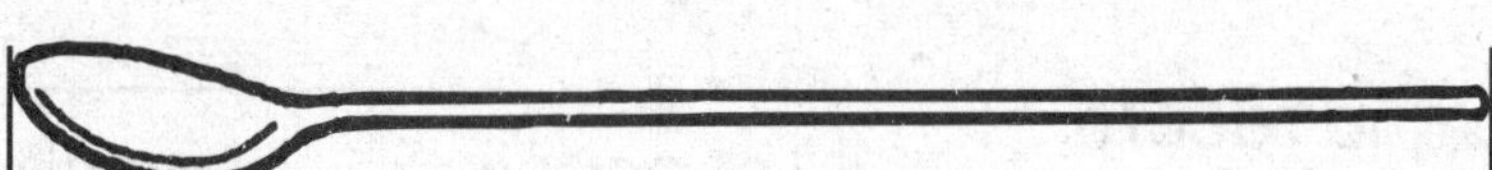

_____ inches

Lesson 8.6 (pp. 409–412)

Measure to the nearest inch.
Then measure to the nearest foot.

Find the real object.	Measure.
1. chair	_____ inches _____ feet

Lesson 8.7 (pp. 413–416)

Find the object. Estimate how many 12-inch rulers will be about the same length as the object.

1. table

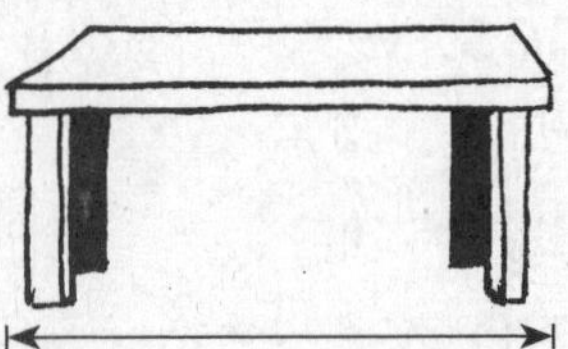

Estimate: _____ rulers, or _____ feet

Lesson 8.8 (pp. 417–420)

Choose the best tool for measuring the real object. Then measure and record the length.

inch ruler
yardstick
measuring tape

1. the length of a door

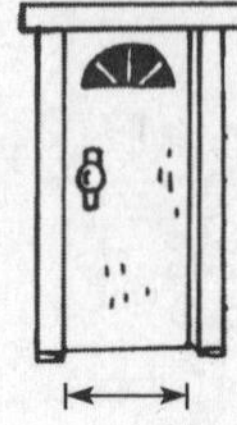

Tool: ______________________

Length: ______________________

Lesson 8.9 (pp. 421–424)

1. Use an inch ruler. Measure and record the lengths of 4 pencils in inches.
2. Write a title for the line plot. Then write the numbers and draw the Xs.

1st pencil: _____ inches
2nd pencil: _____ inches
3rd pencil: _____ inches
4th pencil: _____ inches

_____ _____ _____ _____

____

Chapter 9

School-Home Letter

Dear Family,

My class started Chapter 9 this week. In this chapter, I will learn how to measure using centimeters and meters. I will also solve problems about adding and subtracting lengths.

Love, ______________________

Vocabulary

centimeter Unit of length

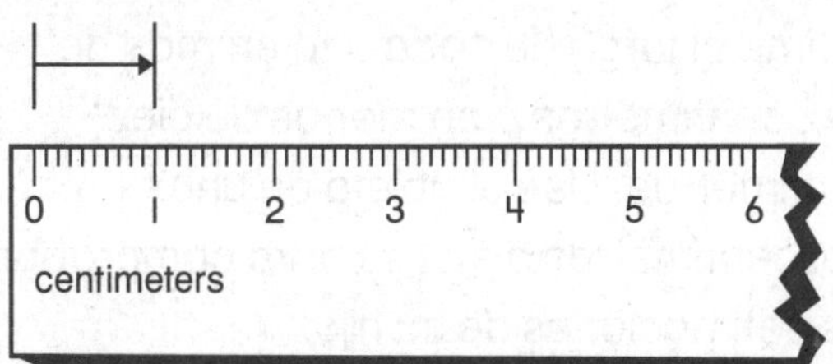

meter 100 centimeters

Home Activity

Show your child an object that is about ten centimeters long. Have your child choose three or four more objects and estimate each length as more than ten centimeters or less than ten centimeters. Use the object that is about ten centimeters long to check your child's estimates.

Literature

Reading math stories reinforces ideas. Look for these books at the library.

How Tall, How Short, How Far Away? by David Adler. Holiday House, 2000.

Length by Henry Arthur Pluckrose. Children's Press, 1995.

Capítulo 9

Carta para la casa

Querida familia:

Mi clase comenzó el Capítulo 9 esta semana. En este capítulo, aprenderé a medir usando centímetros y metros. También resolveré problemas de suma y resta de longitudes.

Con cariño, ____________________

Vocabulario

centímetro unidad de longitud

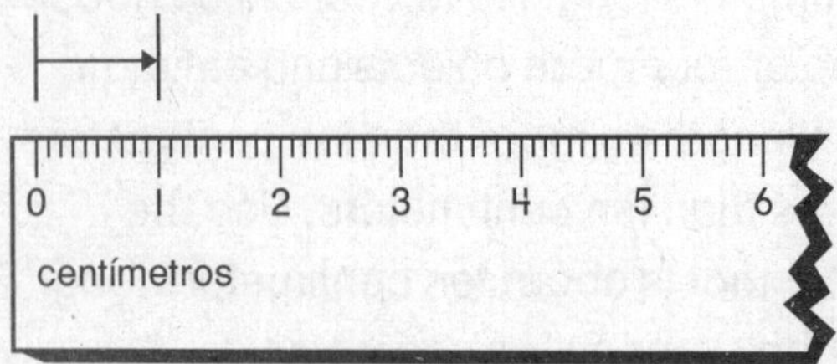

metro 100 centímetros

Actividad para la casa

Muéstrele a su hijo un objeto de unos diez centímetros de largo. Pídale que elija tres o cuatro objetos más y que estime el largo de cada uno en más de diez centímetros o en menos de diez centímetros. Use el objeto de unos diezcentímetros de largo para comprobar las estimaciones de su hijo.

Literatura

Leer cuentos de matemáticas refuerza los conceptos. Busque estos libros en la biblioteca.

How Tall, How Short, How Far Away?
por David Adler.
Holiday House, 2000.

Length
por Henry Arthur Pluckrose.
Children's Press, 1995.

Name ________________________________

Measure with a Centimeter Model

COMMON CORE STANDARD CC.2.MD.1
Measure and estimate lengths in standard units.

Use a unit cube. Measure the length in centimeters.

1.

about _______ centimeters

2.

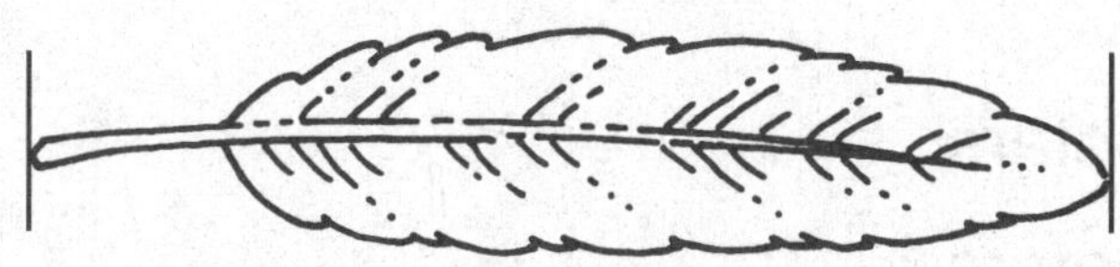

about _______ centimeters

3.

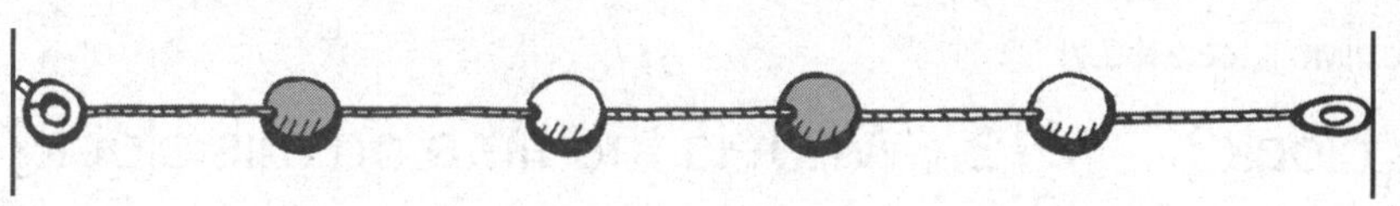

about _______ centimeters

4.

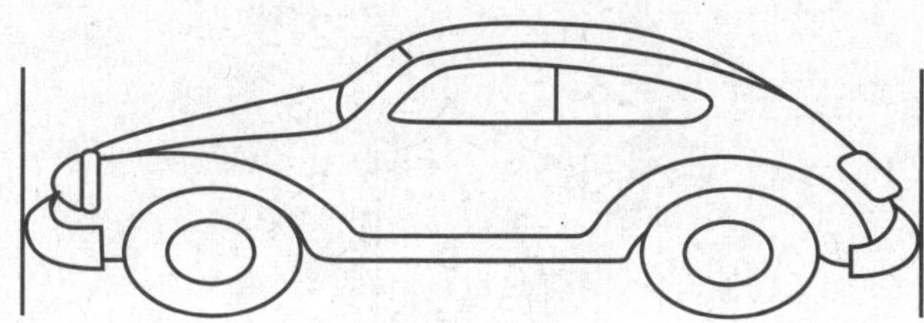

about _______ centimeters

PROBLEM SOLVING

Solve. Write or draw to explain.

5. Susan has a pencil that is 3 centimeters shorter than this string. How long is the pencil?

about _______ centimeters

Lesson Check (CC.2.MD.1)

1. Sarah used unit cubes to measure the length of a ribbon. Which is the best choice for the length of the ribbon?

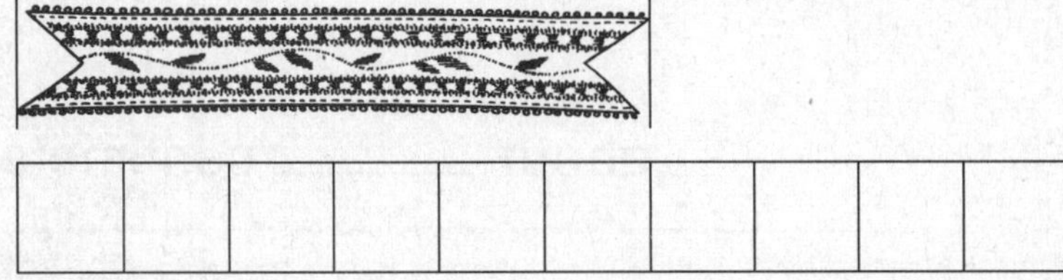

○ 1 centimeter ○ 6 centimeters
○ 4 centimeters ○ 10 centimeters

Spiral Review (CC.2.MD.5, CC.2.MD.6, CC.2.MD.7)

2. What is the time on this clock? (Lesson 7.8)

○ 12:00 ○ 10:00
○ 11:00 ○ 9:00

3. What is the time on this clock? (Lesson 7.9)

○ 8:20 ○ 5:08
○ 5:40 ○ 4:40

4. Dan has a paper strip that is 28 inches long. He tears 6 inches off the strip. How long is the paper strip now? (Lesson 8.5)

○ 16 inches ○ 28 inches
○ 22 inches ○ 34 inches

5. Rita has 1 quarter, 1 dime, and 2 pennies. What is the total value of Rita's coins? (Lesson 7.3)

○ 41¢ ○ 26¢
○ 37¢ ○ 17¢

Name ____________________

Estimate Lengths in Centimeters

COMMON CORE STANDARD CC.2.MD.3
Measure and estimate lengths in standard units.

1. The toothpick is about 6 centimeters long. Circle the best estimate for the length of the yarn.

6 centimeters

9 centimeters

12 centimeters

---

2. The pen is about 11 centimeters long. Circle the best estimate for the length of the eraser.

4 centimeters

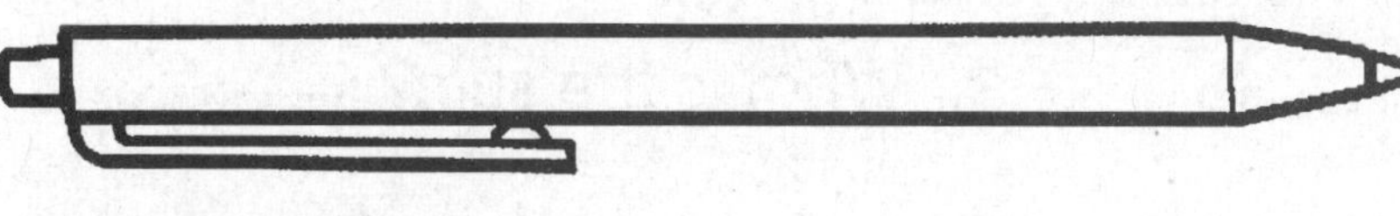

10 centimeters

14 centimeters

---

3. The string is about 6 centimeters long. Circle the best estimate for the length of the crayon.

5 centimeters

9 centimeters

14 centimeters

PROBLEM SOLVING

4. The string is about 6 centimeters long. Draw a pencil that is about 12 centimeters long.

Lesson Check (CC.2.MD.3)

1. The pencil is about 12 centimeters long. Which is the best estimate for the length of the yarn?

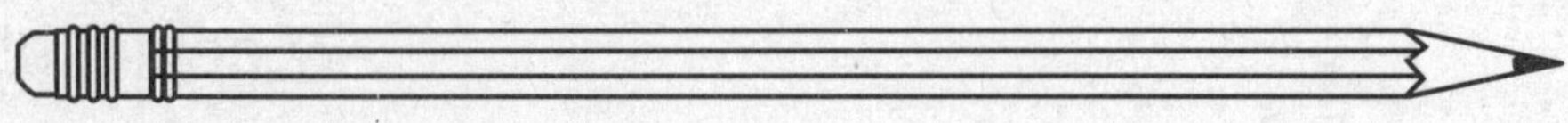

- ○ 5 centimeters
- ○ 12 centimeters
- ○ 10 centimeters
- ○ 24 centimeters

Spiral Review (CC.2.NBT.5, CC.2.MD.5, CC.2.MD.6, CC.2.MD.8)

2. What is the difference? (Lesson 5.5)

$$\begin{array}{r} 58 \\ -\ 23 \\ \hline \end{array}$$

- ○ 35
- ○ 53
- ○ 62
- ○ 81

3. What is the sum? (Lesson 4.8)

$$14 + 65$$

- ○ 42
- ○ 51
- ○ 54
- ○ 79

4. Adrian has a cube train that is 13 inches long. He adds 6 inches of cubes to the train. How long is the cube train now? (Lesson 8.5)

- ○ 7 inches
- ○ 11 inches
- ○ 19 inches
- ○ 27 inches

5. What is the total value of this group of coins? (Lesson 7.1)

- ○ 8¢
- ○ 17¢
- ○ 22¢
- ○ 26¢

Name ______________________________

Measure with a Centimeter Ruler

COMMON CORE STANDARD CC.2.MD.1
Measure and estimate lengths in standard units.

Measure the length to the nearest centimeter.

1.

______ centimeters

2.

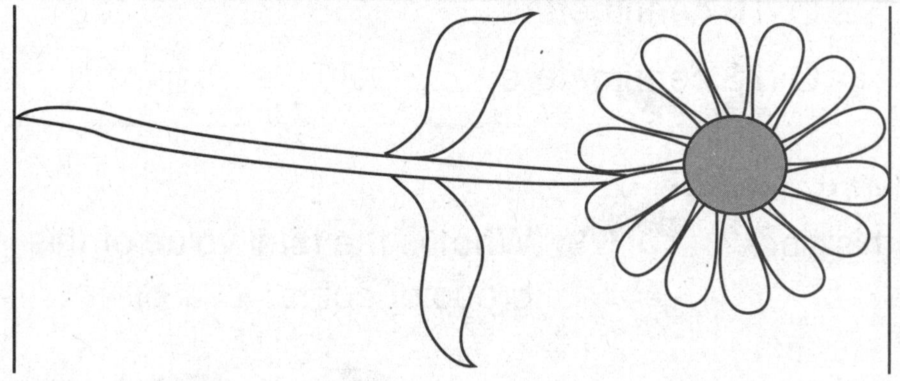

______ centimeters

3.

______ centimeters

PROBLEM SOLVING

4. Draw a string that is about 8 centimeters long. Then use a centimeter ruler to check the length.

TEST PREP

Lesson Check (CC.2.MD.1)

1. Use a centimeter ruler. What is the length of this pencil to the nearest centimeter?

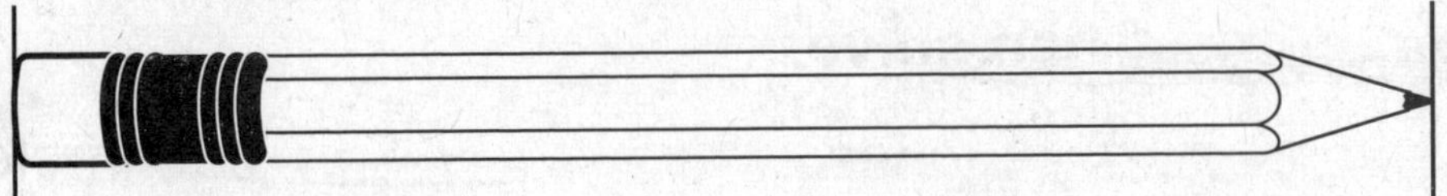

- ○ 5 centimeters
- ○ 6 centimeters
- ○ 10 centimeters
- ○ 12 centimeters

Spiral Review (CC.2.MD.7, CC.2.MD.8, CC.2.MD.9)

2. What is the time on this clock? (Lesson 7.9)

- ○ 1:20
- ○ 2:04
- ○ 3:25
- ○ 4:05

3. What is the total value of this group of coins? (Lesson 7.1)

- ○ 16¢
- ○ 21¢
- ○ 35¢
- ○ 57¢

4. Use the line plot. How many pencils are 5 inches long? (Lesson 8.9)

- ○ 7
- ○ 5
- ○ 2
- ○ 1

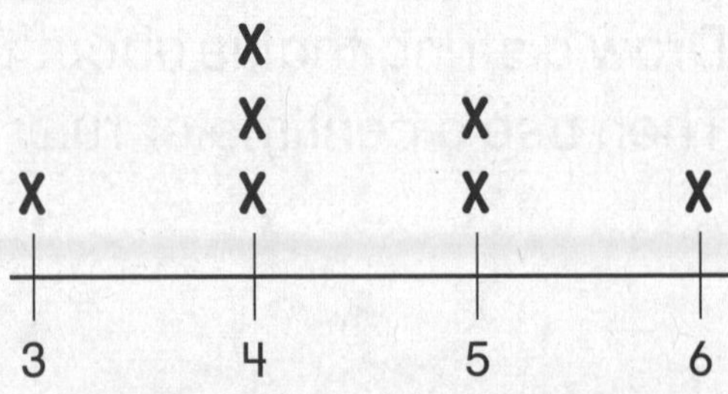

Name ______________________________

Problem Solving • Add and Subtract Lengths

COMMON CORE STANDARDS CC.2.MD.6, CC.2.MD.5
Relate addition and subtraction to length.

Draw a diagram. Write a number sentence using a ▢ for the missing number. Then solve.

1. A straw is 20 centimeters long. Mr. Jones cuts off 8 centimeters of the straw. How long is the straw now?

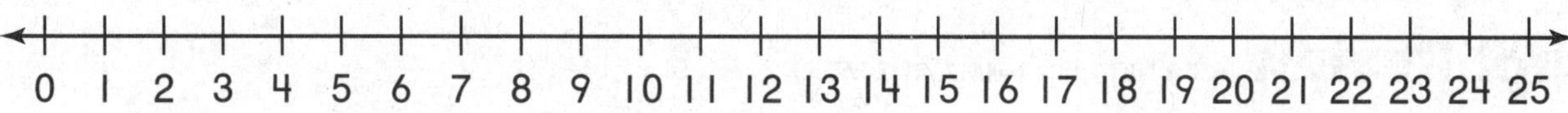

____

The straw is ______ centimeters long now.

2. Ella has a piece of blue yarn that is 14 centimeters long. She has a piece of red yarn that is 9 centimeters long. How many centimeters of yarn does she have altogether?

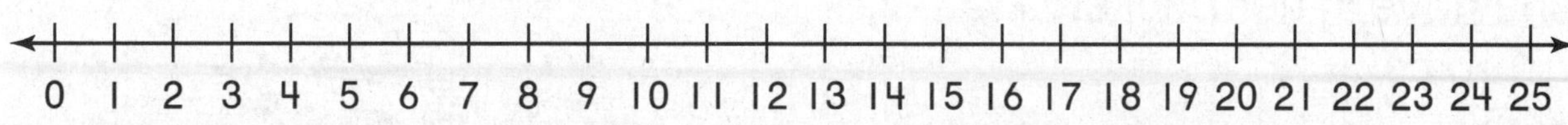

____

She has ______ centimeters of yarn altogether.

Lesson Check (CC.2.MD.6, CC.2.MD.5)

1. Tina has a paper clip chain that is 25 centimeters long. She takes off 8 centimeters of the chain. How long is the chain now?

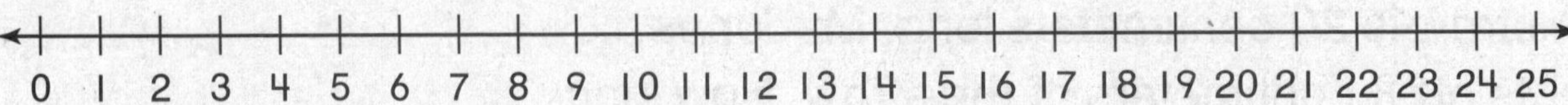

○ 13 centimeters ○ 23 centimeters
○ 17 centimeters ○ 33 centimeters

Spiral Review (CC.2.NBT.7, CC.2.MD.7, CC.2.MD.8)

2. What is the sum? (Lesson 6.3)

$$\begin{array}{r} 327 \\ +\ 145 \\ \hline \end{array}$$

○ 182 ○ 462
○ 262 ○ 472

3. Which is another way to write the time half past 7? (Lesson 7.10)

○ 6:30
○ 7:05
○ 7:30
○ 8:15

4. Molly has these coins in her pocket. How much money does she have in her pocket? (Lesson 7.2)

○ 75¢ ○ 70¢ ○ 65¢ ○ 55¢

Name ______________________________

HANDS ON
Lesson 9.5

Centimeters and Meters

COMMON CORE STANDARD CC.2.MD.2
Measure and estimate lengths in standard units.

Measure to the nearest centimeter.
Then measure to the nearest meter.

Find the real object.	Measure.
1. bookcase	_______ centimeters _______ meters
2. window	_______ centimeters _______ meters
3. map	_______ centimeters _______ meters

PROBLEM SOLVING REAL WORLD

4. Sally will measure the length of a wall in both centimeters and meters. Will there be fewer centimeters or fewer meters? Explain.

____

____

____

TEST PREP

Lesson Check (CC.2.MD.2)

1. Use a centimeter ruler. Which is the best choice for the length of the toothbrush?

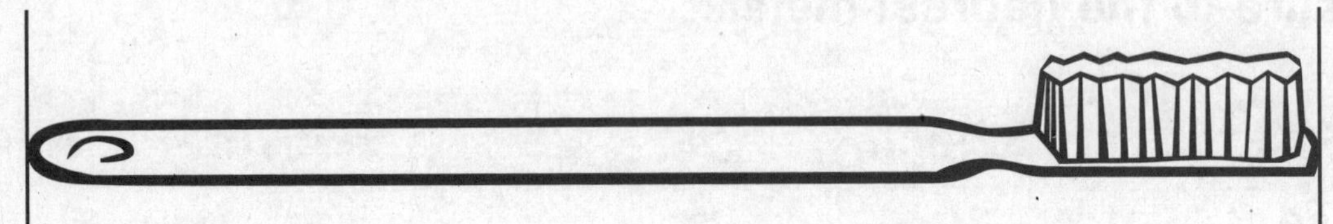

- ○ 4 centimeters
- ○ 14 centimeters
- ○ 20 centimeters
- ○ 25 centimeters

Spiral Review (CC.2.NBT.7, CC.2.MD.2, CC.2.MD.8)

2. Which group of coins has a total value of 65¢? (Lesson 7.4)

- ○ 5 dimes and 3 nickels
- ○ 50 pennies
- ○ 1 quarter and 2 dimes
- ○ 3 dimes and 7 pennies

3. Janet has a poster that is about 3 feet long. Which sentence is true? (Lesson 8.6)

- ○ 3 feet is shorter than 12 inches.
- ○ 3 feet is longer than 12 inches.
- ○ 12 inches is as long as 3 feet.
- ○ 12 inches is longer than 3 feet.

4. What is the sum? (Lesson 6.4)

$$\begin{array}{r} 483 \\ +\ 162 \\ \hline \end{array}$$

- ○ 321
- ○ 421
- ○ 545
- ○ 645

5. Which group of coins has a value of $1.00? (Lesson 7.5)

- ○ 4 dimes
- ○ 3 quarters and 2 nickels
- ○ 4 quarters
- ○ 3 quarters and 3 dimes

Name ___________________________

Estimate Lengths in Meters

COMMON CORE STANDARD CC.2.MD.3
Measure and estimate lengths in standard units.

Find the real object.
Estimate its length in meters.

1. poster

about ______ meters

2. chalkboard

about ______ meters

3. bookshelf

about ______ meters

PROBLEM SOLVING

4. Barbara and Luke each placed 2 meter sticks end-to-end along the length of a large table. About how long is the table?

about ______ meters

TEST PREP

Lesson Check (CC.2.MD.3)

1. Which is the best estimate for the length of a real baseball bat?

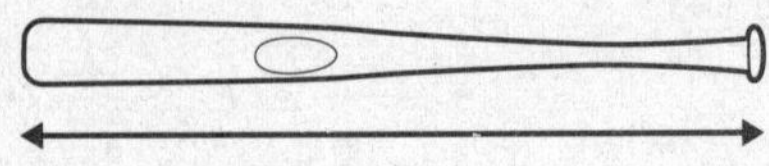

- ○ 1 meter
- ○ 3 meters
- ○ 5 meters
- ○ 7 meters

2. Which is the best estimate for the length of a real couch?

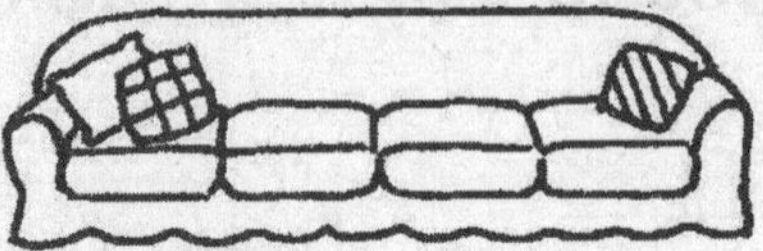

- ○ 8 meters
- ○ 6 meters
- ○ 5 meters
- ○ 2 meters

Spiral Review (CC.2.MD.1, CC.2.MD.8)

3. Sara has two $1 bills, 3 quarters, and 1 dime. How much money does she have? (Lesson 7.7)

- ○ $1.85
- ○ $2.40
- ○ $2.65
- ○ $2.85

4. Use an inch ruler. What is the length of this straw to the nearest inch? (Lesson 8.2)

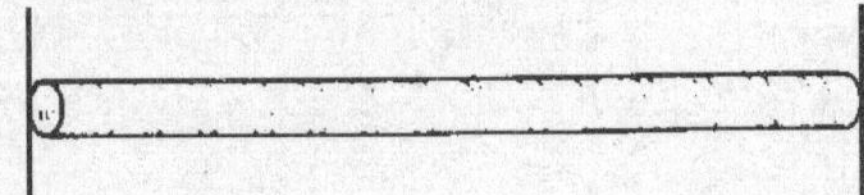

- ○ 4 inches
- ○ 3 inches
- ○ 2 inches
- ○ 1 inch

5. Scott has this money in his pocket. What is the total value of this money? (Lesson 7.6)

- ○ $1.05
- ○ $1.15
- ○ $1.20
- ○ $1.35

Name ______________________________

Measure and Compare Lengths

HANDS ON
Lesson 9.7

COMMON CORE STANDARD CC.2.MD.4
Measure and estimate lengths in standard units.

Measure the length of each object. Write a number sentence to find the difference between the lengths.

1.

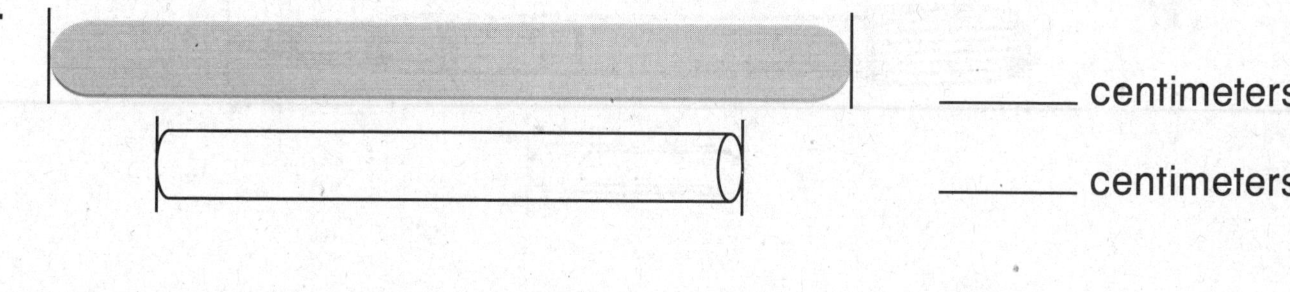

_____ centimeters

_____ centimeters

_____ − _____ = _____
centimeters centimeters centimeters

The craft stick is _____ centimeters longer than the chalk.

2.

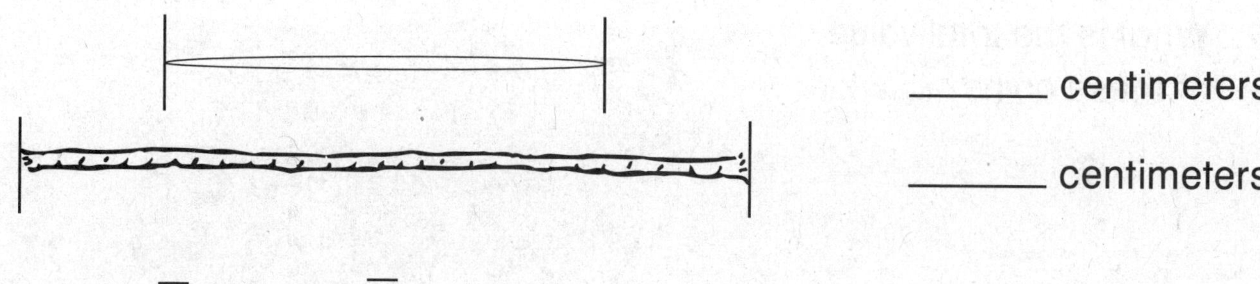

_____ centimeters

_____ centimeters

_____ − _____ = _____
centimeters centimeters centimeters

The string is _____ centimeters longer than the toothpick.

PROBLEM SOLVING

Solve. Write or draw to explain.

3. A string is 11 centimeters long, a ribbon is 24 centimeters long, and a large paper clip is 5 centimeters long. How much longer is the ribbon than the string?

_____ centimeters longer

TEST PREP

Lesson Check (CC.2.MD.4)

1. How much longer is the marker than the paper clip?

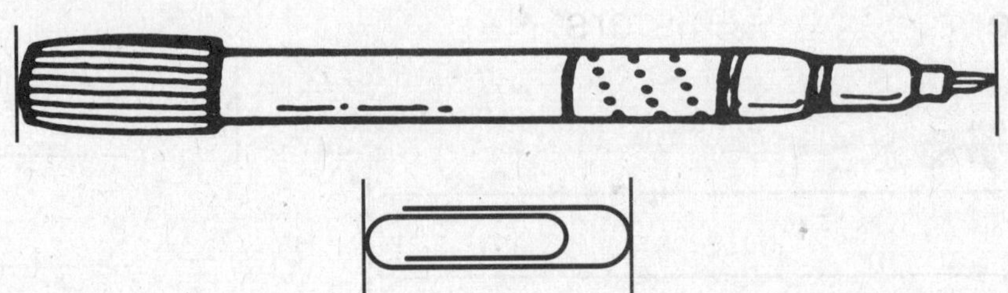

- ○ 11 centimeters longer
- ○ 10 centimeters longer
- ○ 8 centimeters longer
- ○ 5 centimeters longer

Spiral Review (CC.2.MD.3, CC.2.MD.7, CC.2.MD.8)

2. What is the total value of these coins? (Lesson 7.3)

○ 41¢ ○ 66¢ ○ 75¢ ○ 78¢

3. Which is the best estimate for the length of a real chalkboard? (Lesson 8.7)

- ○ 50 feet
- ○ 7 feet
- ○ 7 inches
- ○ 1 inch

4. Cindy leaves at half past 2. At what time does Cindy leave? (Lesson 7.10)

- ○ 2:45
- ○ 2:30
- ○ 2:15
- ○ 1:30

Name ______________________

COMMON CORE STANDARDS CC.2.MD.1, CC.2.MD.2, CC.2.MD.3, CC.2.MD.4

Chapter 9 Extra Practice

Lesson 9.1 (pp. 433–436)

Use a unit cube.
Measure the length in centimeters.

1. 

about ______ centimeters

2. 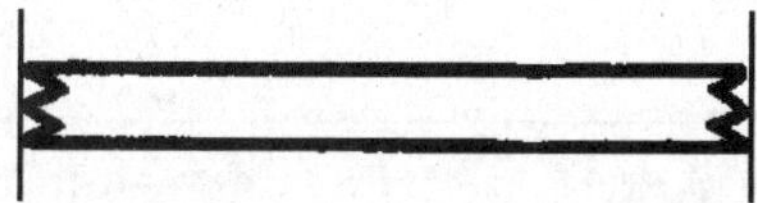

about ______ centimeters

Lesson 9.2 (pp. 437–440)

1. The leaf is about 6 centimeters long. Circle the best estimate for the length of the string.

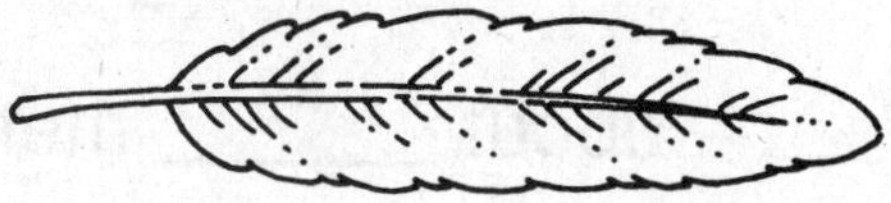

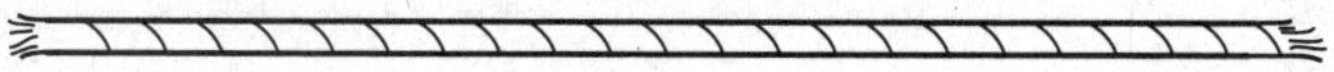

6 centimeters

9 centimeters

12 centimeters

Lesson 9.3 (pp. 441–444)

Measure the length to the nearest centimeter.

1. 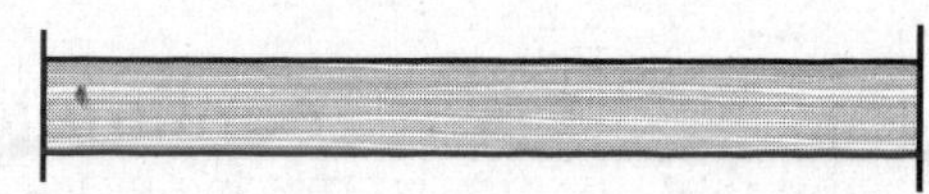

______ centimeters

2. 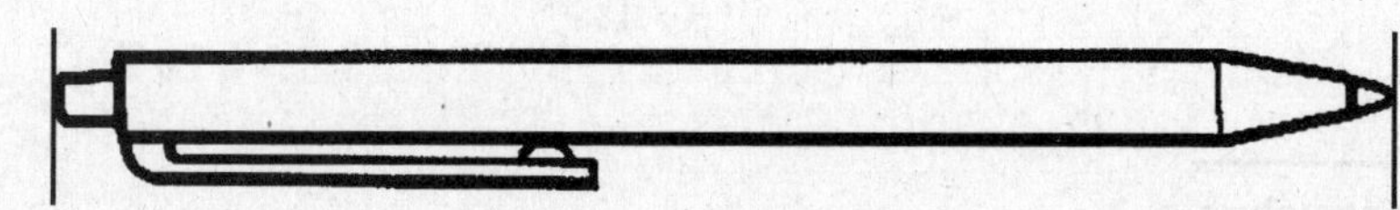

______ centimeters

Lesson 9.5 (pp. 449–452)

Measure to the nearest centimeter.
Then measure to the nearest meter.

Find the real object.	Measure.
I. poster	_______ centimeters _______ meters

Lesson 9.6 (pp. 453–456)

Find the real object.
Estimate its length in meters.

I.

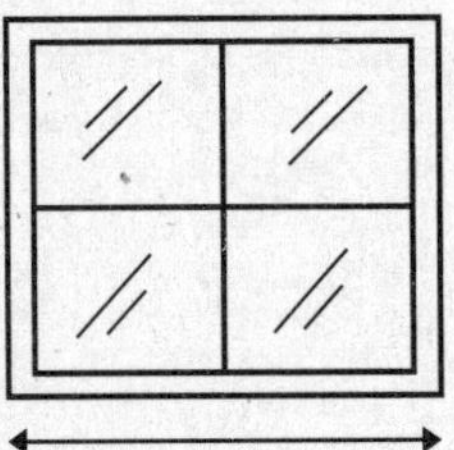

about _______ meters

Lesson 9.7 (pp. 457–460)

Measure the length of each object. Write a number sentence to find the difference between the lengths.

I.

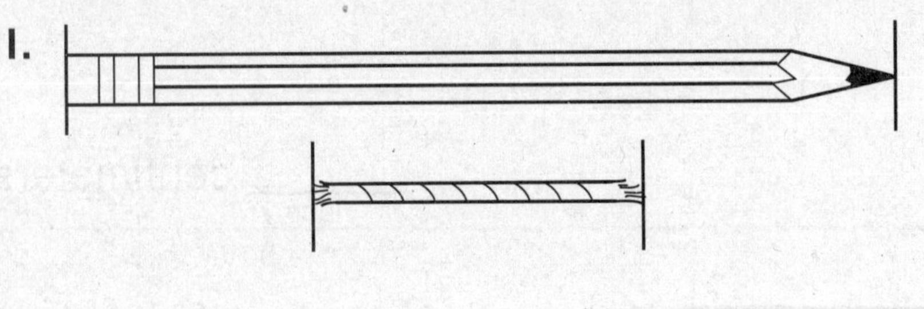

_______ centimeters

_______ centimeters

_______ centimeters − _______ centimeters = _______ centimeters

The pencil is _______ centimeters longer than the string.

Chapter 10

School-Home Letter

Dear Family,

My class started Chapter 10 this week. In this chapter, I will learn about collecting data, making graphs, and interpreting the data.

Love, ______________________________

Vocabulary

picture graph A graph that uses pictures to show data

Apples Sold					
Eric	●	●			
Deb	●	●	●	●	
Alex	●				

Key: Each ● stands for 1 apple.

bar graph A graph that uses bars to show data

Home Activity

Take your child on a walk in your neighborhood. Help your child make a tally chart to record how many people you see driving, walking, and biking. Then talk with your child about the information that is in your tally chart.

How People Are Moving

How Moving	Tally
driving	~~IIII~~ II
walking	IIII
biking	II

Literature

Reading math stories reinforces learning. Look for these books at the library.

Tables and Graphs of Healthy Things
by Joan Freese. Gareth Stevens Publishing, 2008.

Lemonade for Sale
by Stuart J. Murphy. Harper Collins, 1998.

Capítulo 10

Carta para la casa

Querida familia:

Mi clase comenzó el Capítulo 10 esta semana. En este capítulo, aprenderé a recolectar datos, hacer grá cas e interpretar datos.

Con cariño, ______________________________

Vocabulario

pictografía una gráfica que usa ilustraciones para mostrar datos

Manzanas vendidas					
Eric	●	●			
Deb	●	●	●	●	
Alex	●				

Clave: Cada ● representa 2 manzanas.

gráfica de barras una gráfica que usa barras para mostrar datos

Actividad para la casa

Lleve a pasear a su hijo por el vecindario. Ayúdelo a crear una tabla de conteo para anotar cuántas personas ven manejando, caminando y montando en bicicleta. Luego, conversen sobre la información que hay en la tabla de conteo.

Cómo se mueve la gente	
Se mueven	**Conteo**
manejando	~~IIII~~ II
caminando	IIII
en bicicleta	II

Literatura

Leer cuentos de matemáticas refuerza los conceptos. Busque estos libros en la biblioteca.

Table and Graphs of Healthy Things
por Joan Freese. Gareth Stevens Publishing, 2008.

Lemonade for Sale
por Stuart J. Murphy. Harper Collins, 1998.

Name ______________________

Collect Data

COMMON CORE STANDARD CC.2.MD.10
Represent and interpret data.

1. Take a survey. Ask 10 classmates how they got to school. Use tally marks to show their choices.

How We Got to School	
Way	**Tally**
walk	
bus	
car	
bike	

2. How many classmates rode in a bus to school?

_____ classmates

3. How many classmates rode in a car to school?

_____ classmates

4. In which way did the fewest classmates get to school?

____

5. In which way did the most classmates get to school?

____

6. Did more classmates get to school by walking or by riding in a car?

____

How many more? _____ more classmates

TEST PREP

Lesson Check (CC.2.MD.10)

1. Use the tally chart. Which color did the fewest children choose?

- ○ blue
- ○ green
- ○ red
- ○ yellow

Favorite Color	
Color	**Tally**
blue	III
green	~~IIII~~ IIII
red	~~IIII~~ II
yellow	~~IIII~~ I

Spiral Review (CC.2.MD.5, CC.2.MD.6, CC.2.MD.7, CC.2.MD.8)

2. Which group of coins has a value of $1.00? (Lesson 7.5)

- ○ 10 pennies
- ○ 10 nickels
- ○ 10 dimes
- ○ 10 quarters

3. Jared has two ropes. Each rope is 9 inches long. How many inches of rope does he have in all? (Lesson 8.5)

- ○ 10 inches
- ○ 18 inches
- ○ 16 inches
- ○ 21 inches

4. The clock shows the time Lee got to school. At what time did she get to school? (Lesson 7.11)

- ○ 3:40 A.M.
- ○ 3:40 P.M.
- ○ 8:15 A.M.
- ○ 8:15 P.M.

5. Liza finished studying at half past 3. What time did Liza finish studying? (Lesson 7.10)

- ○ 3:30
- ○ 3:15
- ○ 2:45
- ○ 2:15

Name ______________________________

Read Picture Graphs

COMMON CORE STANDARD CC.2.MD.10
Represent and interpret data.

Use the picture graph to answer the questions.

Number of Books Read						
Ryan	Math Grade 2	Math Grade 2	Math Grade 2	Math Grade 2		
Gwen	Math Grade 2	Math Grade 2				
Anna	Math Grade 2	Math Grade 2	Math Grade 2	Math Grade 2	Math Grade 2	Math Grade 2
Henry	Math Grade 2	Math Grade 2	Math Grade 2			

Key: Each Math Grade 2 stands for 1 book.

1. How many books in all did Henry and Anna read? _______ books

2. How many more books did Ryan read than Gwen? _______ more books

3. How many fewer books did Gwen read than Anna? _______ fewer books

4. How many books did the four children read in all? _______ books

PROBLEM SOLVING

Use the picture graph above. Write or draw to explain.

5. Carlos read 4 books. How many children read fewer books than Carlos?

_______ children

Lesson Check (CC.2.MD.10)

1. Use the picture graph. Who has the most fish?

Our Fish					
Jane	🐟				
Will	🐟	🐟	🐟		
Gina	🐟	🐟	🐟	🐟	
Evan	🐟	🐟			

Key: Each 🐟 stands for 1 fish.

- ○ Jane
- ○ Will
- ○ Gina
- ○ Evan

Spiral Review (CC.2.MD.1, CC.2.MD.7, CC.2.MD.8)

2. What is the time on this clock? (Lesson 7.9)

- ○ 1:55
- ○ 3:05
- ○ 2:55
- ○ 11:15

3. Each unit cube is about 1 centimeter long. Which is the best estimate for the length of the paper clip? (Lesson 9.1)

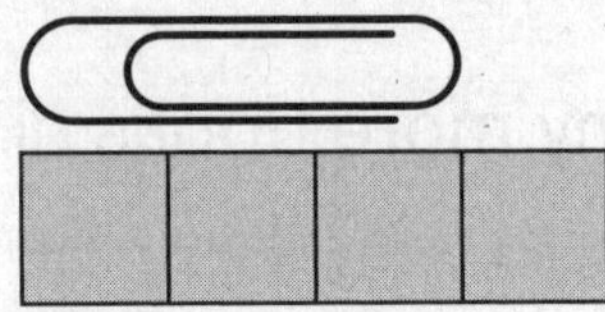

- ○ 1 centimeter
- ○ 3 centimeters
- ○ 4 centimeters
- ○ 8 centimeters

4. What is the total value of this group of coins? (Lesson 7.2)

- ○ 61¢
- ○ 60¢
- ○ 56¢
- ○ 52¢

Name ______________________________

Make Picture Graphs

COMMON CORE STANDARD CC.2.MD.10
Represent and interpret data.

1. Use the tally chart to complete the picture graph. Draw a ☺ for each child.

Favorite Cookie	
Cookie	Tally
chocolate	|||
oatmeal	|
peanut butter	~~||||~~
shortbread	||||

Favorite Cookie					
chocolate					
oatmeal					
peanut butter					
shortbread					

Key: Each ☺ stands for 1 child.

2. How many children chose chocolate? _______ children

3. How many fewer children chose oatmeal than peanut butter? _______ fewer children

4. Which cookie did the most children choose?

____

5. How many children in all chose a favorite cookie? _______ children

6. How many children chose oatmeal or shortbread? _______ children

Lesson Check (CC.2.MD.10)

1. Use the picture graph. How many more rainy days were there in April than in May?

   ○ 2
   ○ 4
   ○ 6
   ○ 12

Number of Rainy Days					
March	☂	☂	☂	☂	☂
April	☂	☂	☂	☂	
May	☂	☂			

Key: Each ☂ stands for 1 day.

Spiral Review (CC.2.MD.1, CC.2.MD.8)

2. Rita has one $1 bill, 2 quarters, and 3 dimes. What is the total value of Rita's money? (Lesson 7.7)

   ○ $1.23 ○ $1.42
   ○ $1.35 ○ $1.80

3. Lucas put 4 quarters and 3 nickels into his coin bank. How much money did Lucas put into his coin bank? (Lesson 7.6)

   ○ $1.15 ○ $1.30
   ○ $1.25 ○ $1.75

4. Use a centimeter ruler. Which is the best choice for the length of this string? (Lesson 9.3)

   ○ 2 centimeters
   ○ 4 centimeters
   ○ 6 centimeters
   ○ 10 centimeters

5. What is the total value of this group of coins? (Lesson 7.1)

   ○ 8¢
   ○ 17¢
   ○ 21¢
   ○ 26¢

Name ___________________________

Read Bar Graphs

COMMON CORE STANDARD CC.2.MD.10
Represent and interpret data.

Use the bar graph.

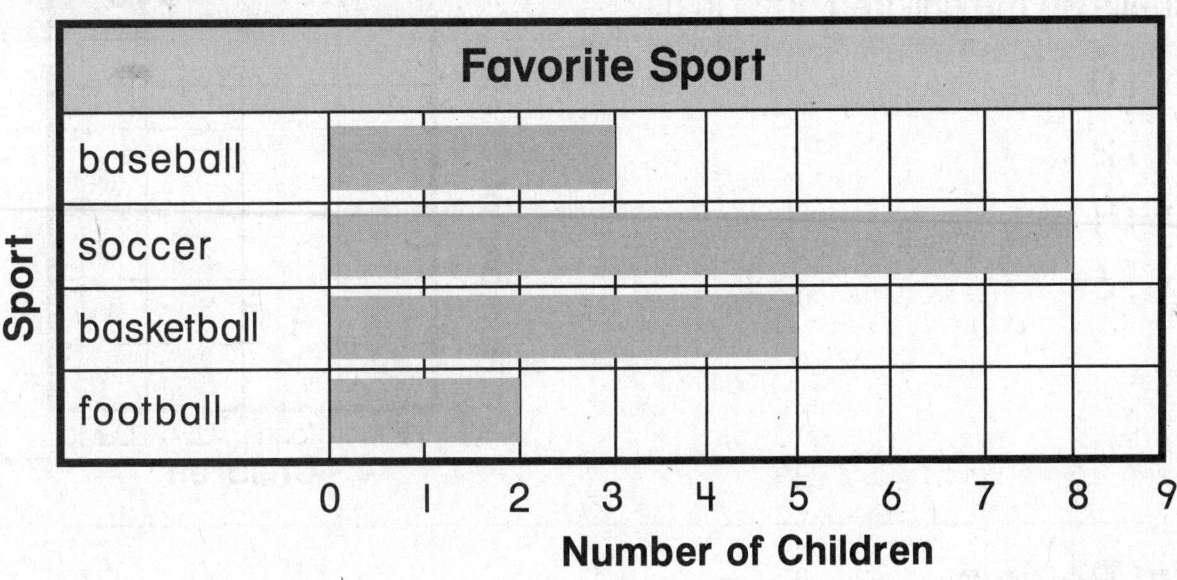

1. How many children chose basketball? _______ children

2. Which sport did the most children choose? _______________

3. How many more children chose basketball than baseball? _______ more children

4. Which sport did the fewest children choose? _______________

5. How many children chose a sport that was not soccer? _______ children

PROBLEM SOLVING REAL WORLD

6. How many children chose baseball or basketball?

_______ children

Lesson Check (CC.2.MD.10)

1. Use the bar graph. How many shells do the children have in all?

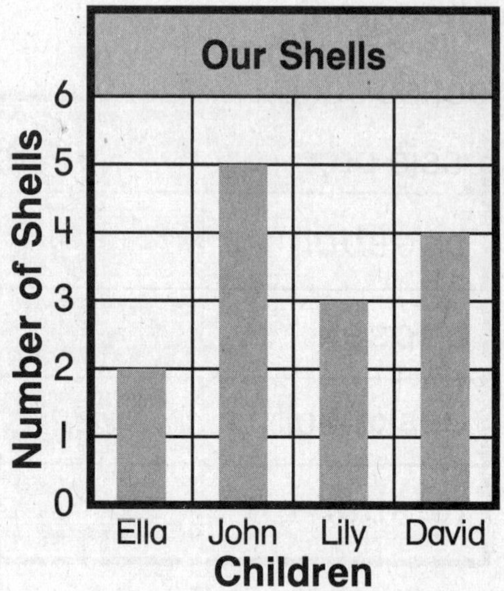

- ○ 10
- ○ 12
- ○ 14
- ○ 16

Spiral Review (CC.2.MD.1, CC.2.MD.8, CC.2.MD.9)

2. Use the line plot. How many twigs are 3 inches long? (Lesson 8.9)

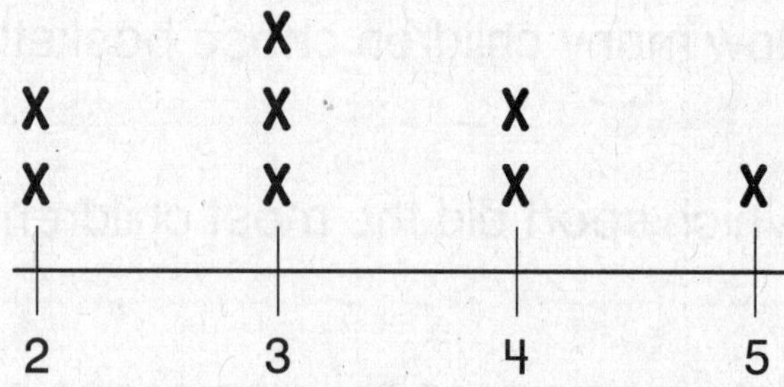

- ○ 8
- ○ 5
- ○ 4
- ○ 3

3. Use a centimeter ruler. Which is the best choice for the length of the yarn? (Lesson 9.3)

- ○ 7 centimeters
- ○ 4 centimeters
- ○ 2 centimeters
- ○ 1 centimeter

4. Noah buys a pencil. He uses 1 quarter and 2 nickels to pay. How much money does the pencil cost? (Lesson 7.4)

- ○ 45¢
- ○ 35¢
- ○ 30¢
- ○ 27¢

Name ______________________________

Make Bar Graphs

COMMON CORE STANDARD CC.2.MD.10
Represent and interpret data.

Maria asked her friends how many hours they practice soccer each week.

- Jessie practices for 3 hours.
- Victor practices for 2 hours.
- Samantha practices for 5 hours.
- David practices for 6 hours.

1. Write a title and labels for the bar graph.

2. Draw bars in the graph to show the data.

______________________										
Jessie										
Victor										
Samantha										
David										
	0	1	2	3	4	5	6	7	8	9 10

____

3. Which friend practices soccer for the most hours each week? ______________

PROBLEM SOLVING

4. Which friends practice soccer for fewer than 4 hours each week?

____

Lesson Check (CC.2.MD.10)

1. Use the bar graph. How many more children chose summer than spring?

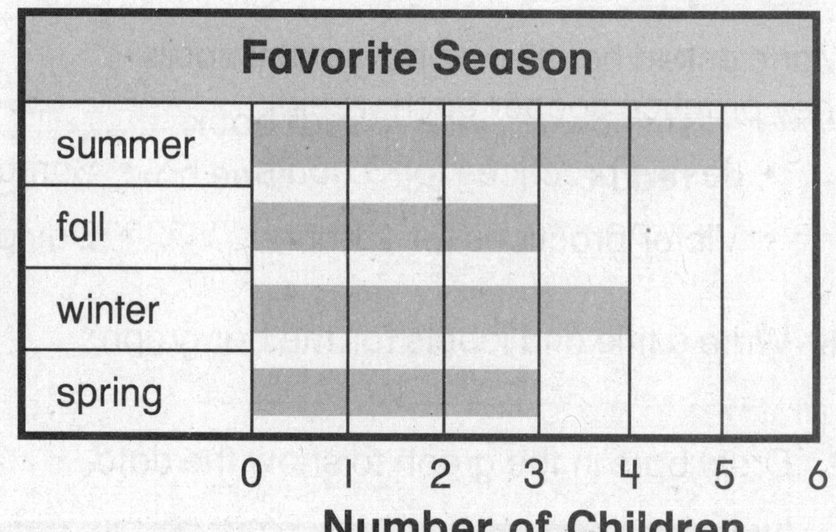

- ○ 2
- ○ 3
- ○ 5
- ○ 8

Spiral Review (CC.2.MD.1, CC.2.MD.5, CC.2.MD.6, CC.2.MD.7, CC.2.MD.8)

2. Rachel's chain is 22 centimeters long. She takes 9 centimeters off the chain. How long is Rachel's chain now? (Lesson 9.4)

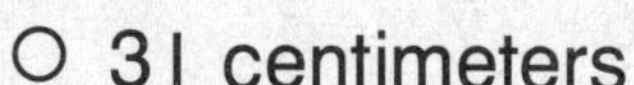

- ○ 31 centimeters
- ○ 29 centimeters
- ○ 17 centimeters
- ○ 13 centimeters

3. Use an inch ruler. What is the length of the string to the nearest inch? (Lesson 8.4)

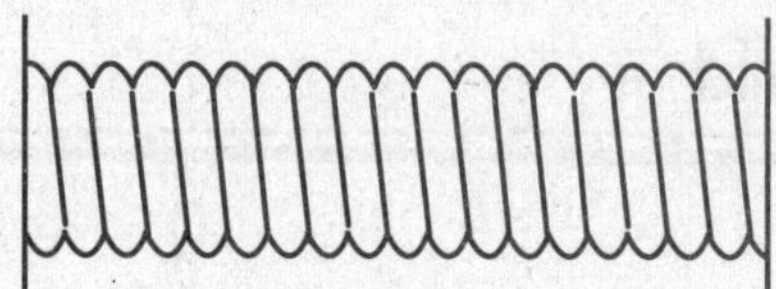

- ○ 1 inch
- ○ 2 inches
- ○ 4 inches
- ○ 6 inches

4. Gail finished studying at quarter past 1. What time did Gail finish studying? (Lesson 7.10)

- ○ 1:15
- ○ 3:50
- ○ 4:30
- ○ 5:45

5. Jill has two $1 bills, 1 quarter, and 1 nickel. How much money does Jill have? (Lesson 7.7)

- ○ $2.35
- ○ $2.30
- ○ $2.05
- ○ $1.30

Name ______________________

Problem Solving • Display Data

COMMON CORE STANDARD CC.2.MD.10
Represent and interpret data.

Make a bar graph to solve the problem.

1. The list shows the number of books that Abby read each month. Describe how the number of books she read changed from February to May.

February	8 books
March	7 books
April	6 books
May	4 books

______________										
February										
March										
April										
May										
	0	1	2	3	4	5	6	7	8	9 10

____

The number of books ______________________________

____

2. How many books in all did Abby read in February and March? _____ books

3. How many fewer books did Abby read in April than in February? _____ fewer books

4. In which months did Abby read fewer than 7 books? ______________

TEST PREP

Lesson Check (CC.2.MD.10)

1. Use the bar graph. Which of the following describes how the number of hours changed from Week 1 to Week 4?

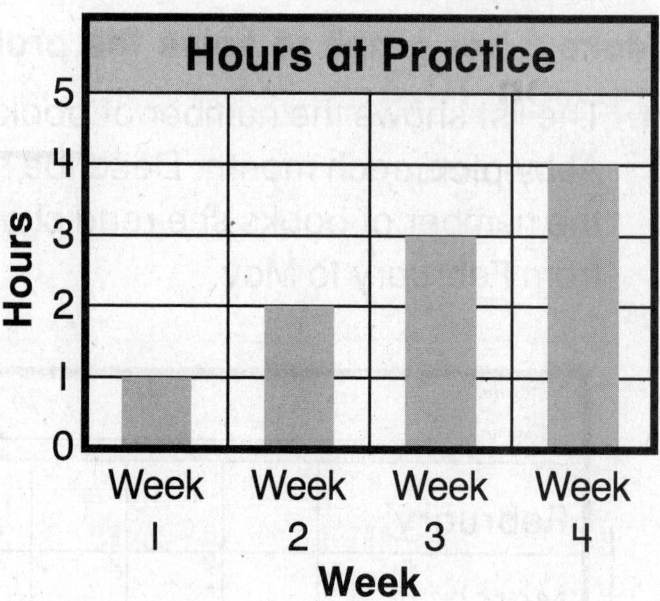

- ○ The number of hours decreased.
- ○ The number of hours increased and then decreased.
- ○ The number of hours increased.
- ○ The number of hours stayed the same.

Spiral Review (CC.2.MD.3, CC.2.MD.8)

2. The string is about 10 centimeters long. Which is the best estimate for the length of the feather? (Lesson 9.2)

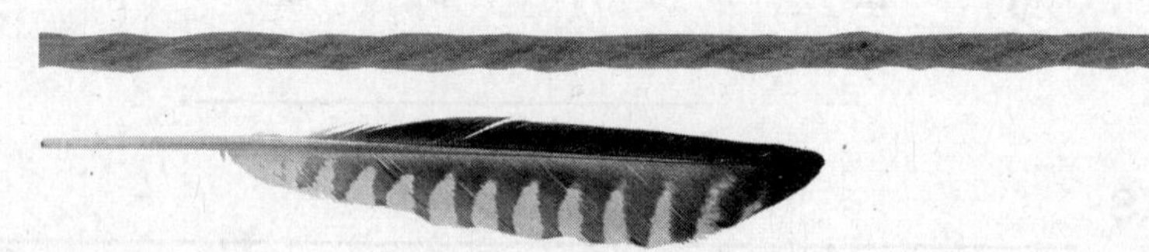

- ○ 2 centimeters
- ○ 5 centimeters
- ○ 10 centimeters
- ○ 20 centimeters

3. What is the total value of this group of coins? (Lesson 7.3)

- ○ 55¢
- ○ 50¢
- ○ 40¢
- ○ 28¢

4. Rick has one $1 bill, 2 dimes, and 3 pennies. How much money does Rick have? (Lesson 7.6)

- ○ $1.72
- ○ $1.53
- ○ $1.40
- ○ $1.23

Name ______________________

COMMON CORE STANDARD CC.2.MD.10

Chapter 10 Extra Practice

Lesson 10.2 (pp. 473–476)

Use the picture graph.

Favorite Flavor					
vanilla	☺	☺	☺		
chocolate	☺	☺	☺	☺	
strawberry	☺	☺	☺	☺	☺
mint	☺	☺			

Key: Each ☺ stands for 1 child.

1. How many children chose chocolate? _______ children
2. Which flavor did the most children choose? ______________
3. How many children in all chose a favorite flavor? _______ children

Lesson 10.3 (pp. 477–479)

1. Use the tally chart to complete the picture graph. Draw a ● for each book.

Number of Books Read	
Name	**Tally**
Maya	||||
Gabe	~~||||~~
Tia	|||
Cathy	|

Number of Books Read					
Maya					
Gabe					
Tia					
Cathy					

Key: Each ● stands for 1 book.

2. Who read more than 4 books? ______________

Lesson 10.4 (pp. 481–484)

Use the bar graph.

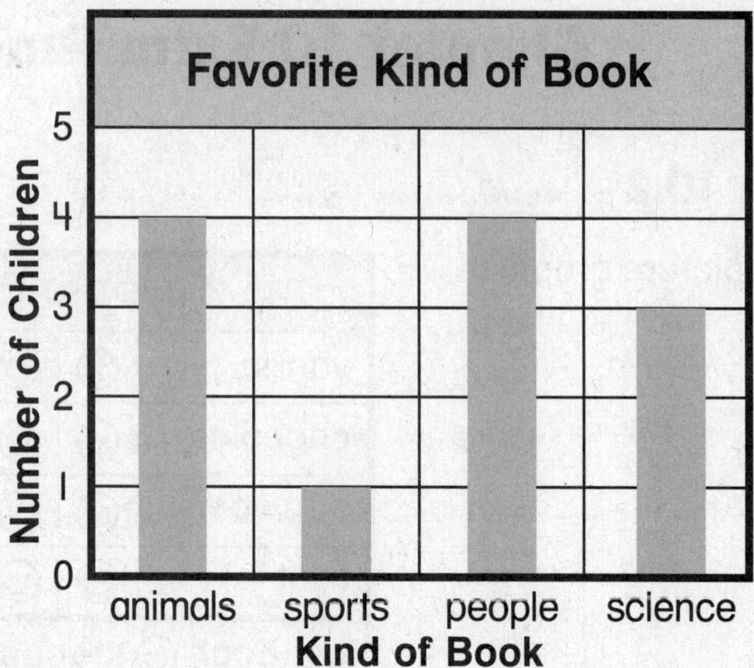

1. Which kind of book did the fewest children choose? ____________

2. How many children in all chose a favorite kind of book? ______ children

Lesson 10.5 (pp. 485–488)

Robin has 5 red beads, 7 blue beads, 8 yellow beads, and 5 green beads.

1. Write a title and labels. Draw bars to show the data.

____________									
red									
blue									
yellow									
green									
	0	1	2	3	4	5	6	7	8 9

____

Chapter 11

School-Home Letter

Dear Family:

My class started Chapter 11 this week. In this chapter, I will learn about three-dimensional and two-dimensional shapes. I will also learn about equal parts of a whole.

Love, ______________________________

Vocabulary

quadrilateral

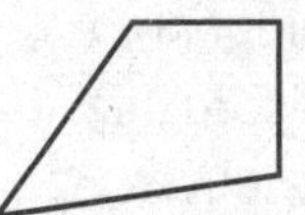

pentagon

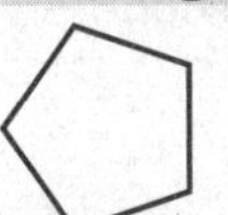

hexagon

cone

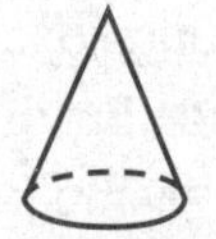

cylinder

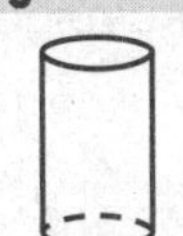

cube

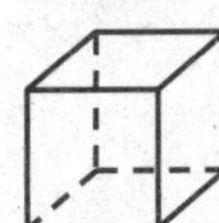

Home Activity

Name a two-dimensional shape: triangle, quadrilateral, pentagon, or hexagon. With your child, look for an object that has that shape.

Repeat the activity using a three-dimensional shape: cube, rectangular prism, sphere, cylinder, or cone.

Literature

Reading math stories reinforces learning. Look for these books at the library.

Shape Up! by David Adler. Holiday House, 1998.

The Village of Round and Square Houses by Ann Grifalconi. Little, Brown and Company, 1986.

Capítulo 11

Carta para la casa

Querida familia:

Mi clase comenzó hoy el Capítulo 11. En este capítulo, aprenderé acerca de las guras bidimensionales y tridimensionales. También aprenderé sobre las partes igualdades de un entero.

Con cariño, ______________________________

Vocabulario

cuadrilátero

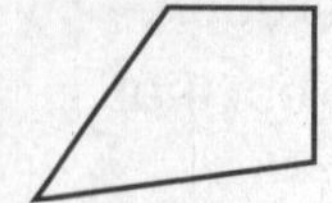

pentágono

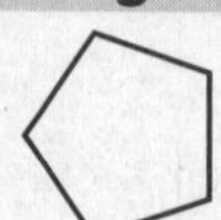

hexágono

cono

cilindro

cubo

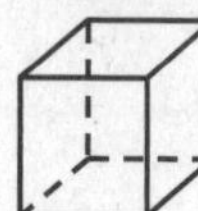

Actividad para la casa

Nombre alguna figura bidimensional, como triángulo, cuadrilátero, pentágono o hexágono. Juntos, busquen una figura que tenga la misma forma. Repitan la actividad con una figura tridimensional, como cubo, prisma rectangular, esfera, cilindro o cono.

Literatura

Leer cuentos de matemáticas refuerza el aprendizaje. Busquen estos libros en la biblioteca.

Shape Up!
por David Adler. Holiday House, 1998

The Village of Round and Square Houses
por Ann Grifalconi. Little, Brown and Company, 1986.

Name ______________________

Three-Dimensional Shapes

COMMON CORE STANDARD CC.2.G.1
Reason with shapes and their attributes.

Circle the objects that match the shape name.

1. cube			
2. cone			
3. rectangular prism			
4. cylinder			

PROBLEM SOLVING

5. Lisa draws a circle by tracing around the bottom of a block. Which could be the shape of Lisa's block? Circle the name of the shape.

cone   cube   rectangular prism

Lesson Check (CC.2.G.1)

1. What is the name of this shape?

○ cube
○ cone
○ cylinder
○ sphere

2. What is the name of this shape?

○ rectangular prism
○ cube
○ sphere
○ cone

Spiral Review (CC.2.MD.3, CC.2.MD.7, CC.2.MD.8)

3. The string is about 6 centimeters long. Which is the best estimate for the length of the crayon? (Lesson 9.2)

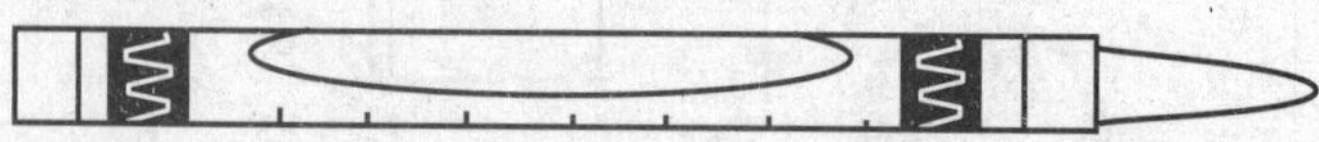

○ 3 centimeters
○ 4 centimeters
○ 9 centimeters
○ 12 centimeters

4. What is the total value of this group of coins? (Lesson 7.1)

○ 3¢
○ 11¢
○ 15¢
○ 16¢

5. What time is shown on this clock? (Lesson 7.8)

○ 6:00
○ 10:06
○ 10:30
○ 11:00

Name ______________________________

Attributes of Three-Dimensional Shapes

COMMON CORE STANDARD CC.2.G.1
Reason with shapes and their attributes.

Circle the set of shapes that are the faces of the three-dimensional shape.

1.

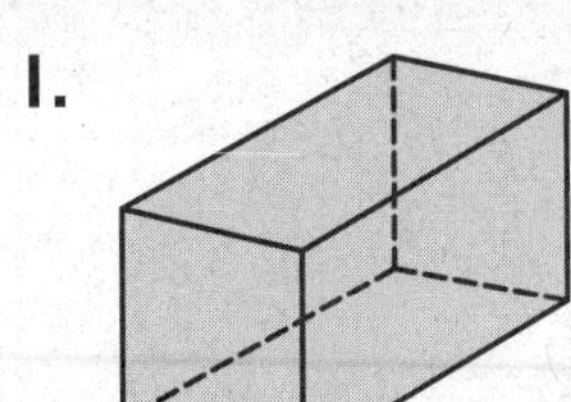

rectangular prism

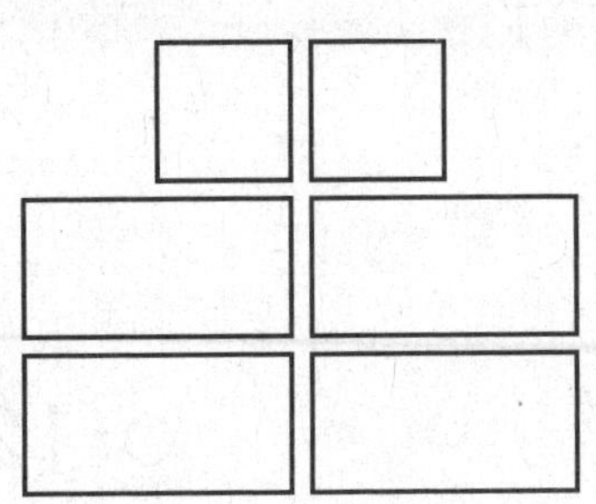

2.

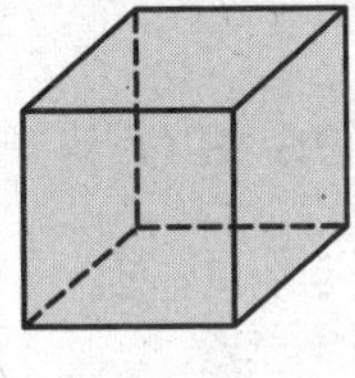

cube

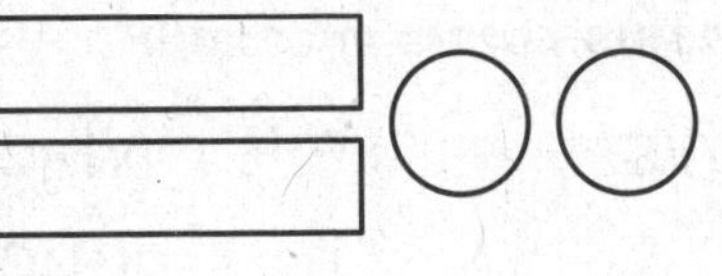

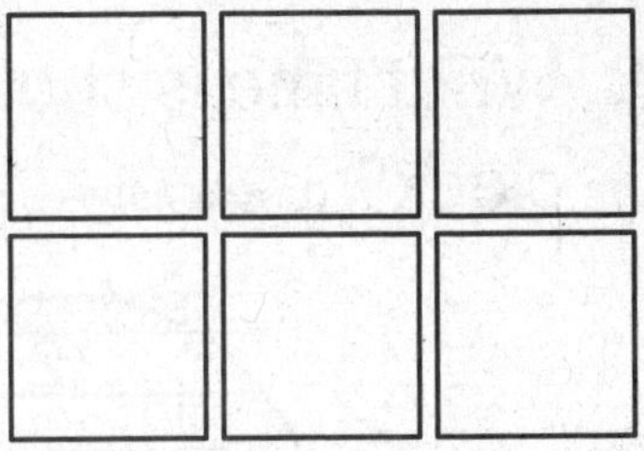

3.

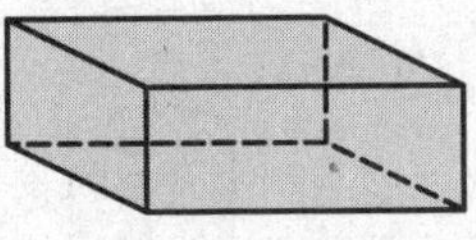

rectangular prism

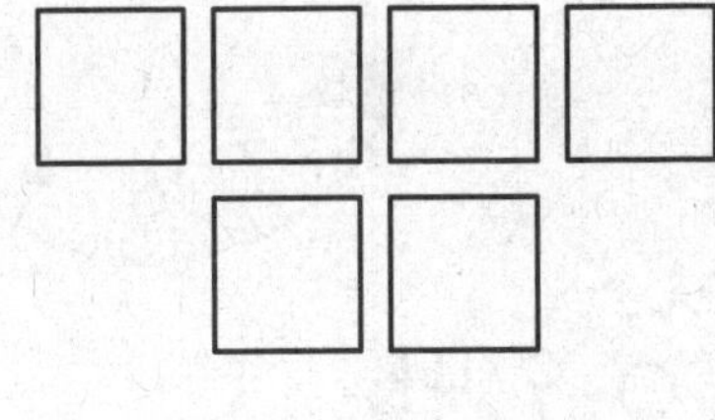

PROBLEM SOLVING REAL WORLD

4. Kevin keeps his marbles in a container that has the shape of a cube. He wants to paint each face a different color. How many different paint colors does he need?

____ different paint colors

Lesson Check (CC.2.G.1)

1. How many faces does a cube have?

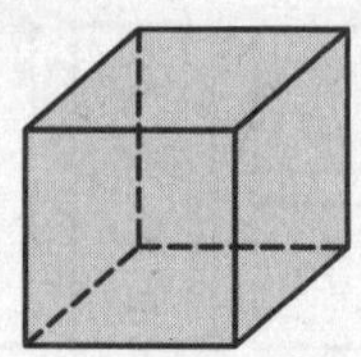

○ 8
○ 7
○ 6
○ 5

2. How many faces does a rectangular prism have?

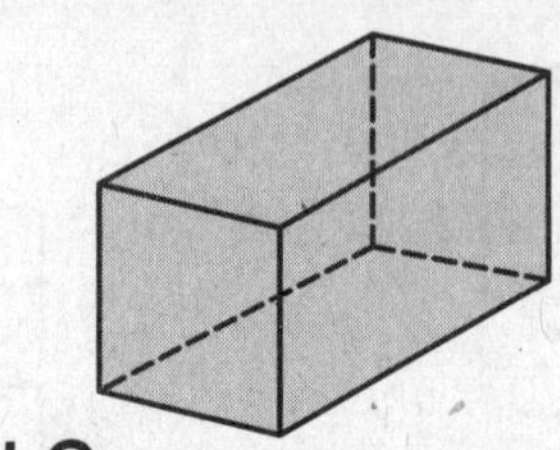

○ 12
○ 10
○ 8
○ 6

Spiral Review (CC.2.MD.7, CC.2.MD.9, CC.2.MD.10, CC.2.G.1)

3. What time is shown on this clock? (Lesson 7.9)

○ 9:45
○ 9:15
○ 9:03
○ 3:45

4. Which of these shapes is a cone? (Lesson 11.1)

○ 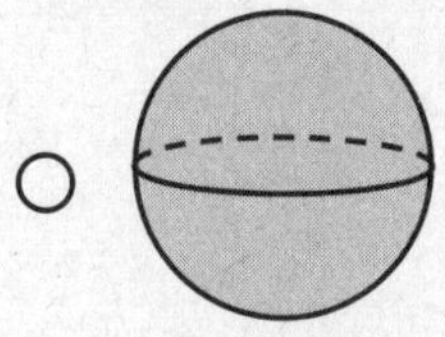
○ 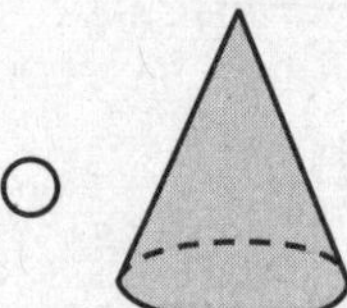
○ 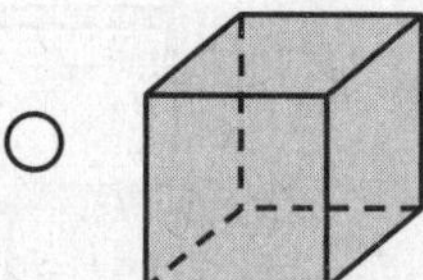
○ 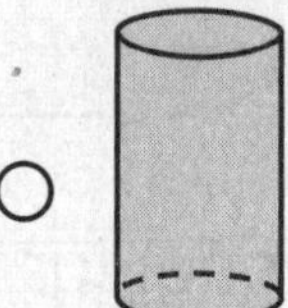

5. Use the line plot. How many books are 8 inches long? (Lesson 8.9)

○ 1
○ 2
○ 6
○ 8

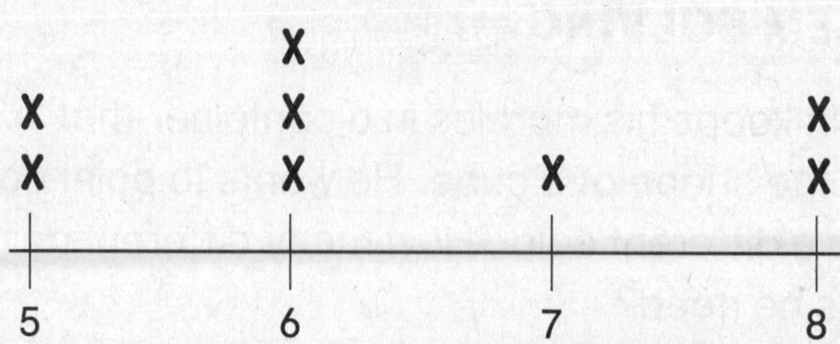

Lengths of Books in Inches

Name ______________________

Two-Dimensional Shapes

COMMON CORE STANDARD CC.2.G.1
Reason with shapes and their attributes.

Write the number of sides and the number of vertices. Then write the name of the shape.

pentagon | triangle | hexagon | quadrilateral

1. 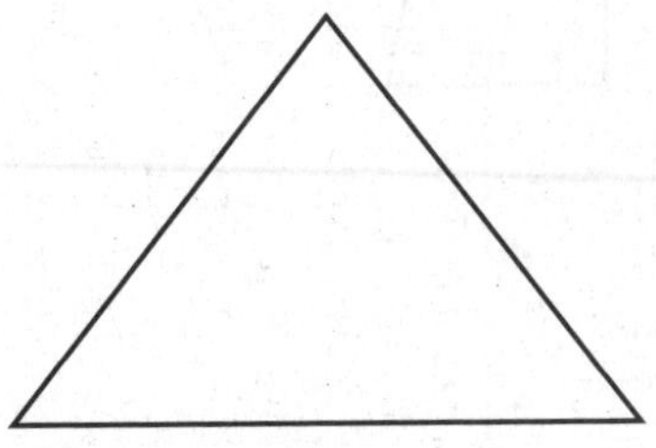

____ sides

____ vertices

____

2. 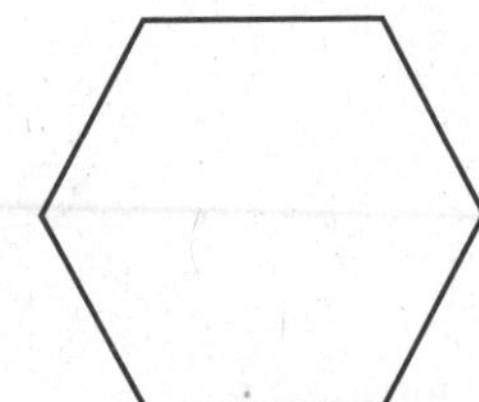

____ sides

____ vertices

____

3. 

____ sides

____ vertices

____

4. 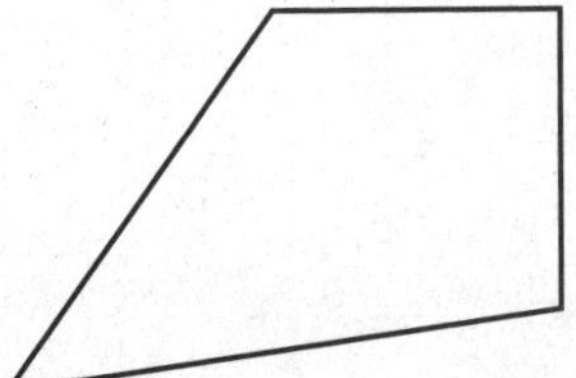

____ sides

____ vertices

____

5. 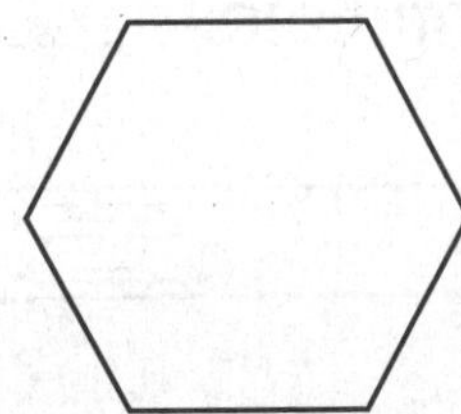

____ sides

____ vertices

____

6. 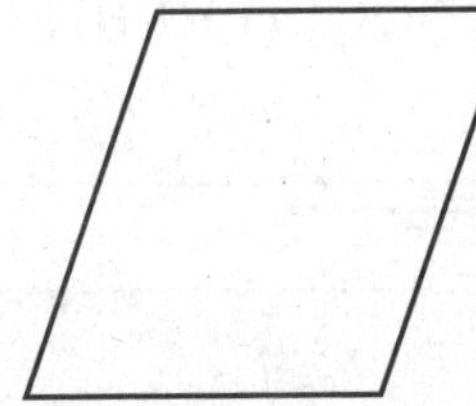

____ sides

____ vertices

____

PROBLEM SOLVING

Solve. Draw or write to explain.

7. Oscar is drawing a picture of a house. He draws a pentagon shape for a window. How many sides does his window have?

____ sides

Lesson Check (CC.2.G.1)

1. How many sides does a hexagon have?

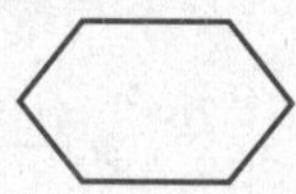

- ○ 3
- ○ 4
- ○ 5
- ○ 6

2. How many vertices does a quadrilateral have?

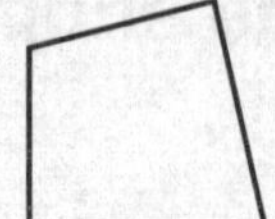

- ○ 6
- ○ 5
- ○ 4
- ○ 3

Spiral Review (CC.2.MD.1, CC.2.MD.10)

3. Use a centimeter ruler. What is the length of the ribbon to the nearest centimeter? (Lesson 9.3)

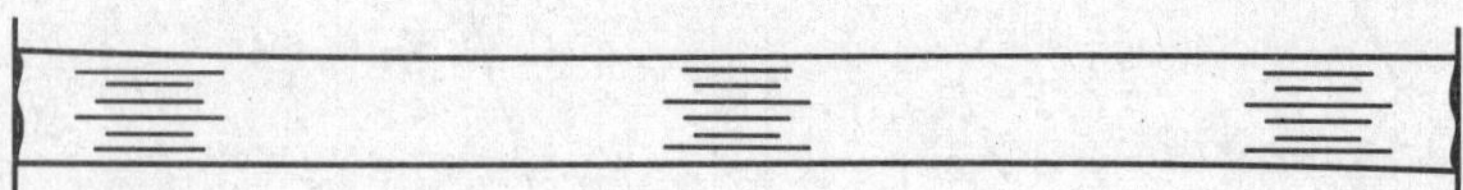

- ○ 10 centimeters
- ○ 14 centimeters
- ○ 16 centimeters
- ○ 18 centimeters

4. Look at the picture graph. How many more children chose apples than chose oranges? (Lesson 10.3)

- ○ 1
- ○ 2
- ○ 4
- ○ 11

Favorite Fruit					
apples	☺	☺	☺	☺	
oranges	☺	☺			
grapes	☺	☺	☺		
peaches	☺	☺			

Key: Each ☺ stands for 1 child.

Name ______________________________

Angles in Two-Dimensional Shapes

COMMON CORE STANDARD CC.2.G.1
Reason with shapes and their attributes.

Circle the angles in each shape.
Write how many.

1.

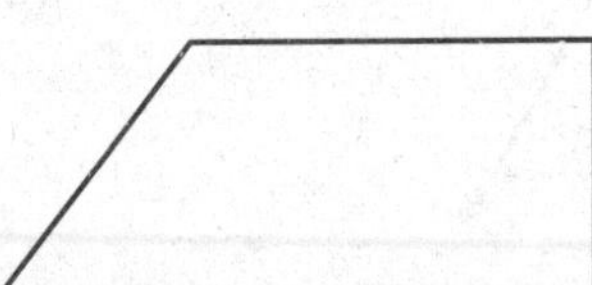

_____ **angles**

2.

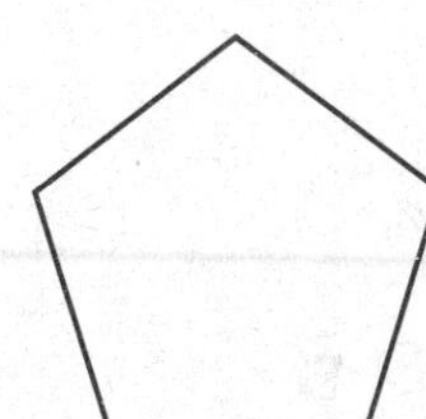

_____ **angles**

3.

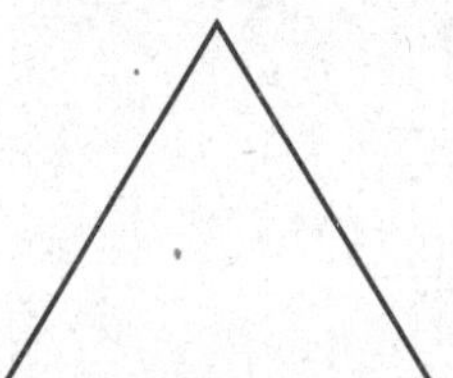

_____ **angles**

4.

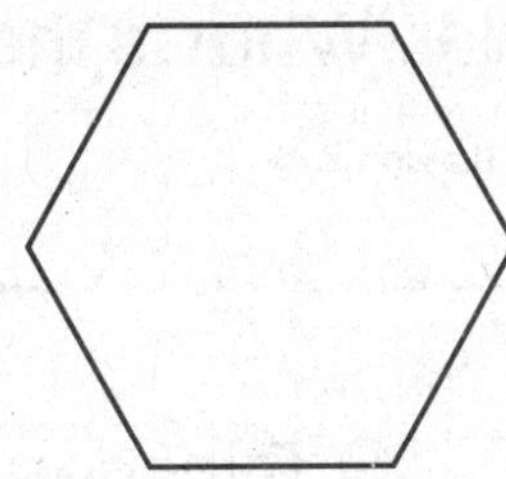

_____ **angles**

PROBLEM SOLVING

5. Logan drew 2 two-dimensional shapes that had 8 angles in all. Draw shapes Logan could have drawn.

Lesson Check (CC.2.G.1)

1. How many angles does this shape have?

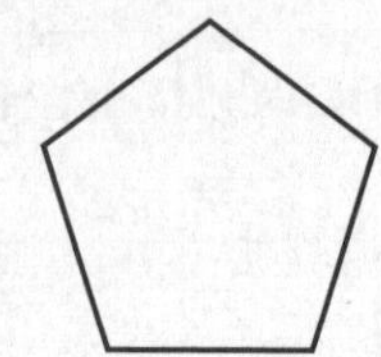

○ 3 ○ 5
○ 4 ○ 6

2. How many angles does this shape have?

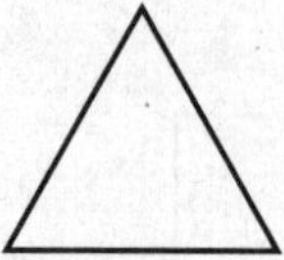

○ 3 ○ 5
○ 4 ○ 6

Spiral Review (CC.2.MD.5, CC.2.MD.6, CC.2.MD.10, CC.2.G.1)

3. Use an inch ruler. What is the length of the string to the nearest inch? (Lesson 8.4)

○ 13 inches ○ 5 inches
○ 11 inches ○ 3 inches

4. Look at the picture graph. How many children chose daisies? (Lesson 10.2)

○ 2
○ 3
○ 4
○ 5

Favorite Flower						
roses	☺	☺	☺	☺		
tulips	☺	☺	☺			
daisies	☺	☺	☺	☺	☺	
lillies	☺	☺				

Key: Each ☺ stands for 1 child.

Name ______________________________

Sort Two-Dimensional Shapes

COMMON CORE STANDARD CC.2.G.1
Reason with shapes and their attributes.

Circle the shapes that match the rule.

1. Shapes with fewer than 5 sides

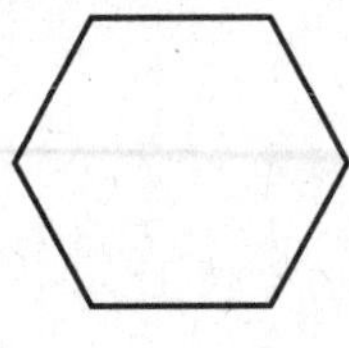
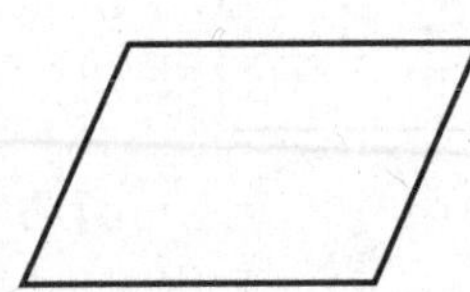
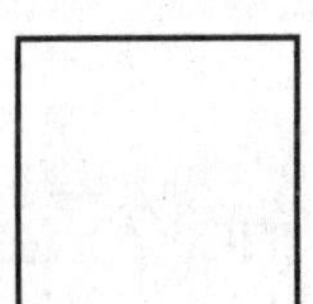
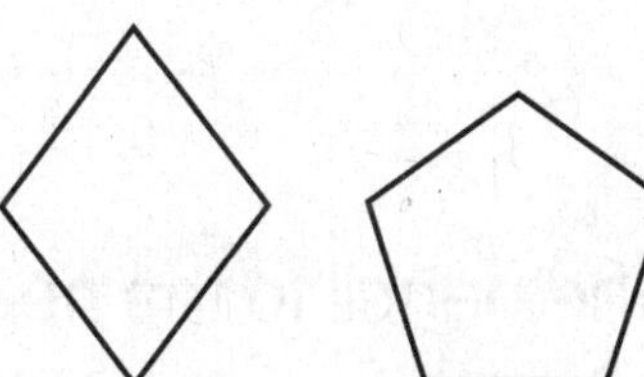

2. Shapes with more than 4 sides

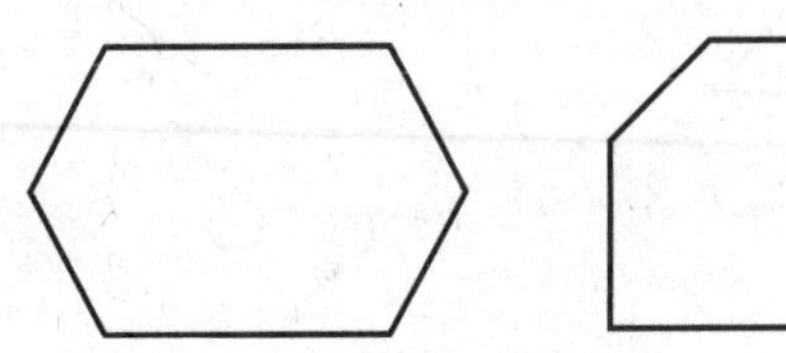
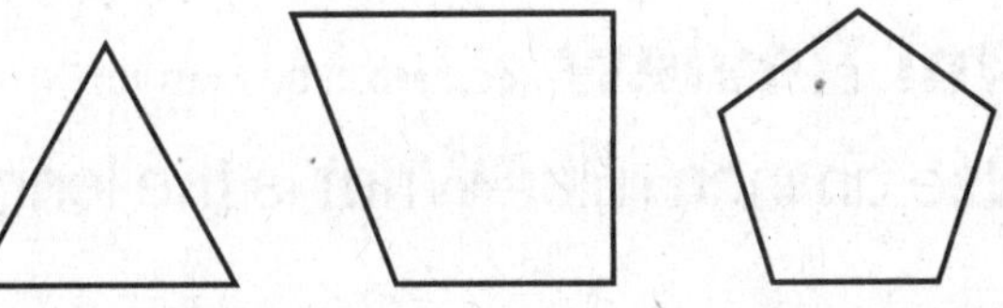

3. Shapes with 4 angles

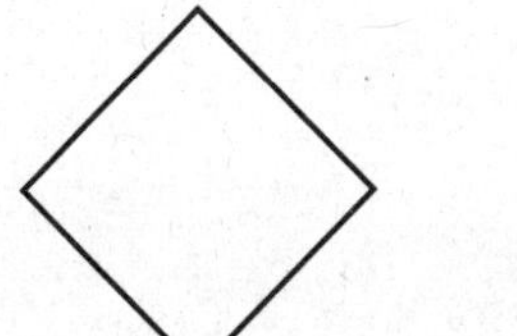
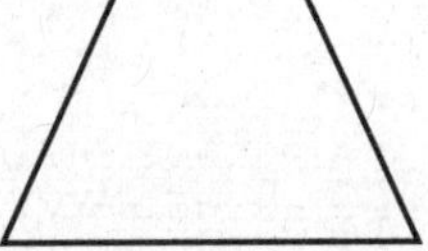
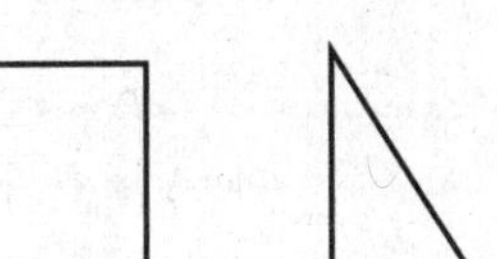

4. Shapes with fewer than 6 angles

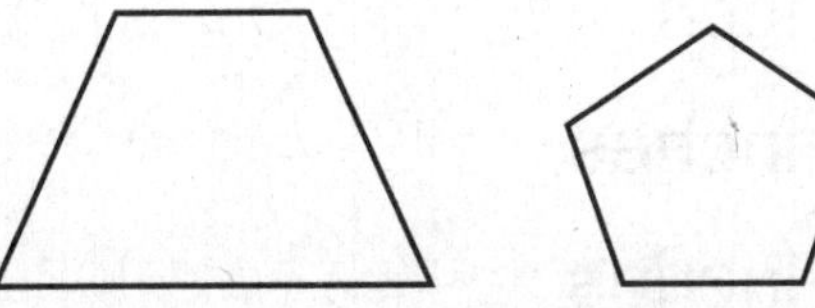

PROBLEM SOLVING

Circle the correct shape.

5. Tammy drew a shape with more than 3 angles.
It is not a hexagon. Which shape did Tammy draw?

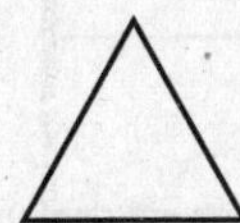
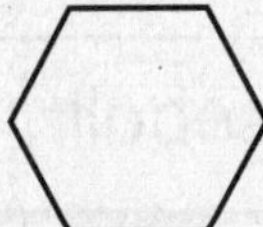

Lesson Check (CC.2.G.1)

1. Which shape has fewer than 4 sides?

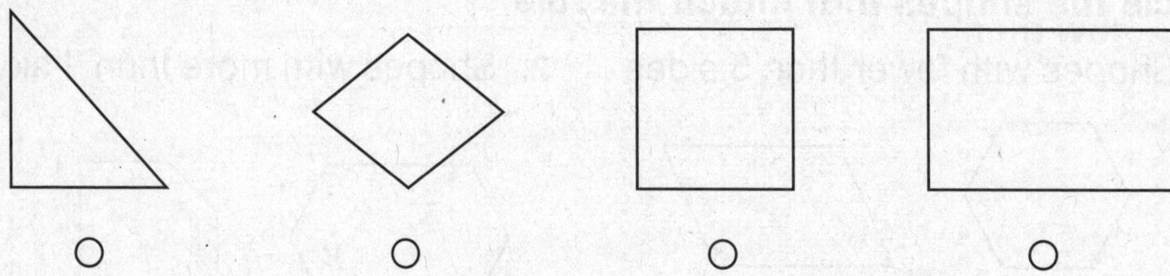

○ ○ ○ ○

Spiral Review (CC.2.MD.1, CC.2.MD.10)

2. Use an inch ruler. What is the length of the pencil to the nearest inch? (Lesson 8.4)

○ 1 inch
○ 2 inches
○ 6 inches
○ 8 inches

3. Use the tally chart. How many children chose basketball as their favorite sport? (Lesson 10.1)

○ 4
○ 5
○ 6
○ 7

Favorite Sport

Sport	Tally
soccer	𝍸
basketball	𝍸 ||
football	||||
baseball	||||

Name ____________________

Partition Rectangles

COMMON CORE STANDARD CC.2.G.2
Reason with shapes and their attributes.

**Use color tiles to cover the rectangle.
Trace around the square tiles.
Write how many.**

1.

Number of rows: _____

Number of columns: _____

Total: _____ square tiles

2.

Number of rows: _____

Number of columns: _____

Total: _____ square tiles

PROBLEM SOLVING

Solve. Write or draw to explain.

3. Nina wants to put color tiles on a square. 3 color tiles fit across the top of the square. How many rows and columns of of squares will Nina need? How many color tiles will she use in all?

Number of rows: _____

Number of columns: _____

Total: _____ square tiles

_____ tiles

Lesson Check (CC.2.G.2)

1. Use color tiles to cover the rectangle. How many tiles did you use?

- ○ 1
- ○ 2
- ○ 3
- ○ 4

Spiral Review (CC.2.MD.10, CC.2.G.1)

2. How many faces does a cube have? (Lesson 11.2)

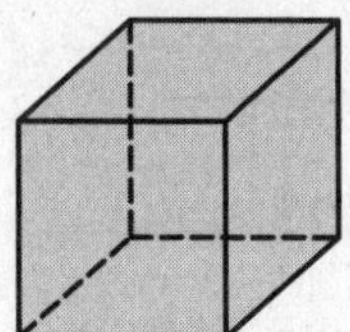

- ○ 4
- ○ 8
- ○ 6
- ○ 10

3. How many angles does this shape have? (Lesson 11.4)

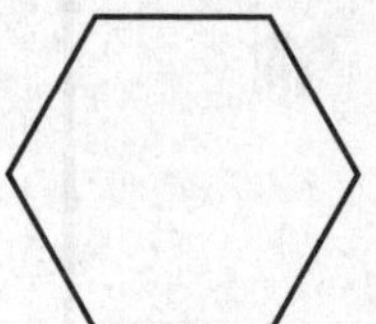

- ○ 6
- ○ 8
- ○ 7
- ○ 10

4. Use the tally chart. How many more children chose art than reading? (Lesson 10.1)

- ○ 10
- ○ 8
- ○ 3
- ○ 2

Favorite Subject

Subject	Tally
reading	卌 III
math	卌 IIII
science	卌
art	卌 卌

Name ______________________

Equal Parts

COMMON CORE STANDARD CC.2.G.3
Reason with shapes and their attributes.

Write how many equal parts there are in the whole.
Write halves, thirds, or fourths to name the equal parts.

1. 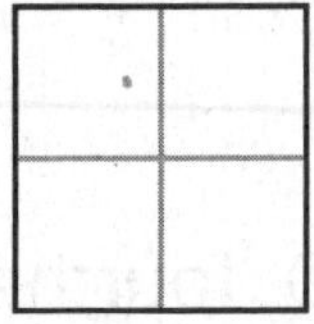

____ equal parts

____

2. 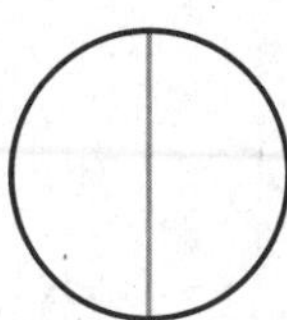

____ equal parts

____

3. 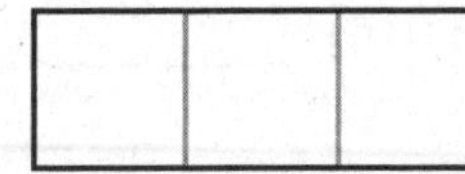

____ equal parts

____

4. 

____ equal parts

____

5. 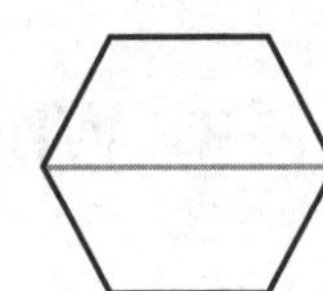

____ equal parts

____

6. 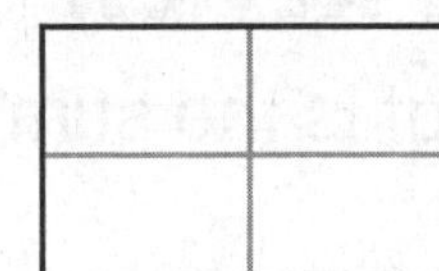

____ equal parts

____

PROBLEM SOLVING

7. Sort the shapes.
   - Draw an X on the shapes that do not show equal parts.
   - Circle the shapes that show halves.

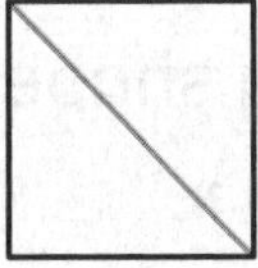
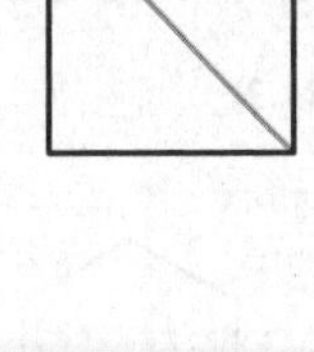
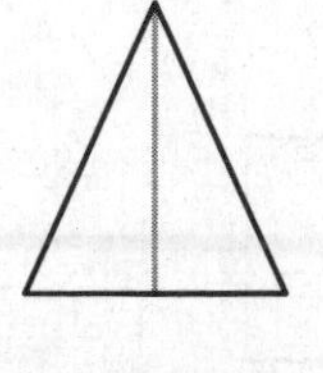

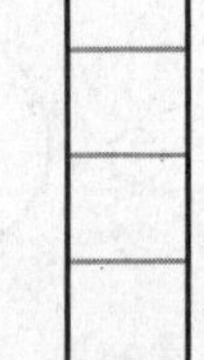

Lesson Check (CC.2.G.3)

1. What are the 3 equal parts of the shape called?

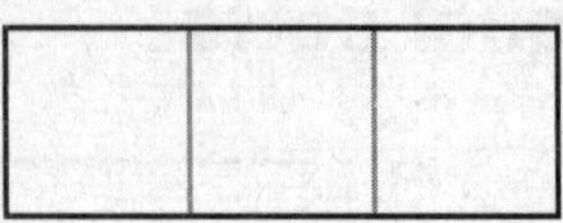

- ○ halves
- ○ fourths
- ○ thirds
- ○ sixths

2. What are the 4 equal parts of the shape called?

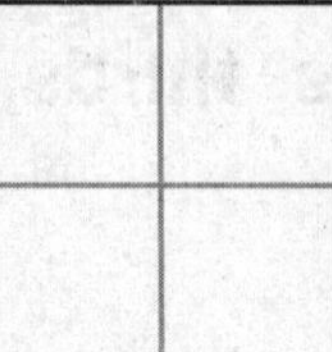

- ○ halves
- ○ fourths
- ○ thirds
- ○ sixths

Spiral Review (CC.2.NBT.5, CC.2.G.1)

3. What is the sum? (Lesson 4.7)

$$\begin{array}{r} 87 \\ +\ 45 \\ \hline \end{array}$$

- ○ 132
- ○ 122
- ○ 112
- ○ 42

4. What is the difference? (Lesson 5.2)

$$\begin{array}{r} 59 \\ -\ 15 \\ \hline \end{array}$$

- ○ 24
- ○ 34
- ○ 44
- ○ 74

5. Which of the following shapes is a quadrilateral? (Lesson 11.3)

○ 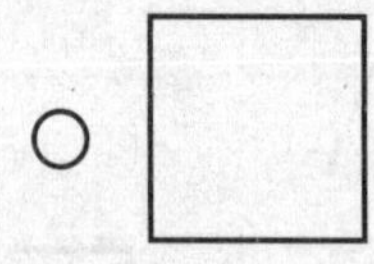
○ 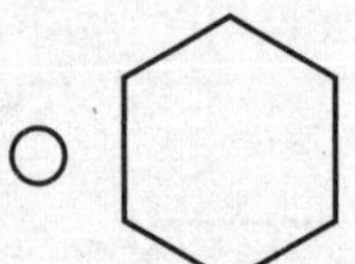
○ 
○ 

6. Which of the following shapes is a hexagon? (Lesson 11.3)

○ 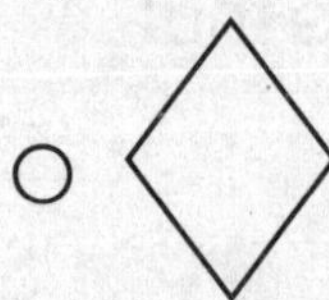
○ 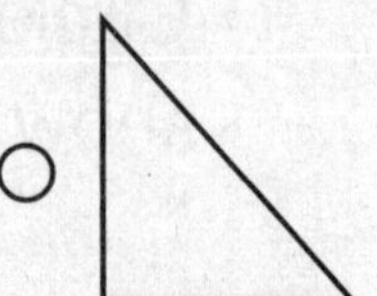
○ 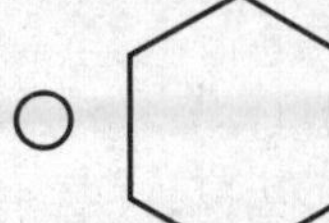
○ 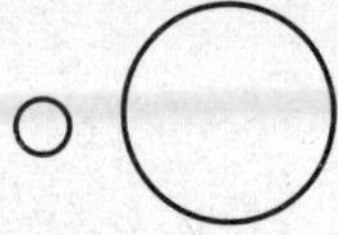

Name ______________________________

Show Equal Parts of a Whole

COMMON CORE STANDARD CC.2.G.3
Reason with shapes and their attributes.

Draw to show equal parts.

1. halves

2. fourths

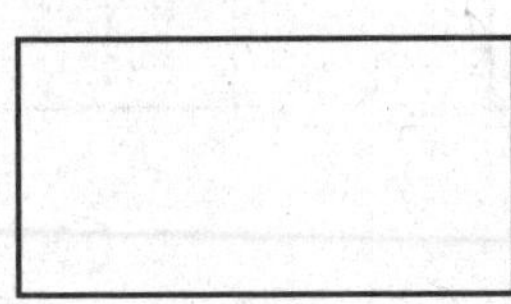

3. thirds

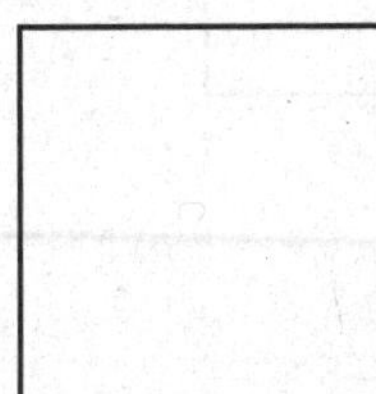

4. thirds

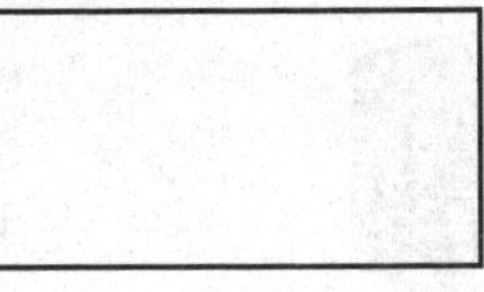

5. halves

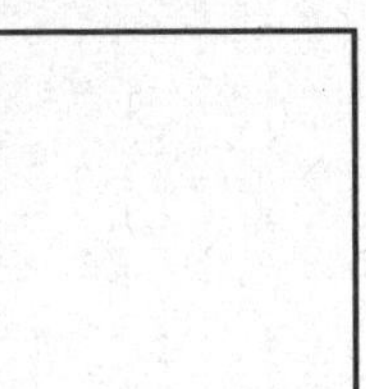

6. fourths

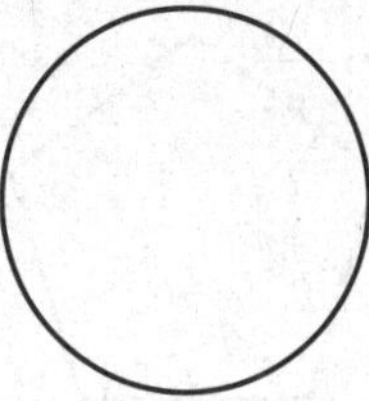

7. fourths

8. halves

9. thirds

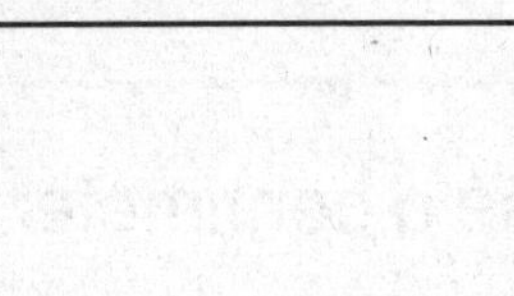

PROBLEM SOLVING

Solve. Write or draw to explain.

10. Joe has one sandwich. He cuts the sandwich into fourths. How many pieces of sandwich does he have?

_____ pieces

Lesson Check (CC.2.G.3)

1. Which shape is divided into fourths?

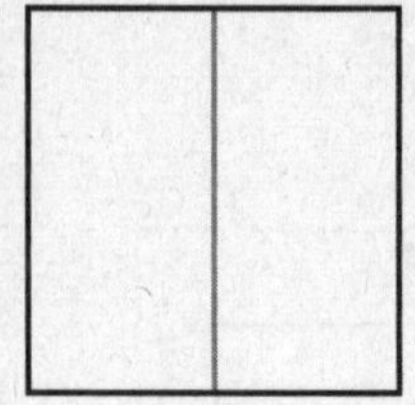  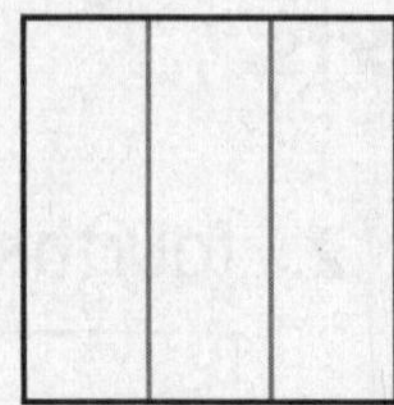 

○ ○ ○ ○

Spiral Review (CC.2.MD.4, CC.2.G.1)

2. How many angles does this shape have? (Lesson 11.4)

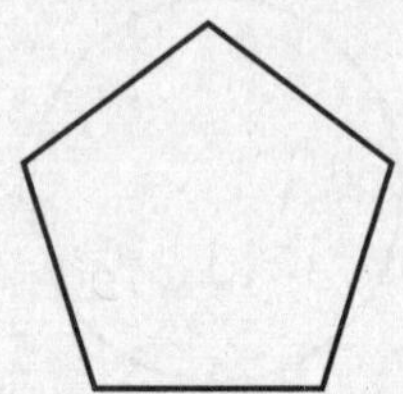

○ 5 ○ 7
○ 6 ○ 8

3. How many faces does a rectangular prism have? (Lesson 11.2)

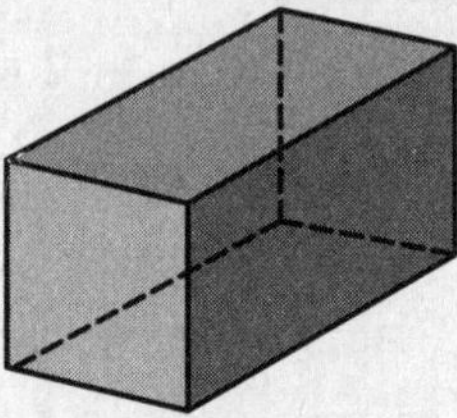

○ 4 ○ 8
○ 6 ○ 12

4. Use a centimeter ruler. Measure the length of each object. How much longer is the ribbon than the string? (Lesson 9.7)

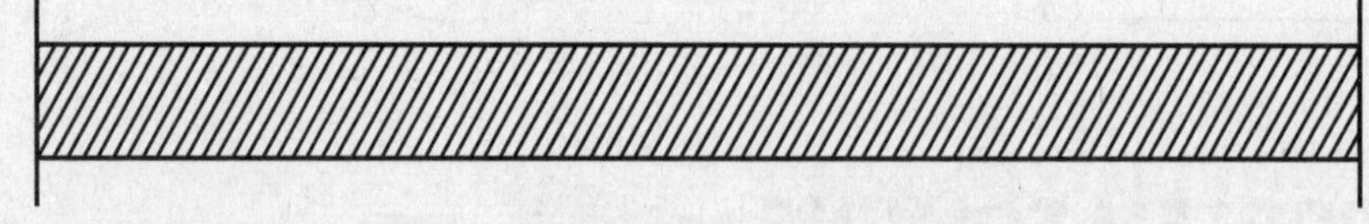

○ 2 centimeters longer
○ 3 centimeters longer
○ 5 centimeters longer
○ 17 centimeters longer

Name ___________________________

Describe Equal Parts

COMMON CORE STANDARD CC.2.G.3
Reason with shapes and their attributes.

Draw to show halves.
Color a half of the shape.

1. 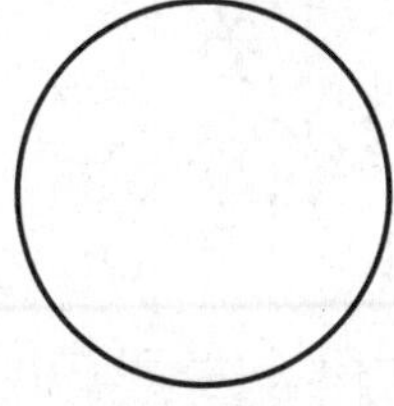

2. 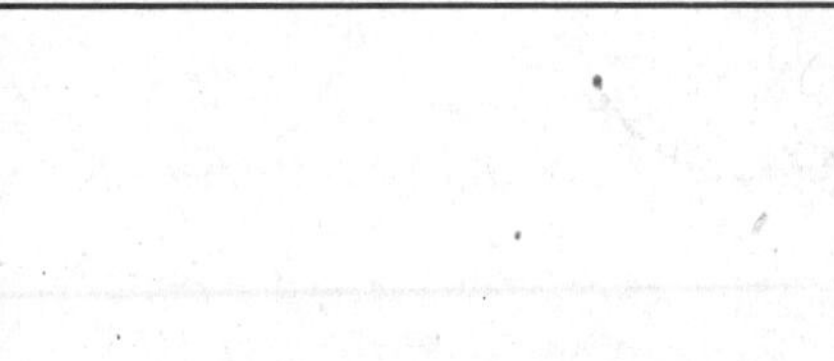

Draw to show thirds.
Color a third of the shape.

3. 

4. 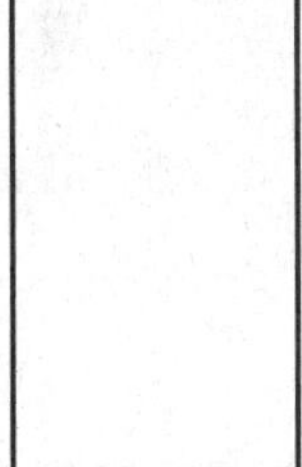

Draw to show fourths.
Color a fourth of the shape.

5. 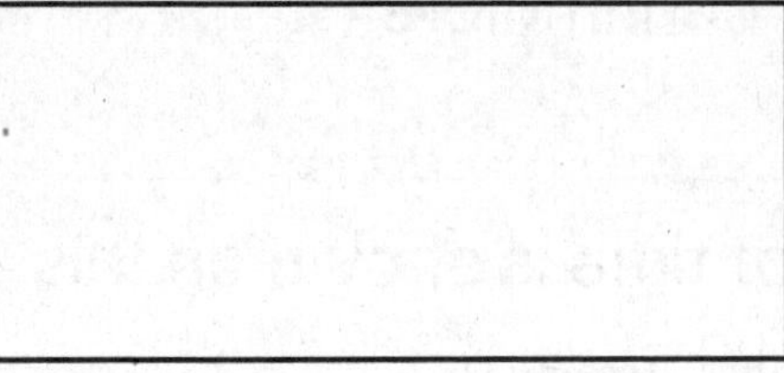

6. 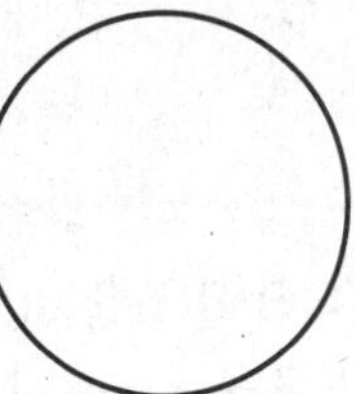

PROBLEM SOLVING

7. Circle all the shapes that have a third of the shape shaded.

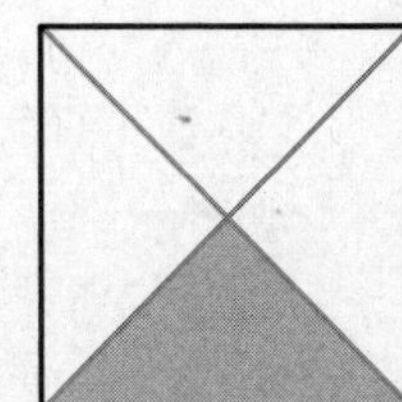
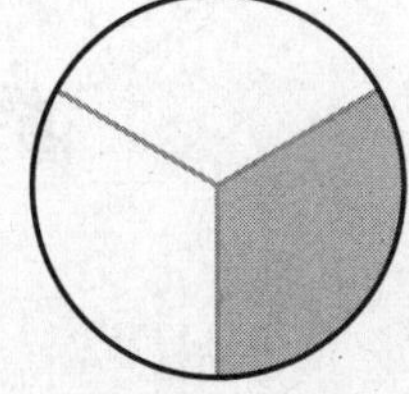
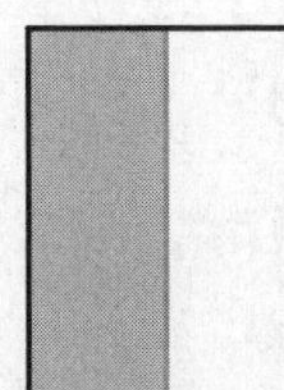
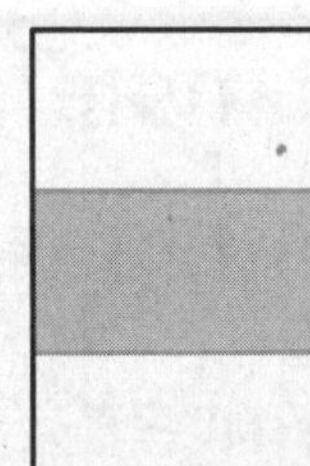
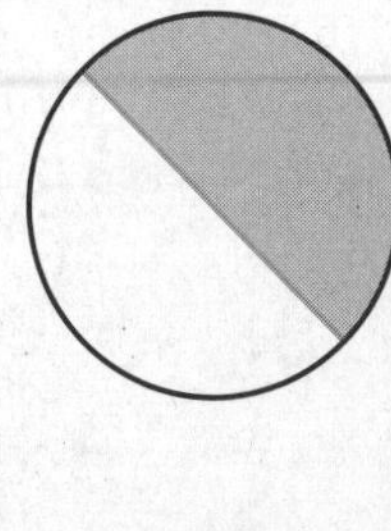

Lesson Check (CC.2.G.3)

1. Which of these has a half of the shape shaded?

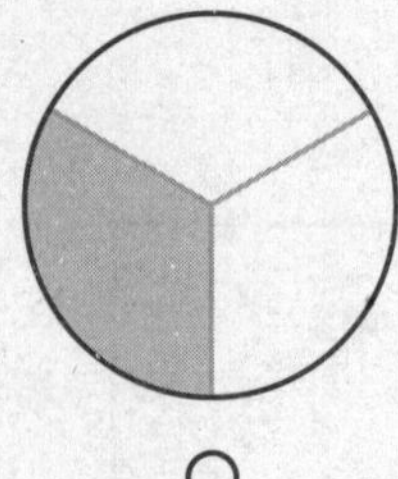
○

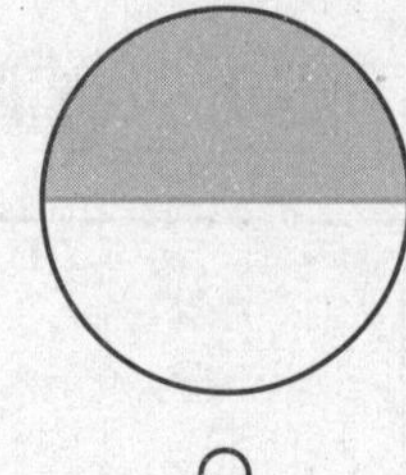
○

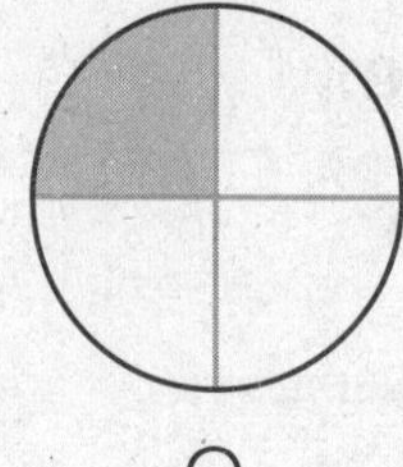
○

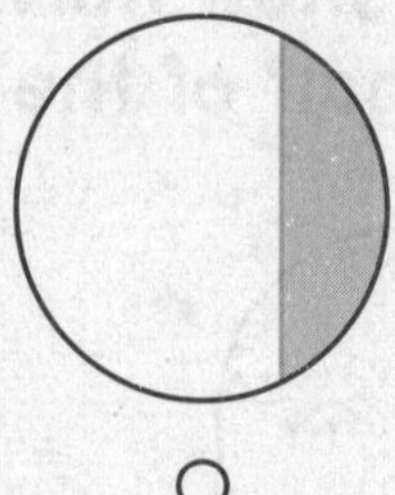
○

Spiral Review (CC.2.MD.1, CC.2.MD.7, CC.2.G.1)

2. What is the name of this shape? (Lesson 11.2)

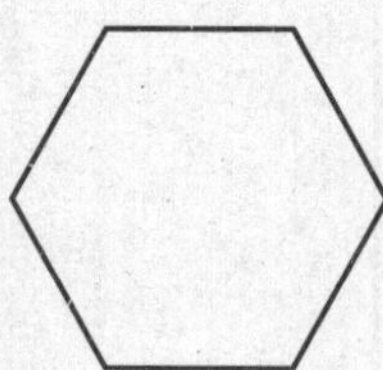

○ hexagon
○ pentagon
○ rectangle
○ triangle

3. Use a centimeter ruler. What is the length of the string to the nearest centimeter? (Lesson 9.3)

○ 2 centimeters
○ 4 centimeters
○ 6 centimeters
○ 8 centimeters

4. The clock shows the time Chris finished his homework. What time did Chris finish his homework? (Lesson 7.11)

○ 2:10 A.M. ○ 6:10 P.M.
○ 2:30 A.M. ○ 2:30 P.M.

5. What time is shown on this clock? (Lesson 7.9)

○ 3:40 ○ 8:15
○ 8:03 ○ 9:15

Name ______________________

Problem Solving • Equal Shares

COMMON CORE STANDARD CC.2.G.3
Reason with shapes and their attributes.

Draw to show your answer.

1. Max has square pizzas that are the same size. What are two different ways he can divide the pizzas into fourths?

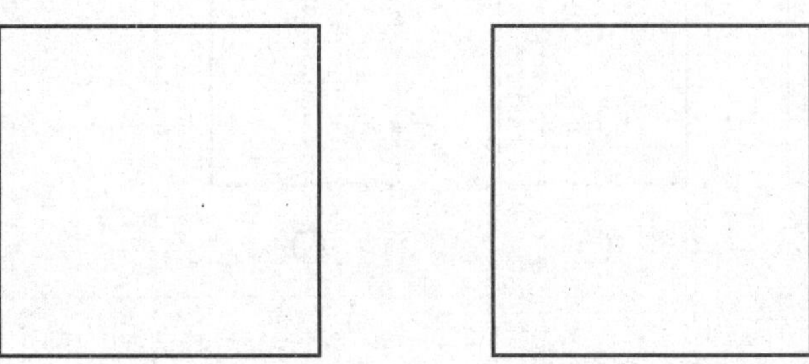

2. Lia has two pieces of paper that are the same size. What are two different ways she can divide the pieces of paper into halves?

3. Frank has two crackers that are the same size. What are two different ways he can divide the cracker into thirds?

Lesson Check (CC.2.G.3)

1. Bree cut a piece of cardboard into thirds like this.

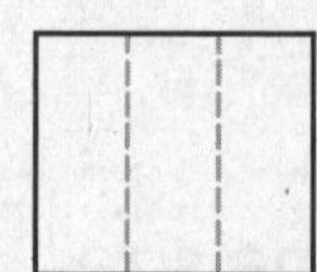

Which of these shows another way to cut the cardboard into thirds?

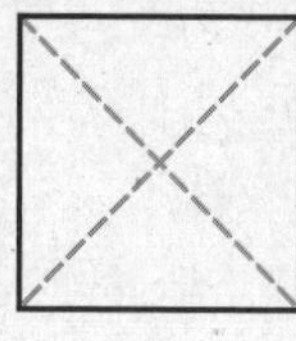 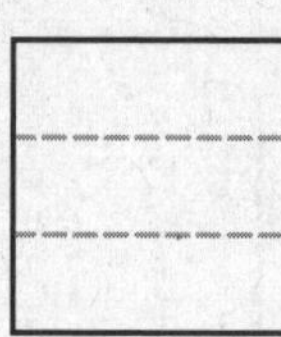 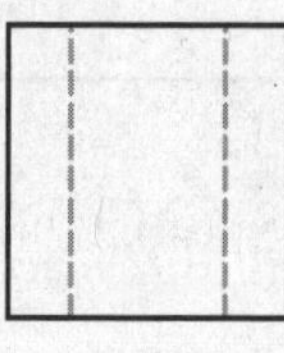 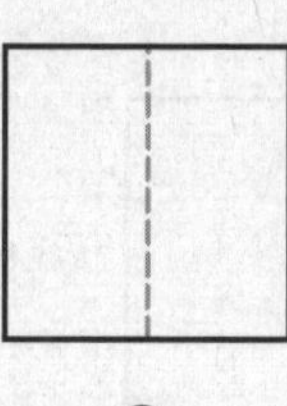

○ ○ ○ ○

Spiral Review (CC.2.MD.7, CC.2.MD.8, CC.2.G.1)

2. Which shape has 3 equal parts? (Lesson 11.7)

○ 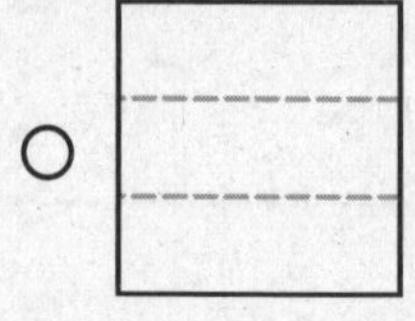 ○ 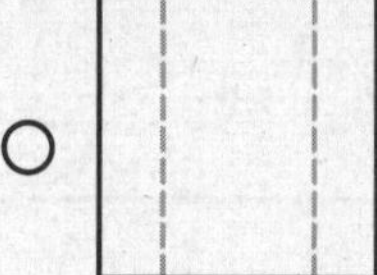

○ 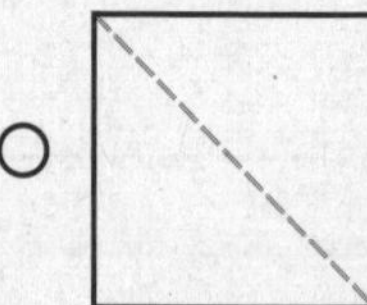 ○ 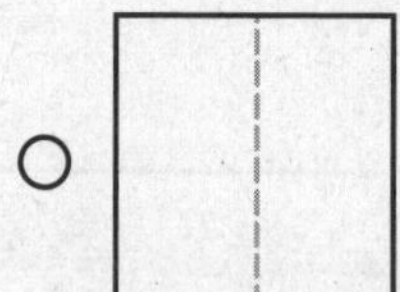

3. How many angles does this shape have? (Lesson 11.5)

○ 3
○ 4
○ 5
○ 6

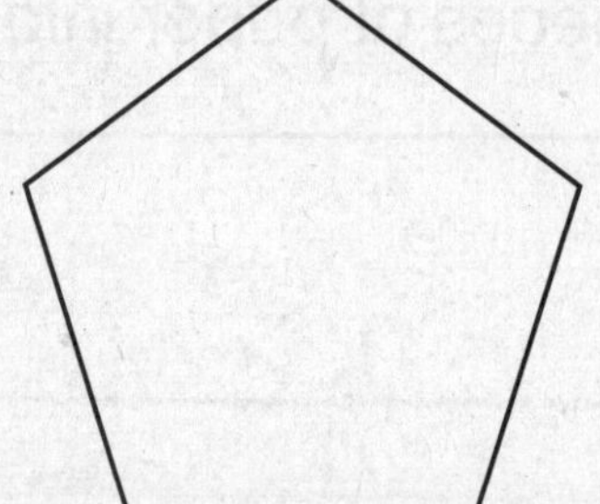

4. What is the best estimate for the width of a door? (Lesson 10.4)

○ 1 foot
○ 3 feet
○ 6 feet
○ 10 feet

5. Which is another way to write 10 minutes after 9? (Lesson 7.10)

○ 8:50
○ 9:10
○ 9:50
○ 10:10

Name ____________________

COMMON CORE STANDARDS CC.2.G.1, CC.2.G.2, CC.2.G.3

Chapter 11 Extra Practice

Lessons 11.1–11.2 (pp. 509–516)

Circle the objects that match the shape name.

1. rectangular prism

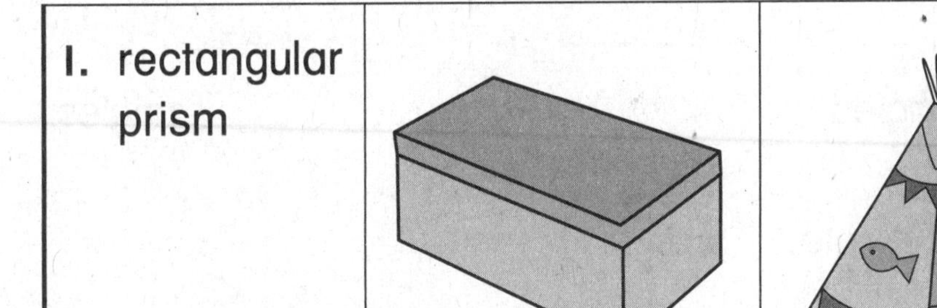

Circle the set of shapes that are the faces of the three-dimensional shape.

2.

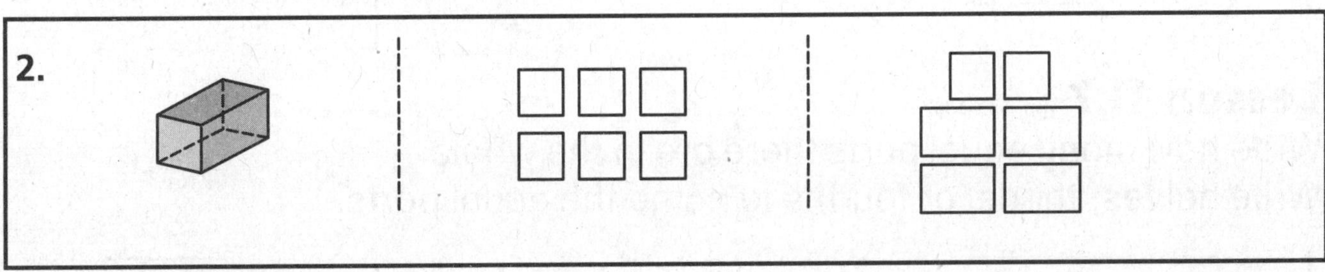

Lesson 11.3 (pp. 517–520)

Write the number of sides and the number of vertices.

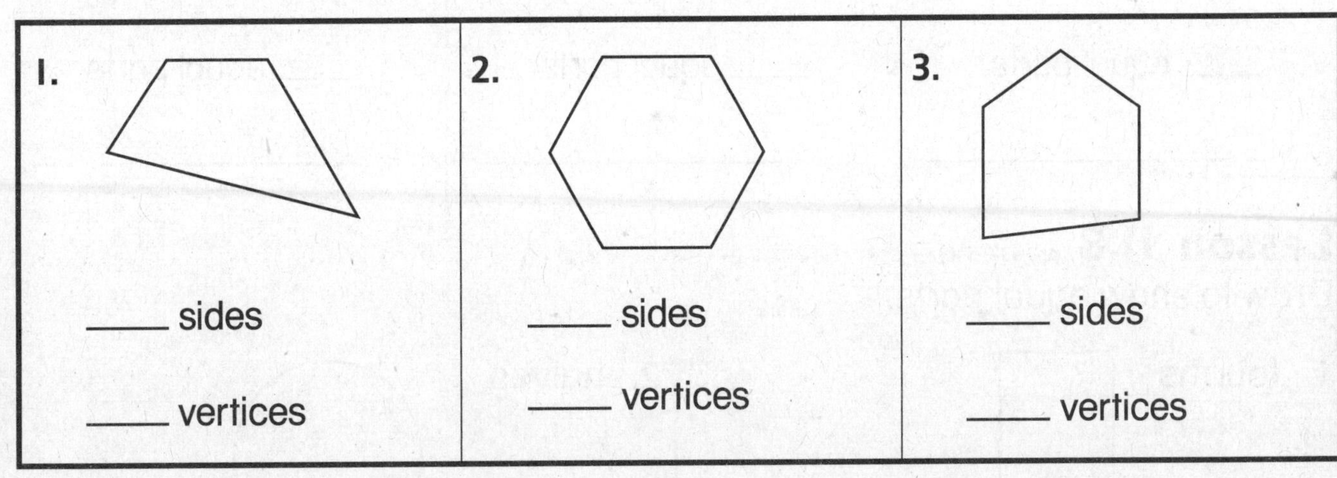

1.	2.	3.
____ sides	____ sides	____ sides
____ vertices	____ vertices	____ vertices

Lesson 11.4 (pp. 521–524)

Circle the angles in each shape. Write how many.

1.

____ angles

2.

____ angles

Lesson 11.5 (pp. 525–528)

Circle the shapes that match the rule.

1. Shapes with fewer than 4 sides

2. Shapes with 5 angles

Lesson 11.7 (pp. 533–536)

Write how many equal parts there are in the whole.
Write halves, thirds, or fourths to name the equal parts.

1.

____ equal parts

____

2.

____ equal parts

____

3.

____ equal parts

____

Lesson 11.8 (pp. 537–540)

Draw to show equal parts.

1. fourths

2. halves

Name ______________________

Find Sums on an Addition Table

Essential Question How do you find sums on an addition table?

Model and Draw

3 + 4 = ?

The sum for 3 + 4 is found where row 3 and column 4 meet.

3 + 4 = 7

column

row

+	0	1	2	3	(4)
0	0	1	2	3	4
1	1	2	3	4	5
2	2	3	4	5	6
(3)	3	4	5	6	(7)
4	4	5	6	7	8

Share and Show

1. Write the missing sums in the addition table.

+	0	1	2	3	4	5	6	7	8	9	10
0	0	1	2	3	4	5	6			9	
1	1	2	3	4	5	6			9		11
2	2	3	4	5	6			9		11	12
3	3	4	5	6			9		11	12	13
4	4	5	6			9		11	12	13	14
5	5	6			9		11	12	13	14	15
6	6			9		11	12	13	14	15	16
7			9		11	12	13	14	15	16	17
8		9		11	12	13	14	15	16	17	18
9	9		11	12	13	14	15	16	17	18	19
10		11	12	13	14	15	16	17	18	19	20

Math Talk Describe a pattern in the addition table.

On Your Own

2. Write the missing sums in the addition table.

+	0	1	2	3	4	5	6	7	8	9	10
0	0	1	2	3	4	5	6	7	8	9	10
1	1	2	3	4	5	6	7	8	9	10	
2	2	3	4	5	6	7	8	9	10		12
3	3	4	5	6	7	8	9	10		12	
4	4	5	6	7	8	9	10		12		
5	5	6	7	8	9	10		12			15
6	6	7	8	9	10		12			15	16
7	7	8	9	10		12			15	16	17
8	8	9	10		12			15	16	17	18
9	9	10		12			15	16	17	18	19
10	10		12			15	16	17	18	19	20

PROBLEM SOLVING REAL WORLD

Solve. Write or draw to explain.

3. Natasha has 13 apples. Some apples are red and some are green. She has more red apples than green apples. How many red apples and how many green apples could she have?

TAKE HOME ACTIVITY • Ask your child to explain how to use the addition table to find the sum of 8 + 6.

Name ___________________________

Estimate Sums: 2-Digit Addition

Essential Question How can you estimate the sum of two 2-digit numbers?

Model and Draw

Estimate the sum of 24 + 38.

Find the nearest ten for each number.

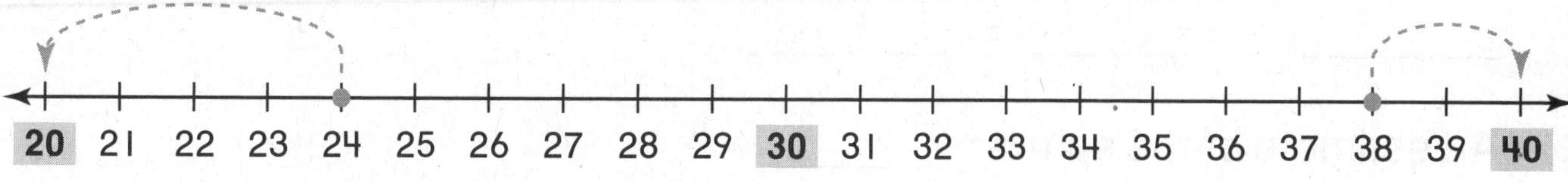

20 + 40 = 60

An estimate of the sum is 60.

Share and Show

Find the nearest ten for each number.

1. Estimate the sum of 18 + 29.

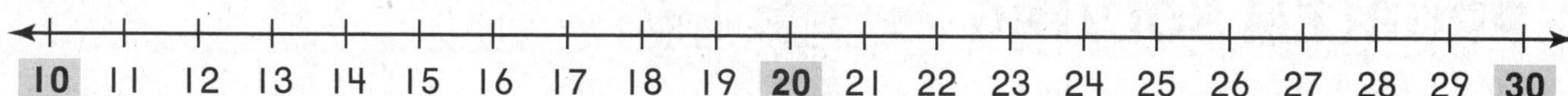

Add the tens to estimate.

_____ + _____ = _____

An estimate of the sum is _____.

Math Talk How did you know which ten is nearest to 18?

On Your Own

Find the nearest ten for each number.
Add the tens to estimate.

2. Estimate the sum of 13 + 28.

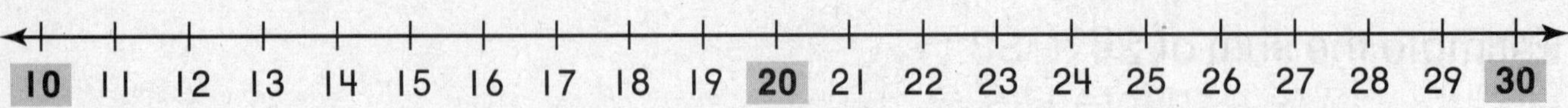

______ + ______ = ______

An estimate of the sum is ______.

---

3. Estimate the sum of 31 + 22.

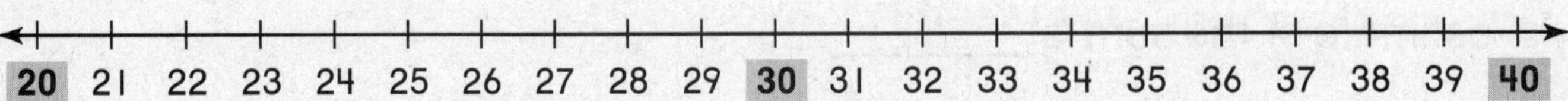

______ + ______ = ______

An estimate of the sum is ______.

PROBLEM SOLVING REAL WORLD

Solve. Write or draw to explain.

4. Mark has 34 pennies. Emma has 47 pennies. About how many pennies do they have altogether?

about ______ pennies

TAKE HOME ACTIVITY • Ask your child to use the number line for Exercise 2 and describe how to estimate the sum of 27 + 21.

Name ______________________

Estimate Sums: 3-Digit Addition

Essential Question How can you estimate the sum of two 3-digit numbers?

Model and Draw

Estimate the sum of 189 + 284.
Find the nearest hundred for each number.

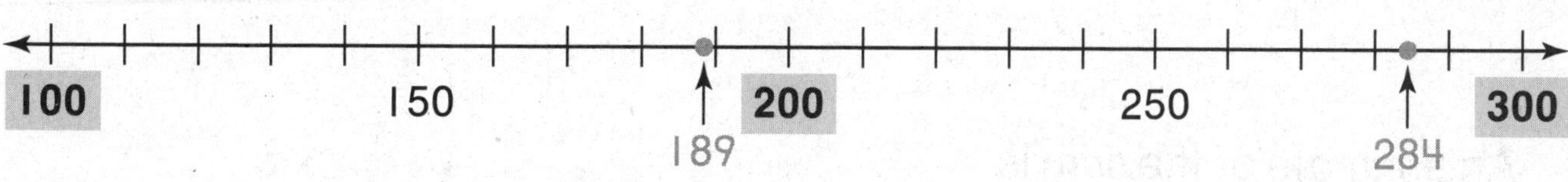

200 + 300 = 500

An estimate of the sum is 500.

Share and Show

Find the nearest hundred for each number.
Add the hundreds to estimate.

1. Estimate the sum of 229 + 386.

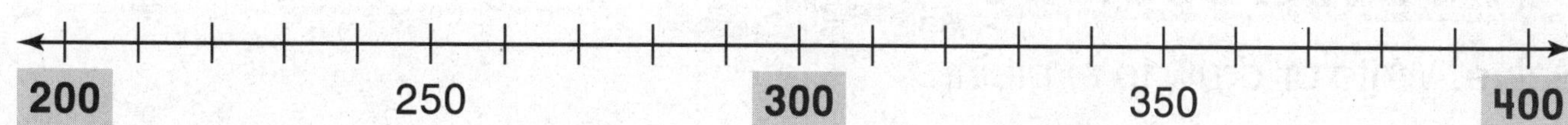

_______ + _______ = _______

An estimate of the sum is _______.

Math Talk How do you know which two hundreds a 3-digit number is between?

On Your Own

Find the nearest hundred for each number.
Add the hundreds to estimate.

2. Estimate the sum of 324 + 218.

_______ + _______ = _______

An estimate of the sum is _______.

3. Estimate the sum of 468 + 439.

_______ + _______ = _______

An estimate of the sum is _______.

PROBLEM SOLVING REAL WORLD

Solve. Write or draw to explain.

4. There are 375 yellow fish and 283 blue fish swimming around a coral reef. About how many fish are there altogether?

about _______ fish

TAKE HOME ACTIVITY • Ask your child to use the number line for Exercise 2 and describe how to estimate the sum of 215 + 398.

Name ______________________

Estimate Differences: 2-Digit Subtraction

Essential Question How can you estimate the difference of two 2-digit numbers?

Model and Draw

Estimate the difference of 62 − 48.
Find the nearest ten for each number.

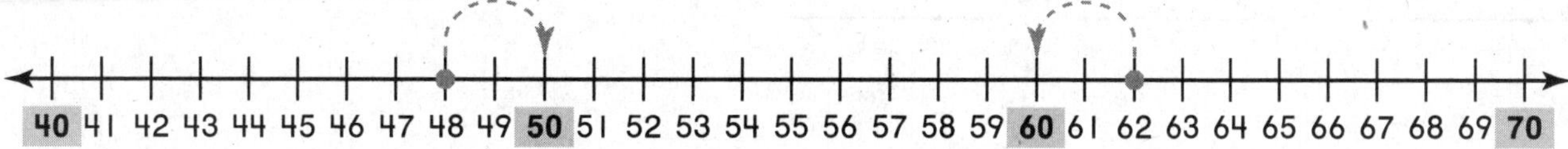

60 − 50 = 10

An estimate of the difference is 10.

Share and Show

Find the nearest ten for each number.
Subtract the tens to estimate.

1. Estimate the difference of 42 − 29.

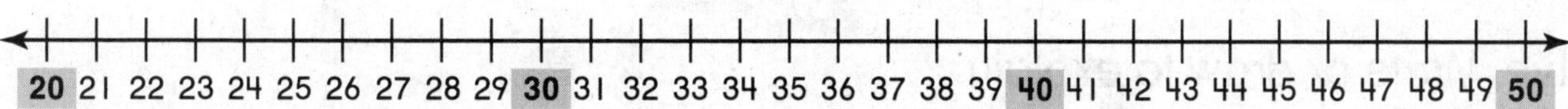

________ − ________ = ________

An estimate of the difference is ________.

Math Talk How do you know which two tens a number is between?

On Your Own

Find the nearest ten for each number.
Subtract the tens to estimate.

2. Estimate the difference of 51 − 39.

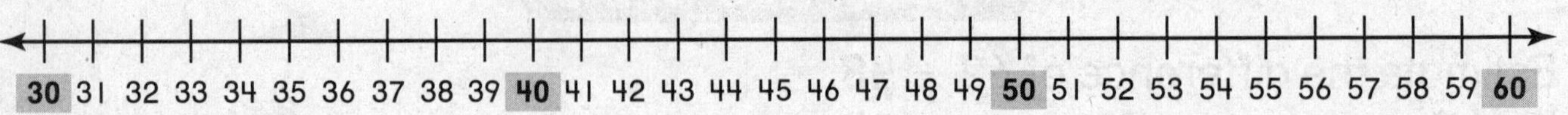

_______ − _______ = _______

An estimate of the difference is _______.

3. Estimate the difference of 79 − 56.

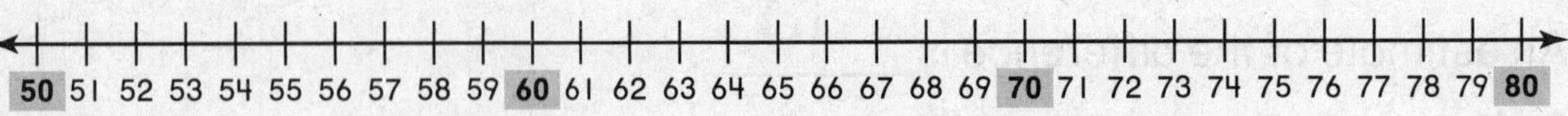

_______ − _______ = _______

An estimate of the difference is _______.

PROBLEM SOLVING REAL WORLD

Solve. Write or draw to explain.

4. A farmer has 91 cows. 58 of the cows are in the barn. About how many of the cows are not in the barn?

about _______ cows

TAKE HOME ACTIVITY • Ask your child to use the number line for Exercise 2 and describe how to estimate the difference of 57 − 41.

Name ____________________

Estimate Differences: 3-Digit Subtraction

Essential Question How can you estimate the difference of two 3-digit numbers?

Model and Draw

Estimate the difference of 382 − 265.
Find the nearest hundred for each number.

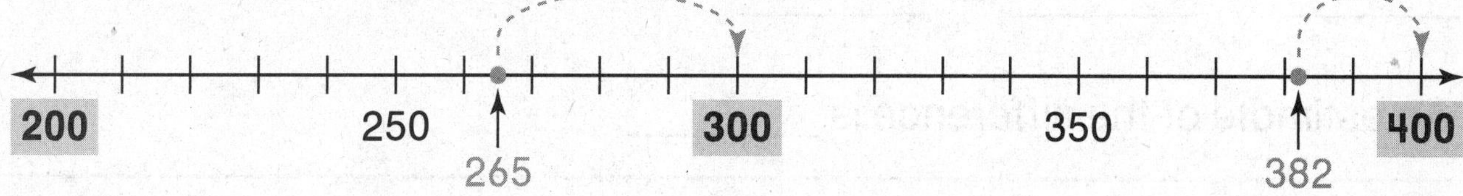

400 − 300 = 100

An estimate of the difference is 100.

Share and Show

Find the nearest hundred for each number.
Subtract the hundreds to estimate.

1. Estimate the difference of 674 − 590.

______ − ______ = ______

An estimate of the difference is ______.

Math Talk How did you know which hundred is nearest to 674?

On Your Own

Find the nearest hundred for each number.
Subtract the hundreds to estimate.

2. Estimate the difference of 791 − 612.

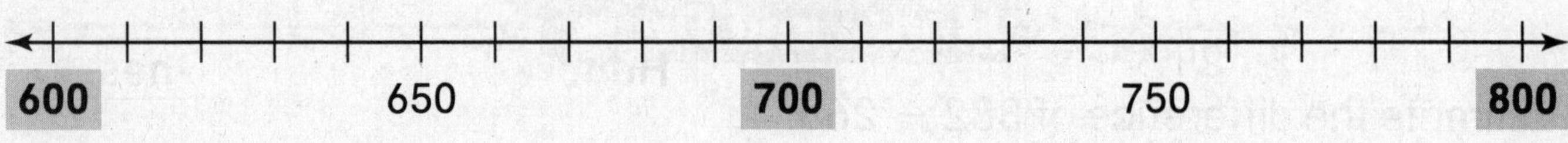

________ − ________ = ________

An estimate of the difference is ________.

3. Estimate the difference of 487 − 309.

________ − ________ = ________

An estimate of the difference is ________.

PROBLEM SOLVING REAL WORLD

Solve. Write or draw to explain.

4. A mail carrier had 819 letters to deliver. Then she delivered 687 letters. About how many letters does she still have to deliver?

about ________ letters

TAKE HOME ACTIVITY • Ask your child to use the number line for Exercise 2 and describe how to estimate the difference of 786 − 611.

Name ______________________________

Order 3-Digit Numbers

Essential Question: How does place value help you order 3-digit numbers?

Model and Draw

You can order 249, 418, and 205 from least to greatest. First, compare the **hundreds**. Next, compare the tens and then the ones, if needed.

Hundreds	Tens	Ones
2	4	9
4	1	8
2	0	5

I compare the hundreds. 249 and 205 are both less than 418.

Which is less, 249 or 205? I compare the tens. 205 is less than 249, so 205 is the least.

205 < 249 < 418

least greatest

Share and Show

Write the numbers in order from least to greatest.

1.

672
515
532

_____ < _____ < _____

2.

787
683
564

_____ < _____ < _____

Math Talk Do you always need to compare the ones digits when you order numbers? Explain.

On Your Own

Write the numbers in order from least to greatest.

3.

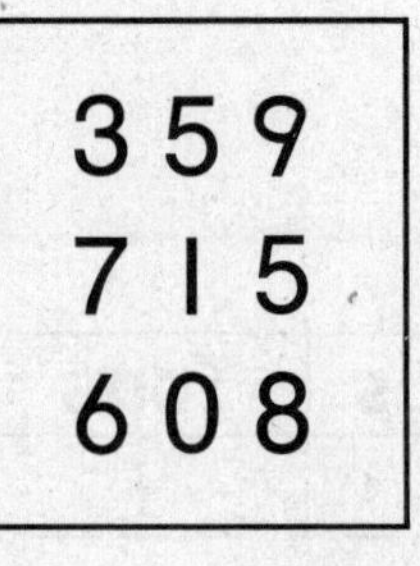

359
715
608

____ < ____ < ____

4.

959
915
908

____ < ____ < ____

5.

343
341
348

____ < ____ < ____

6.

165
746
764

____ < ____ < ____

PROBLEM SOLVING

7. Brenda, Jean, and Pam play a video game. Brenda scores the highest. Jean scores the lowest.

Brenda	863
Jean	767
Pam	?

On the line, write a 3-digit number that could be Pam's score.

767 < ____ < 863

TAKE HOME ACTIVITY • Write three 3-digit numbers. Have your child tell you how to order the numbers from least to greatest.

Name ______________________________

Concepts and Skills

1. Write the missing sums in the addition table.

+	0	1	2	3	4	5	6	7	8	9	10
0	0	1	2	3	4	5		7		9	
1	1	2	3	4	5		7		9		11
2	2	3	4	5		7		9		11	12
3	3	4	5		7		9		11	12	13
4	4	5		7		9		11	12	13	14
5	5		7		9		11	12	13	14	15

Find the nearest ten.

2. Estimate the sum of 24 and 36.

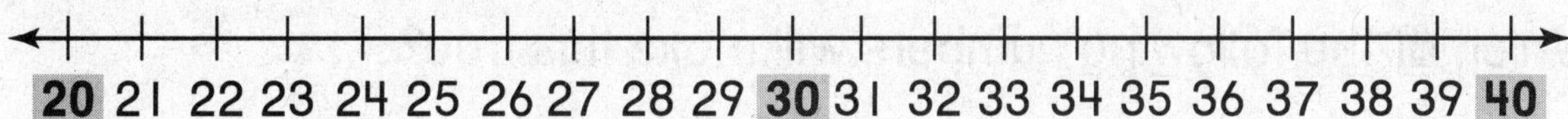

_____ + _____ = _____

An estimate of the sum is _____.

Find the nearest hundred.

3. Estimate the sum of 285 and 122.

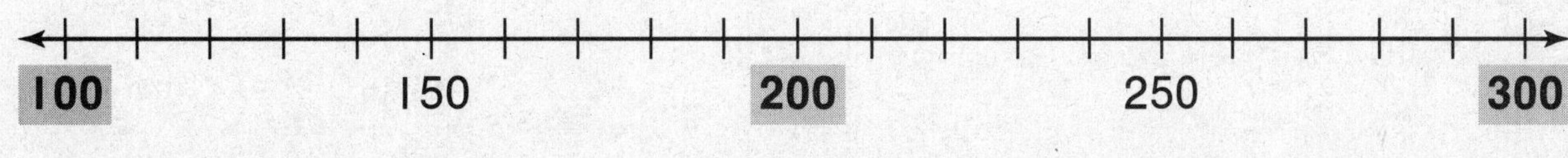

_____ + _____ = _____

An estimate of the sum is _____.

Find the nearest ten.

4. Estimate the difference of 72 − 59.

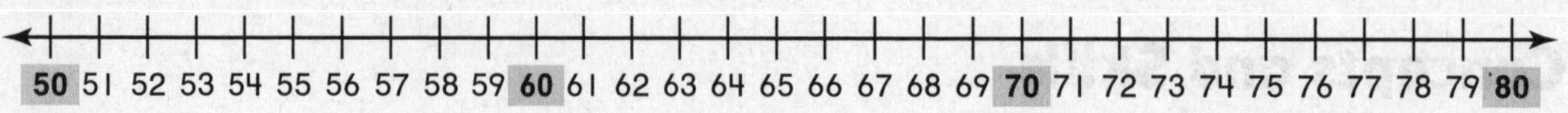

_____ − _____ = _____

An estimate of the difference is _____.

Find the nearest hundred.

5. Estimate the difference of 792 and 619.

_____ − _____ = _____

An estimate of the difference is _____.

6. Which of the following numbers will make this true?

350 < 413 < _____.

- ○ 403
- ○ 398
- ○ 430
- ○ 331

Name ______________________________

Equal Groups of 2

Essential Question: How can you find the total number in equal groups of 2?

Model and Draw

The pet store has 3 fishbowls in the window. There are 2 goldfish in each bowl. How many goldfish are there in all?

I can count the equal groups by twos—2, 4, 6—to find how many in all.

Make 3 groups of 2 counters.

3 groups of 2 is 6 in all.

Share and Show

Complete the sentence to show how many in all.

1.

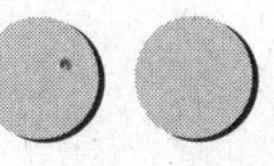

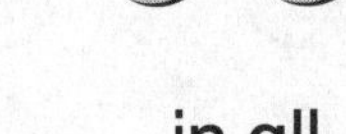

_______ groups of _______ is _______ in all.

2.

_______ groups of _______ is _______ in all.

3.

_______ groups of _______ is _______ in all.

Math Talk How can you use counters to find 2 + 2 + 2 + 2 + 2?

On Your Own

Complete the sentence to show how many in all.

4. 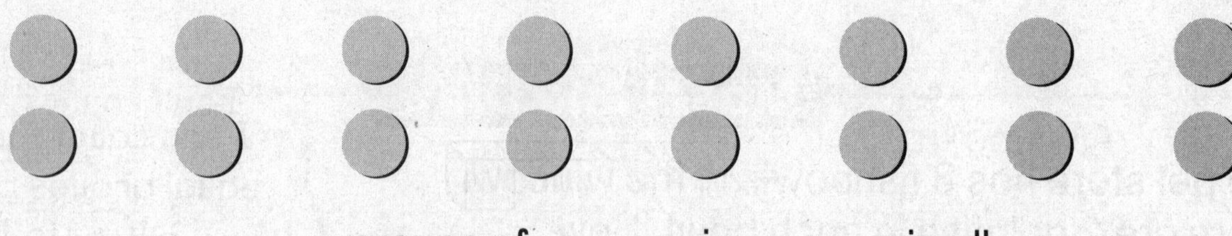

_______ groups of _______ is _______ in all.

5. 

_______ groups of _______ is _______ in all.

6. 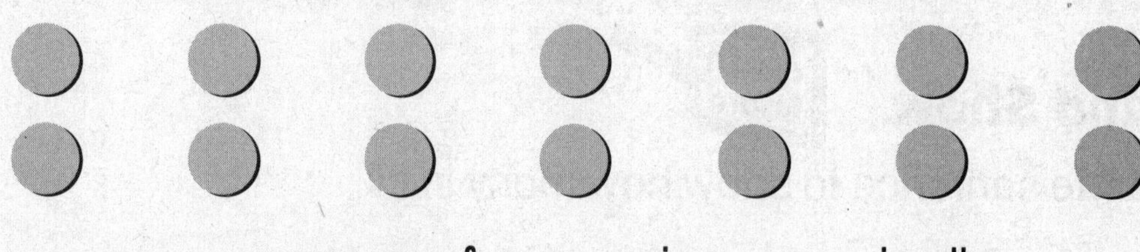

_______ groups of _______ is _______ in all.

7. 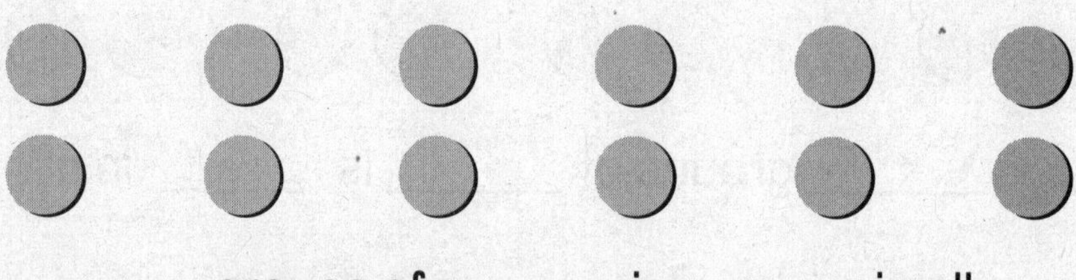

_______ groups of _______ is _______ in all.

PROBLEM SOLVING REAL WORLD

Solve. Write or draw to explain.

8. Coach Baker keeps 2 basketballs in each bin. There are 5 bins. How many basketballs are stored in the bins?

_______ basketballs

TAKE HOME ACTIVITY • Have your child draw groups of two Xs and tell you how to find how many there are in all.

Name ______________________

Equal Groups of 5

Essential Question: How can you find the total number in equal groups of 5?

Model and Draw

Luke made 3 cube trains. He connected 5 cubes in each train. How many cubes did he use in all?

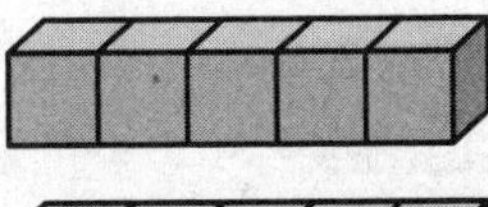
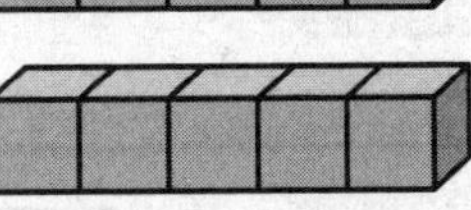
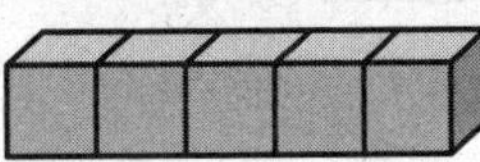

Make 3 groups of 5 cubes.

I can count the equal groups by fives—5, 10, 15—to find how many in all.

3 groups of 5 is 15 in all.

Share and Show

Complete the sentence to show how many in all.

1.

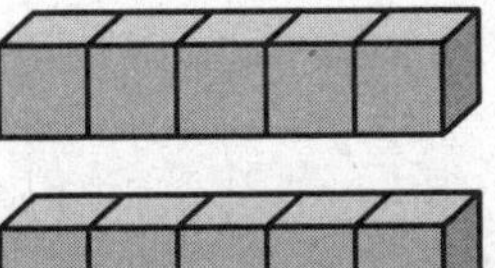

_____ groups of _____ is _____ in all.

2.

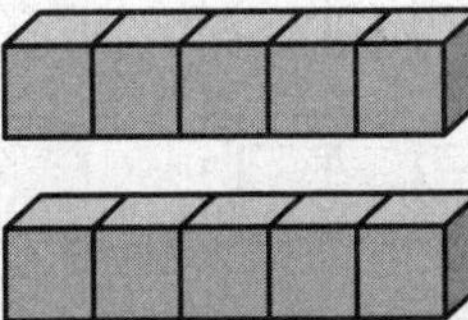

_____ groups of _____ is _____ in all.

3.

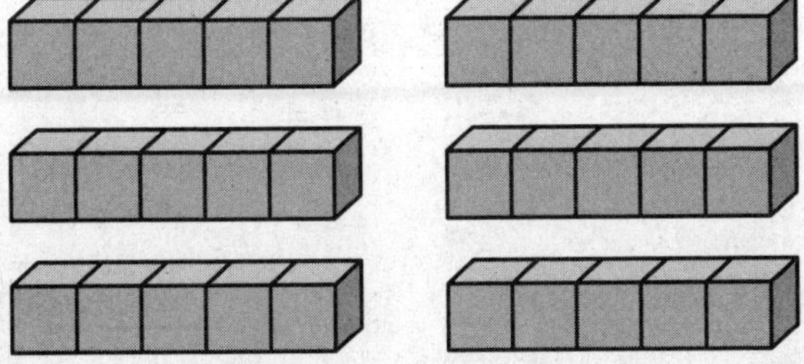

_____ groups of _____ is _____ in all.

Math Talk How can you use addition to find how many in all in Exercise 2?

On Your Own

Complete the sentences to show how many in all.

4. _____ groups of _____ is _____ in all.

5.

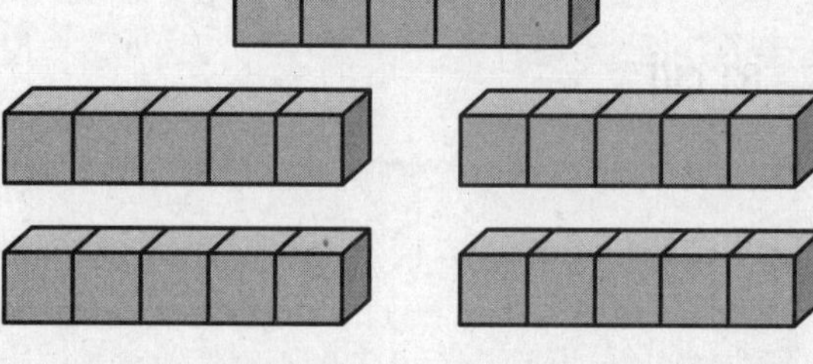

_____ groups of _____ is _____ in all.

6.

_____ groups of _____ is _____ in all.

PROBLEM SOLVING

Solve. Write or draw to explain.

7. Gina fills 6 pages of her photo album. She puts 5 photos on each page. How many photos does Gina put in her album?

_____ photos

TAKE HOME ACTIVITY • Place your hands next to your child's hands. Ask how many groups of 5 fingers. Have your child tell you how to find how many in all. How many fingers in all?

Name ______________________

Equal Groups of 10

Essential Question: How can you find the total number in equal groups of 10?

Model and Draw

There are 4 packs of juice. Each pack has 10 juice boxes. How many juice boxes are there in all?

I can count the equal groups by tens—10, 20, 30, 40—to find how many in all.

Make 4 groups of 10 cubes.

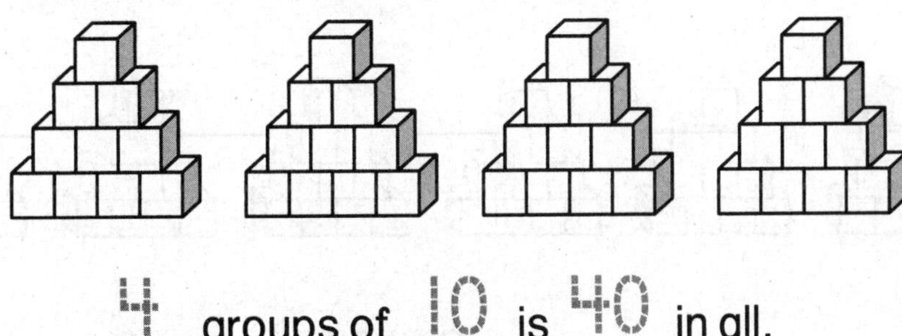

4 groups of 10 is 40 in all.

Share and Show

Complete the sentence to show how many in all.

1.   

_____ groups of _____ is _____ in all.

2. 

_____ groups of _____ is _____ in all.

3. 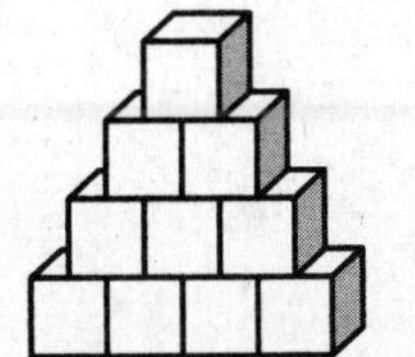 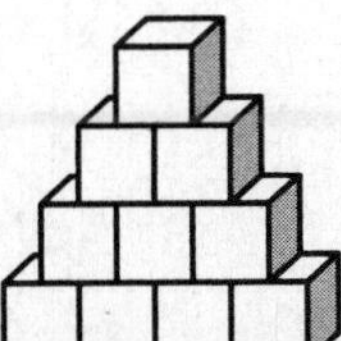   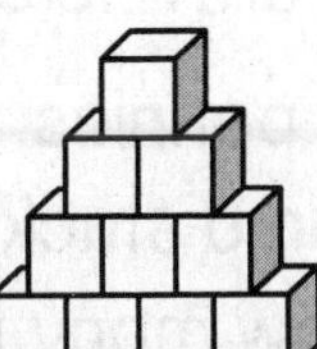 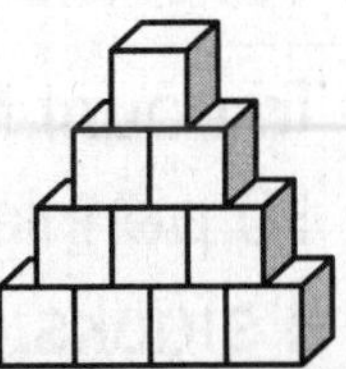

_____ groups of _____ is _____ in all.

Math Talk How many groups of ten are in 70? Explain.

On Your Own

Complete the sentence to show how many in all.

4.

____ groups of ____ is ____ in all.

5.

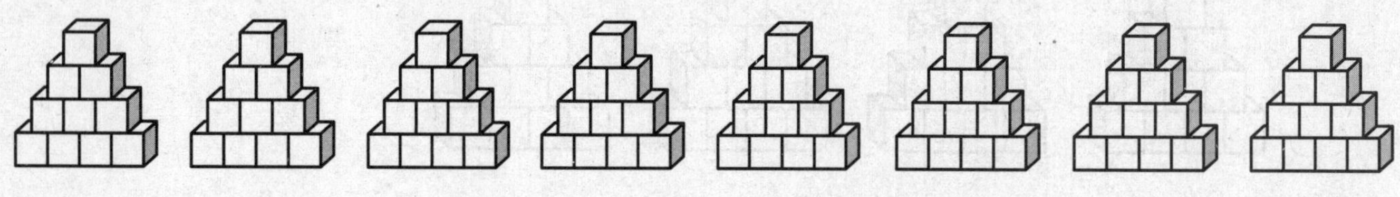

____ groups of ____ is ____ in all.

6.

____ groups of ____ is ____ in all.

PROBLEM SOLVING

Solve. Write or draw to explain.

7. To count his pennies, Travis puts 10 pennies in a stack. He makes 4 stacks. How many pennies does Travis have?

____ pennies

TAKE HOME ACTIVITY • Give your child 30 pieces of macaroni or other small objects. Have your child make groups of 10. Ask how many groups there are. Ask your child to tell you how to find how many in all. How many pieces in all?

Name ________________________________

Size of Shares

Essential Question How can you place items in equal groups?

Model and Draw

When you divide, you place items in equal groups.

Joel has 12 carrots. There are 6 rabbits. Each rabbit gets the same number of carrots. How many carrots does each rabbit get?

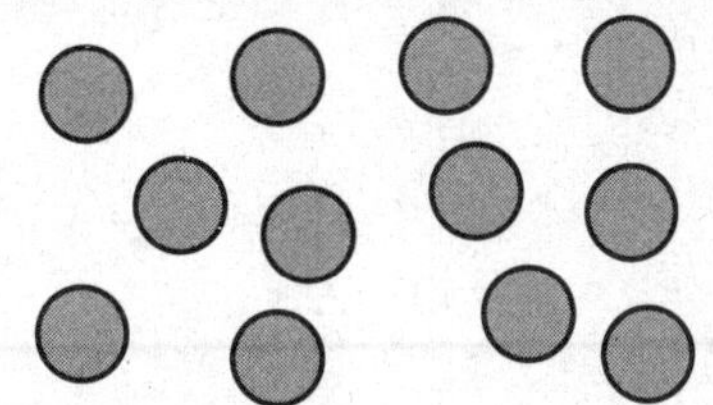

Place 12 counters in 6 equal groups.

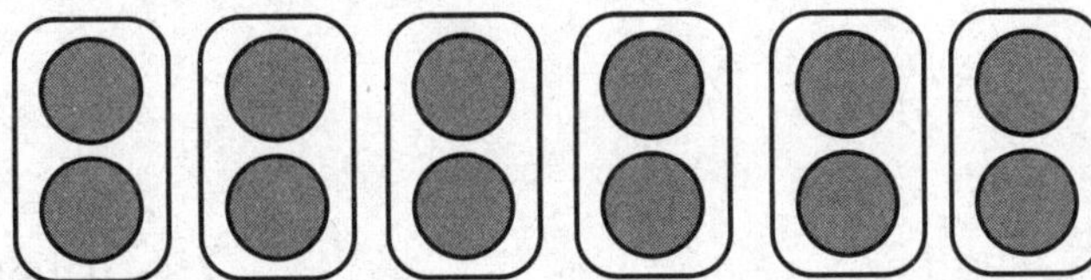

2 counters in each group

So, each rabbit gets 2 carrots.

Share and Show

Use counters. Draw to show your work.
Write how many in each group.

1. Place 10 counters in 2 equal groups.

_____ counters in each group

2. Place 6 counters in 3 equal groups.

_____ counters in each group

Math Talk How did you know how many counters to place in each group for Exercise 2?

On Your Own

Use counters. Draw to show your work.
Write how many in each group.

3. Place 9 counters in 3 equal groups.

_____ counters in each group

4. Place 12 counters in 2 equal groups.

_____ counters in each group

5. Place 16 counters in 4 equal groups.

_____ counters in each group

PROBLEM SOLVING

Solve. Draw to show your work.

6. Mrs. Peters divides 6 orange slices between 2 plates. She wants to have 4 orange slices on each plate. How many more orange slices does she need?

_____ more orange slices

TAKE HOME ACTIVITY • Ask your child to place 15 pennies into 3 equal groups, and then tell how many pennies are in each group.

Name ____________________

Number of Equal Shares

Essential Question How can you find the number of equal groups that items can be placed into?

Model and Draw

There are 12 cookies. 3 cookies fill a snack bag. How many snack bags can be filled?

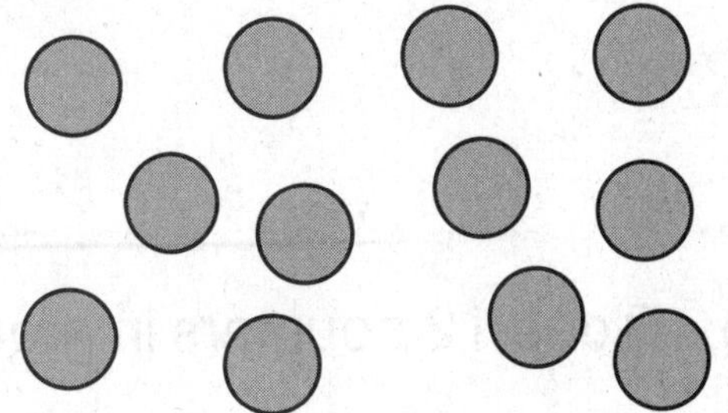

Place 12 counters in groups of 3.

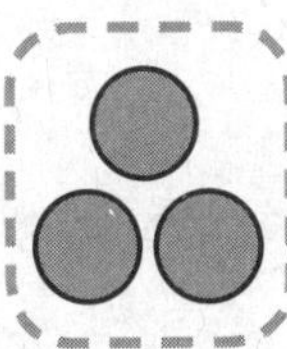 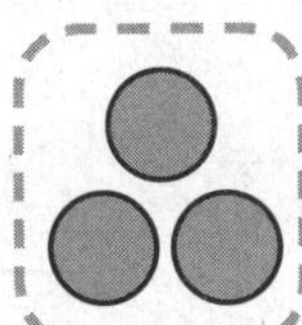 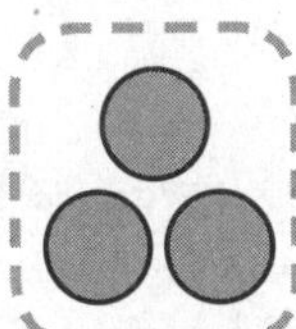 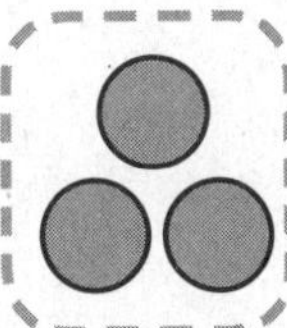

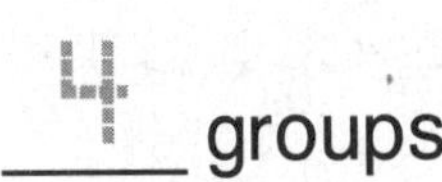

4 groups

So, 4 snack bags can be filled.

Share and Show

Use counters. Draw to show your work.
Write how many groups.

1. Place 8 counters in groups of 4.

_____ groups

2. Place 10 counters in groups of 2.

_____ groups

Math Talk **Describe** how you could find the number of groups of 2 you could make with 12 counters.

On Your Own

Use counters. Draw to show your work.
Write how many groups.

3. Place 4 counters in groups of 2.

_____ groups

4. Place 12 counters in groups of 4.

_____ groups

5. Place 15 counters in groups of 3.

_____ groups

PROBLEM SOLVING

Draw to show your work.

6. Some children want to play a board game. There are 16 game pieces. Each player needs to have 4 pieces. How many children can play?

_____ children

TAKE HOME ACTIVITY • Use small items such as pennies or cereal. Have your child find out how many groups of 5 are in 20.

Name ______________________________

Solve Problems with Equal Shares

Essential Question: How can you solve word problems that involve equal shares?

Model and Draw

You can draw a picture to help you solve problems with equal shares.

There are 10 marbles in each bag. How many marbles are in 3 bags?

__3__ groups of __10__ is __30__ in all.

There are __30__ marbles.

Share and Show

Solve. Draw or write to show what you did.

1. There are 5 oranges in each sack. How many oranges are in 4 sacks?

_____ oranges

2. Sandy can plant 2 seeds in a pot. How many pots will Sandy need in order to plant 6 seeds?

_____ pots

Math Talk Explain how you solved Exercise 2.

On Your Own

Solve. Draw to show what you did.

3. Ben gives each friend 2 crackers. How many crackers does he need for 6 friends?

_____ crackers

4. Mrs. Green can pack 5 books in a box. How many boxes will she need in order to pack 15 books?

_____ boxes

PROBLEM SOLVING

5. Franco used 12 connecting cubes to build towers. All the towers are the same height. Draw a picture to show the towers he could have built.

TAKE HOME ACTIVITY • Ask your child to make up a word problem about 3 boxes of toys with 3 toys in each box. Have your child tell you how to solve the problem.

Name ____________________

Concepts and Skills

Complete the sentence to show how many in all.

1\.

_____ groups of _____ is _____ in all.

2\.

_____ groups of _____ is _____ in all.

3\.

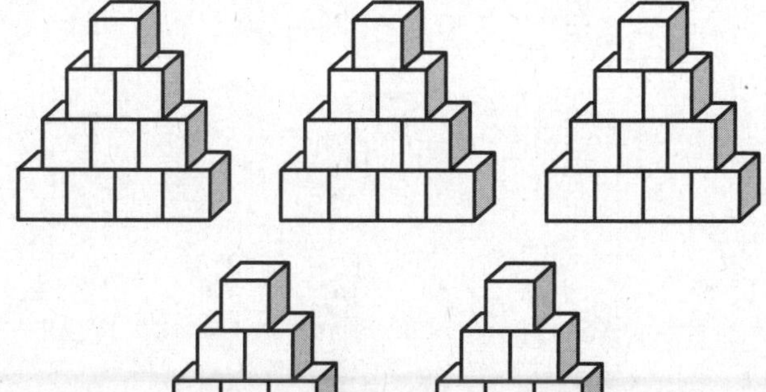

_____ groups of _____ is _____ in all.

Use counters. Draw to show your work.
Write how many in each group.

4. Place 14 counters in 2 equal groups.

_____ counters in each group

Use counters. Draw to show your work.
Write how many groups.

5. Place 12 counters in groups of 2.

_____ groups

Solve the problem.

6. Mrs. Owen puts 3 flowers in each vase.
How many flowers are in 4 vases?

- ○ 7
- ○ 9
- ○ 12
- ○ 16

Name ______________________________

Hour Before and Hour After

Essential Question: How do you tell the time 1 hour before and 1 hour after a given time?

Model and Draw

For these times, the minute hand points to the same place. The hour hands point to different numbers.

The time is 8:00.

The hour hand points to 8.

1 hour before

7:00

The hour hand points to 7.

1 hour after

9:00

The hour hand points to 9.

Share and Show

Write the time shown on the clock. Then write the time 1 hour before and 1 hour after.

1.

______ 1 hour before

______ 1 hour after

2.

______ 1 hour before

______ 1 hour after

Math Talk How are the hands on a clock that shows 8 o'clock the same as the hands on a clock 1 hour after? How are they different?

On Your Own

Write the time shown. Then write the time 1 hour before and 1 hour after.

3.

________ 1 hour before

________ 1 hour after

4.

________ 1 hour before

________ 1 hour after

5.

________ 1 hour before

________ 1 hour after

6.

________ 1 hour before

________ 1 hour after

PROBLEM SOLVING REAL WORLD

7. Tim feeds the cat 1 hour after 7:00. Draw the hour hand and the minute hand to show 1 hour after 7:00. Then write the time.

Tim needs to feed the cat at ________.

TAKE HOME ACTIVITY • Ask your child what the time will be 1 hour after 3:30. What time was it 1 hour before 3:30? Have your child tell you how he or she knows.

Name ______________________________

Elapsed Time in Hours

Essential Question How do you find the number of hours between two times?

Model and Draw

Baseball practice starts at 2:00. Everyone leaves practice at 4:00. How long does baseball practice last?
Use the time line to count how many hours passed from 2:00 P.M. to 4:00 P.M.

_____ hours

Starts at 2:00 **Ends at 4:00**

9:00 A.M. | 10:00 A.M. | 11:00 A.M. | Noon | 1:00 P.M. | 2:00 P.M. | 3:00 P.M. | 4:00 P.M. | 5:00 P.M. | 6:00 P.M.

Share and Show

Use the time line above. Solve.

1. The game starts at 3:00 P.M. It ends at 6:00 P.M. How long does the game last?

   _____ hours

2. The plane leaves at 10:00 A.M. It arrives at 2:00 P.M. How long is the plane trip?

   _____ hours

3. Max goes out at 2:00 P.M. He comes back in at 5:00 P.M. For how long was Max out?

   _____ hours

4. Art class starts at 9:00 A.M. It ends at 11:00 A.M. How long is the art class?

   _____ hours

Math Talk Describe how you used the time line for Exercise 2.

On Your Own

Use the time line below. Solve.

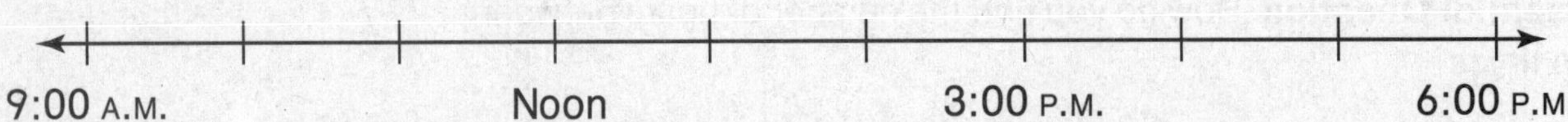

5. Paul's baby sister goes to sleep at 4:00 P.M. She wakes up at 6:00 P.M. How long does the baby sleep?

____ hours

6. Julia goes to a friend's house at noon. She comes home at 3:00 P.M. How long is Julia gone?

____ hours

7. Jeff starts raking leaves at 11:00 A.M. He stops at 1:00 P.M. How long does Jeff rake leaves?

____ hours

8. Mom and Carrie arrive at the shopping mall at 1:00 P.M. They leave at 5:00 P.M. How long are they at the mall?

____ hours

PROBLEM SOLVING REAL WORLD

Solve. Draw or write to explain.

9. Mr. Norton writes the time for classes on the board.

Class	Time
Math	8:30 A.M.
Reading	9:30 A.M.
Music	11:30 A.M.

How long will reading class last?

____ hours

TAKE HOME ACTIVITY • Ask your child how much time passes between 4:30 and 7:30. Have your child explain how he or she arrived at the answer.

Name ______________________________

Elapsed Time in Minutes

Essential Question How do you find the number of minutes between two times?

Model and Draw

You can use subtraction if the times are within the same hour.

Ken starts cleaning his room at 3:15 P.M. He finishes at 3:35 P.M. How long does it take Ken to clean his room?

$$\begin{array}{r} 35 \\ -15 \\ \hline 20 \end{array}$$

So it takes Ken 20 minutes.

Starts at 3:15 P.M. **Ends at 3:35 P.M.**

Share and Show

Subtract to solve. Show your work.

1. Leah starts eating lunch at 12:10 P.M. She finishes at 12:25 P.M. How long does it take for Leah to eat lunch?

   ____ minutes

2. Kwan gets on the school bus at 8:10 A.M. He gets to school at 8:55 A.M. How long is Kwan's bus ride?

   ____ minutes

3. Carla takes her dog to the park at 2:05 P.M. She gets back at 2:40 P.M. How long does Carla walk her dog?

   ____ minutes

4. Ethan starts his spelling homework at 6:25 P.M. He finishes at 6:45 P.M. How long does Ethan work on his spelling?

   ____ minutes

Math Talk How could you check your answers by looking at a clock?

On Your Own

Subtract to solve. Show your work.

5. Mrs. Hall puts a pizza in the oven at 6:10 P.M. She takes it out at 6:30 P.M. How long does the pizza bake?

   ____ minutes

6. The reading test starts at 1:10 P.M. Everyone must stop at 1:25 P.M. How long do the children have to take their test?

   ____ minutes

7. Kelly starts drawing at 8:15 P.M. She finishes her picture at 8:40 P.M. How long does Kelly draw?

   ____ minutes

8. Tony starts reading at 4:30 P.M. He stops reading at 4:45 P.M. How long does Tony read?

   ____ minutes

PROBLEM SOLVING

Show how to use subtraction to solve.

9. Mr. West gets to the bus stop at 9:05 A.M. He looks at the bus schedule.

Bus Arrival Times
8:30 A.M.
9:30 A.M.
10:30 A.M.

How long will Mr. West need to wait for a bus?

____ minutes

TAKE HOME ACTIVITY • Have your child track how many minutes it would take to do math homework if he or she starts at 5:15 P.M. and stops at 5:45 P.M.

Name ______________________________

Capacity • Nonstandard Units

Essential Question How can you measure how much a container holds?

Model and Draw

Use a scoop and rice to estimate and measure how much a can holds.

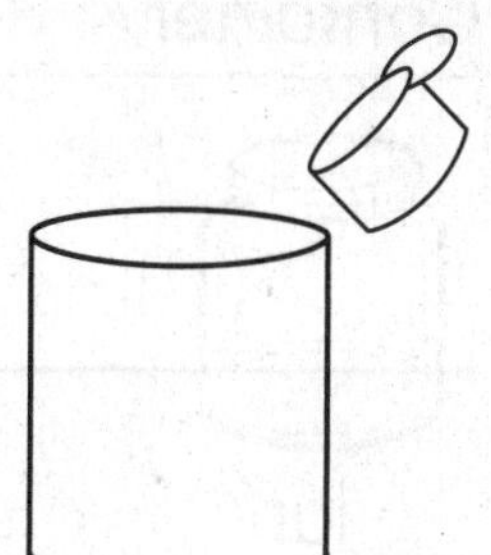

- Estimate how many scoops the can holds.
- Fill a scoop with rice or water.
- Pour it into the can.
- Repeat until the can is full. Keep track of the number of scoops.

Share and Show

How many scoops does the container hold? Estimate. Then measure.

Container	Estimate	Measure
1. mug	about ____ scoops	about ____ scoops
2. vase	about ____ scoops	about ____ scoops
3. paper cup	about ____ scoops	about ____ scoops

Math Talk Explain how you can tell which of the containers on this page is the largest.

On Your Own

How many scoops does the container hold?
Estimate. Then measure.

Container	Estimate	Measure
4. jar	about ____ scoops	about ____ scoops
5. milk carton	about ____ scoops	about ____ scoops
6. bowl	about ____ scoops	about ____ scoops

PROBLEM SOLVING REAL WORLD

Solve.

7. The red bowl holds 5 scoops of rice. The blue bowl holds twice as much rice as the red bowl. How many scoops of rice do the two bowls hold in all?

____ scoops in all

TAKE HOME ACTIVITY • Have your child use a paper cup to estimate how much various containers hold. Then check his or her estimate by measuring how much each container holds.

Name ____________________

Describe Measurement Data

Essential Question What measurement data can a line plot show?

Model and Draw

A line plot shows data on a number line.

Each X on this line plot stands for the length of 1 desk.

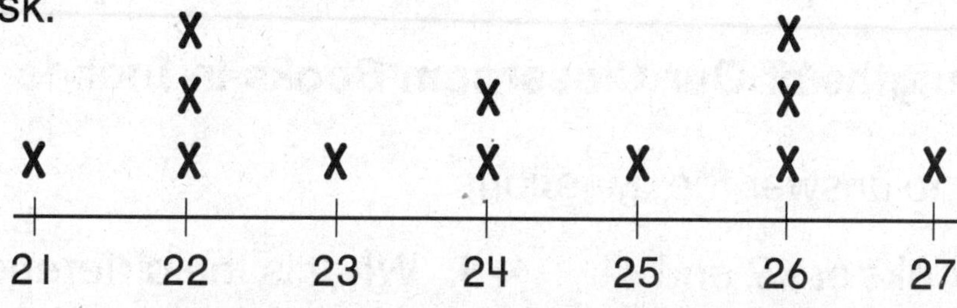

Lengths of Our Desks in Inches

12 desks were measured.

Two desks are 24 inches long.

The longest desk is 27 inches long.

The shortest desk is 21 inches long.

Share and Show

Write 3 more sentences to describe what the line plot above shows.

1. ____________________

2. ____________________

3. ____________________

Math Talk Suppose you measured another desk. If the desk was 23 inches long, how could you show this on the line plot above?

On Your Own

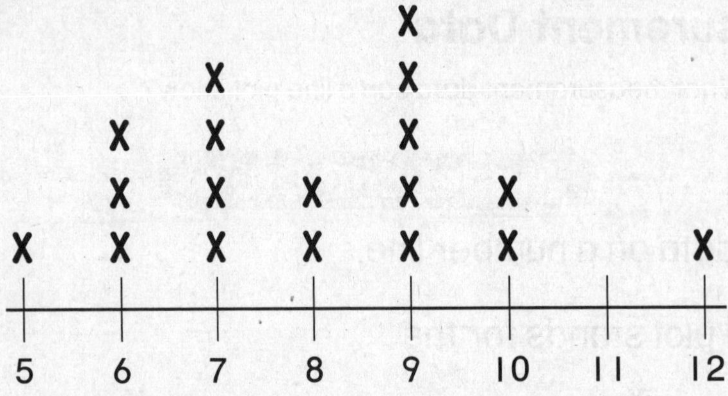

Lengths of Our Classroom Books in Inches

Use the line plot to answer the questions.

4. How many books are 9 and 10 inches in length?

____ books

5. What is the difference in length between the shortest and longest book?

____ inches

Write another question you can answer by looking at the line plot. Answer your question.

6. Question ______________________________

____

Answer ______________________________

PROBLEM SOLVING

7. Look at the table to the right. It shows Tom's books and their lengths. Add the data for the books to the line plot at the top of the page.

Book	Length
Reading	11 inches
Math	12 inches
Spelling	9 inches

TAKE HOME ACTIVITY • **Ask your child to explain how to read the line plot on this page.**

Name ______________________

Checkpoint

Concepts and Skills

Write the time shown on the clock. Then write the time 1 hour before and 1 hour after.

1. 

1 hour before ________

1 hour after ________

2. 

1 hour before ________

1 hour after ________

2:00 P.M. — 3:00 P.M. — 4:00 P.M. — 5:00 P.M. — 6:00 P.M. — 7:00 P.M. — 8:00 P.M.

Use the time line above. Solve.

3. A movie begins at 2:00 P.M. It is over at 5:00 P.M. How long is the movie?

   ______ hours

4. Madison arrives at a friend's house at 3:00 P.M. She leaves at 7:00 P.M. How long does she stay?

   ______ hours

Subtract to solve. Show your work.

5. Will arrives at the library at 1:15 P.M. He leaves at 1:50 P.M. How long is Will at the library?

_____ minutes

6. Andrew begins reading at 3:20 P.M. He stops reading at 3:45 P.M. How long did Andrew read?

_____ minutes

How many scoops does the container hold? Estimate. Then measure.

7. 

plastic cup

Estimate: about _____ scoops

Measure: about _____ scoops

8. What is the difference in height between the shortest and tallest plants?

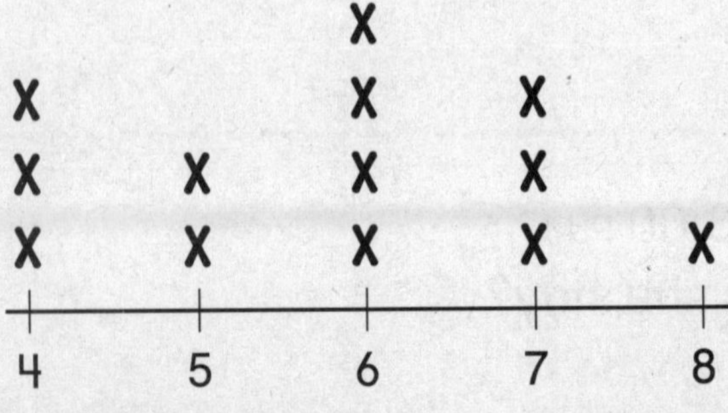

- ○ 3 inches
- ○ 4 inches
- ○ 5 inches
- ○ 6 inches

Name ______________________

Fraction Models: Thirds and Sixths

Essential Question How can you identify thirds and sixths?

Model and Draw

__3__ equal parts or __3__ thirds

__6__ equal parts or __6__ sixths

__1__ part of 3 equal parts or __1__ third

__1__ part of 6 equal parts or __1__ sixth

Share and Show

Color the strips. Show two different ways to show 1 third.

1.

2.

Color the strips. Show two different ways to show 1 sixth.

3.

4.

Math Talk How are 3 thirds and 6 sixths alike?

On Your Own

Color the strips. Show two different ways to show 2 thirds.

5. | | | |

6. | | | |

Color the strips. Show two different ways to show 2 sixths.

7. | | | | | | |

8. | | | | | | |

Color the strips. Show two different ways to show 3 sixths.

9. | | | | | | |

10. | | | | | | |

PROBLEM SOLVING REAL WORLD

Solve. Write or draw to explain.

11. A sub sandwich is cut into sixths. Tim eats two parts of the sandwich. How many parts are left?

_______ parts left

TAKE HOME ACTIVITY • Have your child draw a picture that shows a slice of cheese divided into thirds.

Name ______________________________

Fraction Models: Fourths and Eighths

Essential Question How can you identify **fourths** and **eighths**?

Model and Draw

4 equal parts or 4 fourths

8 equal parts or 8 eighths

1 part of 4 equal parts or

1 fourth

1 part of 8 equal parts or

1 eighth

Share and Show

Color the strips. Show two different ways to show 1 fourth.

1.

2.

Color the strips. Show two different ways to show 1 eighth.

3. 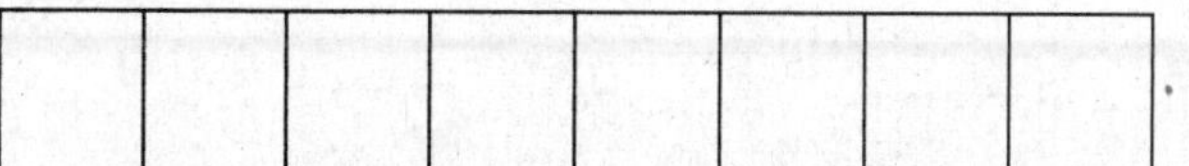

4. 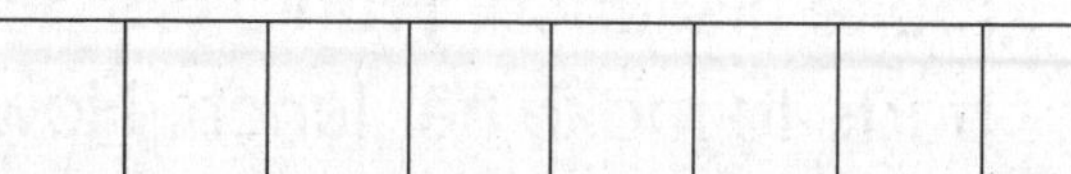

Math Talk How are 4 fourths and 8 eighths alike?

On Your Own

Color the strips. Show two different ways to show 2 fourths.

5. | | | | |

6. | | | | |

Color the strips. Show two different ways to show 3 eighths.

7. | | | | | | | | |

8. | | | | | | | | |

Color the strips. Show two different ways to show 5 eighths.

9. | | | | | | | | |

10. | | | | | | | | |

PROBLEM SOLVING REAL WORLD

Solve. Write or draw to explain.

11. A loaf of bread is cut into eighths. Jake uses 2 parts to make his lunch. Fran uses 3 parts to make her lunch. How many parts of the loaf are left?

_______ parts left

TAKE HOME ACTIVITY • **Have your child draw a picture to show a slice of cheese divided into fourths.**

Name ________________________________

Compare Fraction Models

Essential Question How can you use fraction models to make comparisons?

Model and Draw

fourth	fourth	fourth	fourth

half	half

I fourth (<) I half

Share and Show

Color to show the fractions. Write <, =, or >.

1.

I half	half	half

2 fourths	fourth	fourth	fourth	fourth

I half ◯ 2 fourths

2.

I fourth	fourth	fourth	fourth	fourth

I eighth	eighth	eighth	eighth	eighth	eighth	eighth	eighth	eighth

I fourth ◯ I eighth

Math Talk Look at the strips above. Is I half greater than or less than 3 fourths? How do you know?

On Your Own

Color to show the fractions. Write <, =, or >.

3.

I third	third	third	third			

I sixth	sixth	sixth	sixth	sixth	sixth	sixth

I third ◯ I sixth

4.

3 sixths	sixth	sixth	sixth	sixth	sixth	sixth

I half	half	half

3 sixths ◯ I half

PROBLEM SOLVING REAL WORLD

Solve. Draw to show your answer.

5. Barry cut a cheese stick into halves and ate a half. Marcy cut a cheese stick into fourths and ate a fourth. Which child ate more cheese?

_______________ ate more.

TAKE HOME ACTIVITY • **Ask your child to draw a picture that shows a square divided into fourths.**

Name ______________________________

Concepts and Skills

Color the strips. Show two different ways to show 1 third.

1. | | | |

2. | | | |

Color the strips. Show two different ways to show 2 sixths.

3. | | | | | | |

4. | | | | | | |

Color the strips. Show two different ways to show 2 fourths.

5. | | | | |

6. | | | | |

Color the strips. Show two different ways to show 4 eighths.

7. | | | | | | | | |

8. | | | | | | | | |

Color to show the fractions. Write >, <, or =.

9. 1 half

half	half

3 fourths

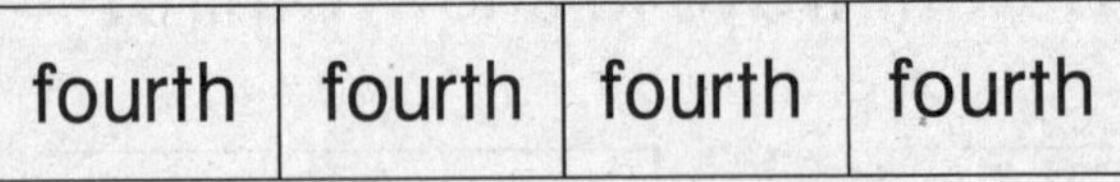

10. 1 third

third	third	third

2 sixths

sixth	sixth	sixth	sixth	sixth	sixth

11. A pizza has 6 slices. Six friends share the pizza equally. What fraction of the pizza does each friend eat?

- ○ 1 third
- ○ 2 thirds
- ○ 1 sixth
- ○ 2 sixths